IS THE GOOD CORPORATION DEAD?

IS THE GOOD CORPORATION DEAD?

Social Responsibility in a Global Economy

Edited by
John W. Houck
and
Oliver F. Williams

ROWMAN & LITTLEFIELD PUBLISHERS, INC.

HD
60
.I77
1996

ROWMAN & LITTLEFIELD PUBLISHERS, INC.

Published in the United States of America
by Rowman & Littlefield Publishers, Inc.
4720 Boston Way, Lanham, Maryland 20706

3 Henrietta Street
London WC2E 8LU, England

Copyright © 1996 by Rowman & Littlefield Publishers, Inc.

British Cataloging in Publication Information Available

Library of Congress Cataloging-in-Publication Data
Is the good corporation dead? : social responsibility in a global
economy / edited by John W. Houck and Oliver F. Williams.
    p.   cm.
Includes bibliographical references and index.
1. Social responsibility of business.   2. International business
enterprises—Moral and ethical aspects.   3. Corporations—Moral and
ethical aspects.   I. Houck, John W.   II. Williams, Oliver F.
HD60.I77   1996   658.4'08—dc20   95-52589   CIP

ISBN 0–8476–8208–0 (cloth : alk. paper)
ISBN 0–8476–8209–9 (pbk. : alk. paper)

Printed in the United States of America

♾ ™ The paper used in this publication meets the minimum requirements of
American National Standard for Information Sciences—Permanence of
Paper for Printed Library Materials, ANSI Z39.48–1984.

Contents

Preface

Part I: The Death of the Good Corporation

It was unquestioned after World War II to about the 1980s that this was the American Century, whether militarily, diplomatically, economically, technologically or philosophically. At the center, spewing forth material comforts and technical ideas, along with full employment and adequate retirement, was the American Corporation: GM, AT&T, GE, CBS, NBC, 3M, HP—the list goes on almost ad infinitum. But at the center of centers was IBM, combining highly technical equipment with business savvy, a highly educated work force with a fierce service mentality, and unblemished profitability with genuine concern for loyal employees. IBM was indeed the Athens or Florence of Corporate America. But something happened, and this became quickly a symbol for the journalist Robert J. Samuelson of *Newsweek:*

> IBM's fall from grace is more than a big business story. It also represents last rites for the "Good corporation." This was our ideal of what all American companies might become. They would marry profit making and social responsibility, economic efficiency and enlightened labor relations. IBM was the model. It seemed to do everything right, and its present troubles (including its first layoffs) have shattered the vision with unmistakable finality.

But does Samuelson have it right that the Good Corporation, combining profitability with Corporate Social Responsibility (CSR), is dead on arrival in our new global economy? It is this important question that is the subject of this volume.

In his new essay for this volume, Samuelson sees CSR as the

corporate response to the Great Depression, with its average unemployment rate of 18 percent during the 1930s, reaching its peak unemployment rate of 25 percent during 1932, and the nostalgic yearning for the individualism of the farming and small-town countryside. The modern corporation would be responsive to the legitimate concerns of the public, workers, and retirees—a sort of organizational security blanket that would salve the wounds of job insecurity and bigness. CSR received a boost after World War II, given the leadership role the United States had in the Cold War struggle with the Soviet Union and Red China: Could corporate capitalism, committed to efficiency and profitability, be responsive to the then perceived needs that Soviet or Chinese socialism "claimed" it was better able to satisfy? Meanwhile, the list of needs lengthened. As Samuelson puts it: "Companies were supposed to provide job security for their employees . . . to provide health insurance and pension benefits . . . to create the kind of working environment that would inspire workers' loyalty and a reciprocal sense of obligation between employees and the company." Later, environmental and affirmative action concerns were added to the mix, then day-care for employee children and rehabilitation for alcohol and drug abuse.

CSR, in addition, was harnessed as the answer to widespread antipathy for centralized big government: "The notion was that because corporations would be able to supply more of this, the state could come and intervene in a relatively modest way—not modest in comparison with U.S. history, but modest in comparison with other modern industrial societies which were attempting to do the same thing." Government's role, like unemployment insurance, social security, Medicare and Medicaid, Aid to Dependent Children, was to be sure hefty but limited by the Good Corporation and its works.

What went wrong with this master plan which seemed so necessary and workable? Samuelson places the blame on the paradox of too much success, both organizationally and financially, causing corporations to lose their capacity for "leanness and meanness," necessary qualities in the new era of global competition and downsizing. Samuelson cautions that we should not exaggerate the extent of the change: "I am not saying that it is a complete jungle out there for workers . . . [clearly though] our psychology and anxiety levels have changed." He warns that there are no easy answers, nor does it appear in these days of tight budgets and deficit reductions that government will be able to take up the slack left by the death of the Good Corporation.

Part II: Redefining Corporate Responsibility: The Challenge

Several respected business observers and ethicists were asked to debate Samuelson's thesis about the death of the good corporation: Richard De George of Kansas, Ronald Green of Dartmouth, James Post of Boston University, Howard Rosen of the Competitiveness Policy Council in Washington, D.C., Prakash Sethi of CUNY, Lee Tavis of Notre Dame and Marina Whitman of the University of Michigan and late of General Motors. A consensus developed that because of the new global dimension, business was experiencing important challenges, including how much to load on business beside survival and profit making, like CSR's lengthening agenda.

Difficult questions are raised in deciding just what responsibility means in today's business climate. Some argue that morality and society's interests are served best by allowing the free market to produce and allocate resources; in this view, if the market encourages behavior that is undesirable to society, then the law is the appropriate tool to correct the situation. For those who take this position, market and legal signals are sufficient, and no moral or social constraints are appropriate. The basic responsibility of corporate leaders operating with this market mind-set is expressed well by one of its leading spokespersons, Milton Friedman: "to make as much money as possible while conforming to the basic rules of the society, both those embodied in law and those embodied in ethical custom." For Friedman, "ethical custom" means the honesty, fidelity, and integrity required for the market mechanism to function. Ethical custom does not include bringing human and social values into economic decisions, but the integration of these concerns into the economic affairs of the corporation is precisely what is advocated by those concerned with the social responsibility of business. Friedman argues that bringing human values into economic decisions will lead ultimately to a transfer of power from the market mechanism to the political mechanism, and that such excessive governmental power brings with it all the evils of socialism. Thus, he labels CSR as a "fundamentally subversive doctrine."

But the opponents of Friedman's position are in the majority of our seven essayists, as expressed by Ronald Green:

> Its basic intent [CSR] is to provide a moral alternative to Friedman's classical view. The core idea is that business firms and, by extension, business managers have an affirmative moral obligation beyond their

duties to shareholders and their legally mandated duties to other corporate stakeholders to improve the social environment. Few advocates of the idea of corporate social responsibility argue that a corporation must bankrupt itself or seriously erode its economic performance in the pursuit of this objective.

But while Friedman's doctrine has few takers among our essayists, there is no dearth of willingness to explore critically CSR.

Richard De George, a longtime philosopher with a profound interest in business, opens the debate by voicing skepticism about CSR: "Although the myth of corporate social responsibility serves a certain function in the United States, it is of limited application here and in the international business area. It is not about to disappear and will undoubtedly continue to function for some time to come. Yet because it tends to hide or obscure a company's moral obligations, there is reason to prefer an approach that makes these obligations clear." He goes on to advocate more traditional principles of morality, adapted to the business world, that would build on our twenty-five hundred years of experience with ethical choices and dilemmas, going back to the Greeks.

Ronald Green of Dartmouth recounts the case study of how a major drug research laboratory took on the task of developing an effective treatment for river blindness, a debilitating ailment that hits millions in the Third World. It was a venture that held out little hope for substantial, if any, financial return; it was a classic face-off between the traditional business mentality and those supportive of CSR. Green rebuts the opponents of this venture by pointing out "how naive it can be to urge companies to concentrate on maximizing profit and to ignore endeavors that engage the moral imagination of key stakeholders," like medical doctors, researchers, and stakeholders who are critical of the further progress of the corporation but who give their allegiance to their professions, i.e., chemistry, biology, etc., and their standards of refereed conduct.

An empirical approach is taken by the author James Post to explore the core values of managerial ranks in this time of huge corporate transformation; it is resulting in a reexamination of how well the large corporation is doing in "its most basis function—to provide good jobs to a substantial portion of the American work force." Several changes were found:

1. life-long security of employment is history;
2. employment security is predicated upon performance and not on seniority;

3. employees of corporations will have to take larger responsibility for training themselves to be flexible and adaptable;
4. employees will bear a larger responsibility for health care and retirement.

While many of these changes are unsettling, James Post argues that there are grounds for optimism that corporate America can reinvent the good corporation.

Howard Rosen of the Competitiveness Policy Council details the impact on CSR of the economic trends of the last fifty years: while aggregate global wealth through production and trade has grown considerably, median income in the United States has been stagnant for the last twenty years. His conclusion is guarded: "In spite of increased globalization, firms should be able to remain socially responsible without placing their workers or home-country citizens at an economic disadvantage."

Like Richard De George, S. Prakash Sethi, a longtime observer of business, going back to his *Up Against the Corporate Wall* (1971), is not enthusiastic about the various incrustations that have grown up around CSR, many of which are misleading about what makes for goodness in business life. He offers a detailed alternative to CSR, which he believes is "more objective and can be applied systematically in defining the nature and extent of corporate social performance in terms of corporate activities that are voluntarily undertaken, . . . flexible enough to incorporate normative value-based standards and explicitly recognize the role of noneconomic considerations and constituencies in shaping societal expectations of corporate behavior."

Lee Tavis is a veteran researcher on the impact of U.S. corporations, exercising their market and technical power, in the Third World. Here he compares how CSR will do in two different economic climates: the United States and Germany, each marked distinctively by different expectations of the good corporation in the current intensity of international competition. The discretionary power and options of managers are described, with special emphasis on the economically weak countries and people.

The final essay is by Marina v.N. Whitman who has combined a distinguished concern in economics with a vice-presidency at General Motors. She brings to her economic analyses the testing of on-the-job experience at the pinnacle of corporate America; she sees the contemporary transformation, caused by changes like global competition and the information revolution, to be painful but necessary. She states the challenge: "The common task we face is not to say farewell to the good corporation, but to help reinvent it in a form suitable for the twenty-first century."

Part III: Religious Perspectives on Corporate Social Responsibility

The five essays in this part are written by authors well-versed in religious-social-business thought, who tackle a difficult aspect of this immensely challenging issue: What can religious thought say about corporate social responsibility? Further, how should religion speak to contemporary issues embedded in our global society? Still further, should religion only raise questions or should it go on to advocating specific solutions and policies?

R. H. Tawney, in his *Religion and the Rise of Capitalism* (1926), in criticizing church leadership of the past, had something to say to these questions:

> Granted that I should love my neighbor as myself, the questions which, under modern conditions of large-scale organization, remain for solutions are: Who precisely *is* my neighbor? and How exactly am I to make my love for him effective in practice? . . . Traditional social doctrines had no specifics to offer, and were merely repeated, when, in order to be effective, they should have been thought out again from the beginning and formulated in new and living terms.

Seventy years ago, Tawney wrote these words, and the problems he raised still stalk religion today. It is not all that clear that religion has thought through its basic message to the global corporation and communicated in terms that are likely to be heard and understood in the corporate corridors.

The first essay is by J. Philip Wogaman, a leading authority on ethics in the Protestant churches. He is the senior minister of the Foundry United Methodist Church in Washington, D.C., a church frequented by President Clinton and Senator Dole, and was for twenty-five years a professor of Christian ethics at Wesley Theological Seminary, likewise in Washington. He is a respected but critical observer of corporate America. His thesis is that "the free market mechanism, for all its benefits in other respects, is unable to set and preserve adequate standards of corporate ethics." He does not believe CSR has much chance at survival without some intervention by government, church groups or other groups such as the press or public-spirited ones to advance socially responsible conduct in global business.

Wogaman is careful to remind the business community that although church groups are critical of corporate behavior, especially in shareholder resolutions, this criticism derives from a positive acceptance of the corporation as a form of global economic organization. This point is crucial, for many in the business world are convinced that religious groups sponsoring shareholder resolutions are intent upon interfering with the free-enterprise system. He draws from the writings of the World Council of Churches and the Catholic church to support his contention that "it is naive to regard business ethics, as practiced by individual businesspeople, as a sufficient guarantee of moral standards in a free-market situation. Different markets afford different degrees of latitude for 'ethical behavior'." He makes a compelling case for strong, countervailing pressure from outside business, like government, religion, interest groups and the press, to enlarge the business perspective.

The second article, by Gerald F. Cavanagh, S.J., an early writer on business ethics, presents an overview of the history of the last twenty-five years in corporate social responsibility: much progress in environmental concerns and in hiring and promoting minorities and women but the "global marketplace has brought sudden and dramatic changes in the world view of and in methods of operating for U.S. business." Business is hustling to respond to these conditions by a new mix of responsibilities and values: efficiency and downsizing, effectiveness and accountability, teamwork and management development, and new trends in dealing with customers and the public. He is optimistic that corporate social responsibility, "with a little help from its friends" in religion and government, will survive as a useful concept and as a challenge to corporate conduct.

Gerald Cavanagh sees religion as playing a key role in the formation and development of business leaders. The important theme of the writings of theologians in social theory and Catholic social encyclicals is the dignity and the social and religious character of the person. To thrive and develop individually, people need others and naturally come together in various groupings—families, church groups, neighborhood associations, professional associations, social clubs, unions, corporations, and so on, with corporations playing a key role in forming the conscience of business managers and leaders.

Michael Novak continues his twenty-year study of the relationship between the church, the state and the business corporation, a lively but contentious partnership of strong wills that Novak calls "democratic capitalism," which is understood to be composed of three powerful groups: political, moral-cultural, and economic. Thus, for example, a U.S. corporation is sustained in meaning and value not simply by some theory of free enterprise but rather by a theory of democratic capitalism. In Novak's view, there is a role for religious leaders and theologians (members of the moral-cultural system) to criticize, protest, and persuade the corporate leaders (members of the economic system). Yet up to now he has not been impressed with statements by church leaders and theologians on economic matters because, in his judgment, these statements demonstrate little understanding of the economic system and its achievements. However, when John Paul II's celebratory encyclical, *Centesimus Annus* was published in 1991, Novak found there a positive study of the business corporation to shed "practical light and truth about the person" working and managing. Novak proposes several further values that both religion and business can share:

1. To establish within the culture of the firm a sense of community and respect for the dignity of persons;
2. To protect the political soil of liberty;
3. To exemplify respect for law;
4. To win the allegiance of the majority;
5. To overcome the principle of envy;
6. To communicate often and fully with their investors, shareholders, pensioners, customers, and employees;
7. To contribute to making the surrounding society, its own habitat, a better place.

Oliver Williams is the author of *The Apartheid Crisis* (1984), an early study of how corporate America responded to the apartheid laws of South Africa. In his chapter in this volume he traces the impact of religious thought and action on stockholders and corporate governance. The hope of some religiously motivated advocates was that stockholders' votes would cause U.S. firms to leave South Africa (disinvest), which, in turn, would either pressure the white rulers to change their racist policies or would create a climate for further direct action. Individual stockholders as well as institutions were asked to take a stand on the question of investments in South Africa. For those persons and institutions that are avowedly Christian, the issue was more pressing: How does one translate the biblical injunction "to love one's neighbor" in this difficult and complex arena?

Williams argues that the appropriate Christian response to U.S. investments in South Africa is a synthesis of religious commitment with political and economic judgment. Although many have contended that the biblical witness to avoid evil precluded investing in an apartheid regime, a biblical standpoint must be informed, not only by Jesus' avoidance of evil but also by the reality of sin and the vocation to work for a just world. He points out that if it can be shown that the political and economic welfare of Blacks will be enhanced by foreign investments in South Africa, then these investments are moral. Williams argues that the stewardship ethics—using corporate power to advance Black welfare—holds the most promise for ending this terrible situation.

The final essay in Part III is written by Dennis McCann, a specialist in exploring the impact of religious thought on vital, contemporary institutions and cultures. He asks specifically, What role should the world's major religious traditions play in promoting corporate social responsibility? His answer avoids focusing only on the Western Tradition; rather, he widens the scope by exploring both Classical Hinduism from South Asia and Confucianism from East Asia:

> Recent history suggests that business ethics in a global economy can and ought to be religiously pluralistic and grounded in a hermeneutical perspective that takes the world's religious traditions seriously as living witnesses to the moral aspirations of humanity. Business executives who expect to make a significant contribution to the development of a global economy would be well advised to familiarize themselves with the history of religions.

Part IV: The Socially Responsible Corporation: Converting Theory into Practice

For many decades, observers of corporate behavior and models used the term "socially responsible" to describe the corporation which did more than market a product, make a lot of money or avoided financial losses. But what is included in the idea of social responsibility for corporations? Several business executives attempt to answer; their perspectives come from some of our largest to the more modest sized corporations; through the most technologically advanced products to a wide spectrum of services. There is a fascinating array of answers but what is common to all is their unalloyed enthusiasm for the concept if not the practice of CSR, and their stories detail the important challenge of converting the theory of CSR into day-to-day validity.

Robert Galvin of Motorola sees business corporations as being responsible when they create wealth:

> I respectfully suggest that if business does not create wealth, nothing else will work in our society. History supports this suggestion. Until the Industrial Revolution, literally, the only way one party survived rather than another was to take away, misuse, or abuse the resources of the day and then move on to the next place once the resources had been depleted. But we are learning how to take resources and use them in a multiplying way, a renewing way, in a fashion that creates wealth which then directly or indirectly benefits and adds value to all the other subsystems of society.

William Lehr, Jr., who was a senior executive with one of our most visible corporations, Hershey Chocolate, recounts the history of that corporation in its role as a good neighbor in its home city. Its sense of being socially responsible has evolved from being a highly paternalistic neighbor, building community recreation facilities, to wanting a more contemporary sense of public reputation for good business and ethical standards.

> Like the rest of corporate America, we are not immune to the temptation to take shortcuts, a temptation that increases as competition intensifies. In an environment of employee cut-backs and internal competition for fewer available jobs and promotions, the desire to take the easy way, not necessarily the right way, dramatically increases. However, we understand and believe also that the consequences of unethical conduct are severe. A good name and reputation for fairness and quality that have taken a company a hundred years to build can be destroyed in one day. Therefore, we believe our commitment to ethics must be as strong, if not stronger than ever. Quite simply, we know it makes good business sense.

In a similar vein of equating a socially responsible firm with being a good neighbor is the story by the CEO of a major bank, David Fox of Northern Trust of Chicago, thirty-eighth largest in the United States. He was especially concerned about assisting employees through difficulties in their neighborhoods: "Our employee-assistance program came about when we recognized that people were being distracted by elder care issues, gangs, drugs or alcohol abuse, or domestic violence and did not know where to turn. Employees motivated our decision to construct in our new operations building a corporate child-care center, the first of its kind in downtown Chicago."

Douglas Ford is the president of Amoco Oil Company. He recounts the mission of his company is to make a profit for stakeholders while maintaining a strong allegiance to Amoco's social and ethical "values and responsibilities":

1. We insist on honest, fair, and trustworthy behavior—or integrity—in all our activities.
2. We respect the individual rights and dignity of all people because our individual and collective actions and talents create our competitive advantage.
3. We believe that technology is a key to the success of our organization.
4. We pledge to protect the environment and the health and safety of employees, the users of our products, and the communities in which we operate.
5. We are committed to customer satisfaction and mutually beneficial business relationships.
6. We challenge ourselves to continually improve—or progress.

It is interesting to compare Amoco's principles with those stated by James Sullivan, the vice chairman of Chevron Corporation, another worldwide oil company:

Society's needs are multiplying, even as most corporations are scaling back in size, humanpower, and resources. Social issues are becoming more global and more complex, but I do believe that corporate social responsibility is alive and, in some cases, thriving in the form of creative solutions, new partnerships, and the continuing respect for individual values.

It was left to Paul Henkels, chairman of a large engineering and construction firm for gas transmission, electrical facilities and telecommunications, to raise alarm warnings about the future. He recounts that intense competition, especially in contract bidding, can lead to lost business unless compromises of quality are made:

Sometimes it is specified that the cable be buried twenty-four inches, sometimes thirty inches, sometimes forty-two inches. Unless an inspector is there to observe, which is not often, he does not know how deep a cable has been buried. We could have taken a chance and subcontracted from some of the successful bidders and maybe gotten away with burying that cable twelve or eighteen inches. However, our company has a reputation for quality and integrity, and we were not going to do that. Among other things, we were not going to tell our people to work with lower standards; we have other work that has been gained through our good reputation, and we would suffer greatly if we started to compromise our quality.

We are most grateful for the financial assistance provided by two businesspeople, John Caron and William Lehr, Jr., both intensely interested in the idea of ethical sensitivity in corporate practice. Two editors at Rowman & Littlefield Publishers, Julie Kuzneski and Jennifer Ruark, were critical in moving this project to completion. Most importantly, our debt of thanks goes to the Center's executive coordinator, Madeline Day, whose tireless competence and commitment at every step of the long way made this volume possible—and, at the same time, the day sunnier!

Part I

The Death of the Good Corporation

1

The Good Corporation: R.I.P.

Robert J. Samuelson

As an introduction, let me clarify that I am not an economist; I am not related to Paul Samuelson, author of the classic economics textbook. I am a journalist and a reporter. The motto of my profession, attributed to an anonymous British TV personality, is "The secret of our business: first you simplify, then you exaggerate."

The column I wrote was meant to be a kind of an obituary for the good corporation. What I mean by the good corporation is a large business enterprise that marries social responsibility and economic efficiency. The history of this concept of the corporation reveals that the origins of the good corporation go back to the early decades of this century, especially the 1920s. American executives in the decades of 1910–29 were trying to accommodate trends in public opinion that were violently antibusiness and reflected, I think, a reaction to the emergence of large-scale business enterprises in the United States. These big companies went against the whole character of the country during its first seventy-five or a hundred years, which basically was built on farming—a rural population and an independent citizenry who had control, at least in theory, over their own lives and were not subject to the whim of concentrated power. Concentrated power traditionally had been seen as a kind of political phenomenon but, with the emergence of these large corporations at the end of the nineteenth century, suddenly there was this economic phenomenon that seemed to subvert the basic idea of individualism in America. The idea of corporate social responsibility, it seems to me, was a social and political reaction by business leaders. They were trying to accommodate a new form of economic enterprise—an inevitable part of modern industrial society—with the basic values and beliefs of the United States.

The Recent History of the Good Corporation

The full flowering of the good corporation did not occur until after World War II. The basic impulses were the same but they were elaborated further in the sense that companies were trying to minimize what they viewed as excessive government regulation and trying to map out an alternative to widespread unionization. They thought they could do both by showing that they could behave spontaneously in a socially responsible, acceptable manner so that public opinion would hold that companies were a good thing for the country and did not have to be regulated in a harsh, draconian way.

This notion that you could marry economic efficiency and profitability with social responsibility was also bound up in the idea of postwar American management. Postwar signifies the era after World War II—almost the last half century. The basic notion was that the central task of modern management was somehow to make companies responsible and efficient at the same time. By making them efficient and highly profitable, there would always be sufficient economic resources—cash flow, profits, whatever—to help accomplish some of these other social objectives. This was the basis of the social contract that people instinctively and intuitively came to after World War II. The idea of a good corporation, a socially responsible corporation, was elastic. There was no real hard and firm definition of what it was supposed to do. But in its essential task it reflected the legacy of the Great Depression: the average unemployment during the 1930s was 18 percent and peak unemployment in 1932 was 25 percent. Companies were supposed to provide job security for their employees. Beyond that, companies were supposed to provide health insurance and pension benefits for their employees and to create the kind of working environment that would inspire workers' loyalty and a reciprocal sense of obligation between the employees and the company. The general idea was to provide a sense that companies, acting spontaneously, could do the right thing.

As the postwar period progressed, additional obligations—formal and informal—were put onto the corporation and the business community in general. Regulations of one sort or another, informal obligations to help out with social problems in the local communities, to be more responsive to some of the new workplace concerns that emerged—taking care of day care for your kids, drug abuse and alcohol, rehabilitation—these were a few. They were the core ideas of the good corporation.

The good corporation was not simply a business phenomenon. It was a social phenomenon and a consciousness that permeated, in my view, society in general. It was the way we were going to construct a modern welfare state in the United States, according to values that were peculiarly American. The good corporation was going to allow us to create a welfare state with a modest amount of government, in contrast to the welfare states that were created in Europe that had—at least compared to the American model—a large amount of government. This would be done by having well-managed corporations take care of their employees and provide the vast bulk of what people in most of the rest of the world would think of as welfare benefits—job security, health insurance, pension coverage for old age, and a basic sense of social stability—that modern societies—almost universally—want and think they are entitled to receive.

In other societies, many of these tasks were handled by explicit programs of social insurance, regulations requiring companies to do this or that, or prohibiting the firing of employees except under certain circumstances. In the United States we did not feel and do not feel comfortable with a large expansion of state power. Thus, the notion that all this would occur more or less spontaneously was very soothing to the American view of things. It helped minimize the very big, disruptive ideological debates about how people get the things they want without getting something that most people do not want—big, intrusive government. The notion was that because corporations would be able to supply most of this, the state could come in and intervene in a relatively modest way—not modest in comparison with its past role, but modest in comparison with other modern industrial societies that were attempting to do the same thing. There would be unemployment insurance for the unemployed in recessions, although in the 1960s we thought we were going to get rid of recessions. The poor would have Medicaid which would be a form of government health insurance. The old would have Medicare which would insure them after they finished their years of employment. We would have social security, created in the 1930s to provide a safety net for those older Americans who, perhaps, had not saved enough or who did not have benefits from private pensions. In the main, people viewed these things informally as an integrated system. The government was going to take care of those who were not taken care of by the good corporation.

When we think of the good corporation, we think of IBM and Delta Airlines and Time-Life and Sears and the large companies that had dominated their industry, were consistently profitable—in many cases highly profitable—and were able to carry out these programs. But I have implied that the same consciousness was going to spread throughout most businesses. I do not think anybody really believed that all companies were going to become like IBM, which in retrospect is probably a good thing. But what they did believe was that there was a certain informal logic at work. The best managed corporations would always be the best managed corporations, and they would always have the highest salaries, the best fringe benefits, and the most unassailable job security. But other companies in other industries would learn to emulate, imitate, and learn from the best practices of the best corporations. Then they would improve their profitability, their efficiency, and begin to imitate what better corporations had done so that if the job security was never exactly what it was at IBM, it would still increase in general. Health insurance might not be quite as good at all companies as it was at IBM but it would still be pretty good. Beyond imitation, the competitive market would also force companies to do this. As more and more companies adopted these practices, any company that wanted to hire somebody would have to, in effect, offer similar benefits, otherwise they would not be able to hire anybody. The people would go other places. Companies would imitate but they would also be compelled by the marketplace to adopt more enlightened practices. By this process, American companies would provide spontaneously much of what was wanted in terms of social services without the heavy arm of government.

Although I have written the obituary for the good corporation, I do not want to imply that what I said was original. If anything, all this column did was put down on paper what I think most people already realized had happened. But although the system did not evolve in the way that we imagined, we should not believe that it has been an utter and complete failure. This is not the case. In fact, the kind of benefits we thought would emerge have, to a large extent—though not universally—emerged. The difference between now and say 1945, 1950 or even 1955, has been dramatic; not only our expectations have changed but also the basic social and economic realities that people now take for granted.

The Private Welfare State

In 1950, 17 million Americans had private health insurance. In 1980, 187 million Americans had private health insurance. Most of that was provided by the employers. In other words, we went from a situation in which almost nobody had employer-based health insurance to a situation in which most people with full-time jobs do have health insurance as a benefit. In 1940, 17 percent of full-time workers had employer-based pensions. By 1970, the figure stood at 52 percent. Again, the situation changed from one in which very few people had company-based pensions to one in which the majority of workers had company-based pensions.

Prospects for job security have also changed. Many people have the impression that almost every company in the United States, in the last four or five years, has had to downsize, restructure, rightsize—or whatever the latest cliché is for throwing people out of work. There is a sense that nobody's job is safe anymore. That perception is probably true in a literal sense, but it is not true that career jobs have disappeared. In 1991, half of the men forty-five to fifty-four years old had been with their current employer twelve or more years. Almost 25 percent had been there twenty or more years. Somebody who is forty-five, who may have been with one company for twelve years, may, if he stays, have spent twenty-five or thirty years there by the time he has finished. Most Americans do not stay at one company for their entire career. In their twenties most are still shopping around for some company or job in which they feel comfortable. President Clinton likes to cite this figure that an average American in a lifetime is going to change jobs six or seven times. This statistic apparently comes from a survey done by the Labor Department which shows that by the time a person is twenty-nine he or she will have changed jobs six or seven times. However, there is a big difference between having six or seven different jobs by the time a person is twenty-nine and having six or seven jobs by the time he is sixty-five. If people had six or seven jobs between thirty and sixty-five, we would have a turbulent labor market in which nobody could expect to hold the same job for more than five or ten years. But a lot of this early job-shifting is basically done to accommodate work during college years, to decide what you do not like, to work during the summer, departure over disagreements with employers. Much of it is the normal process of postadolescence in America and should not be taken as an enormous sign of great turbulence in our labor markets. There is some, but we should not exaggerate it.

The notion of the good corporation has cost us two things. One is peace of mind. What we thought we were creating with the good corporation and its imitators was a stable economic system that would allow us all peace of mind. People would change jobs essentially when they wanted to, not because they were forced to change jobs. We would have some of the traditional insecurities taken care of collectively through companies or through the government health programs and income support in our old age. All these kinds of insecurities would be erased. We have lost that because even if you have a secure job—which most middle-aged, middle-class Americans do—you no longer can be certain that the job is going to be secure for the next several years.

We have also lost our notion of the welfare state. It is now clear that, barring some miracle, the convergence between private and public welfare that we had informally imagined is not going to occur. The private sector is not going to provide universal job security or cover all but a small minority for health care and pensions. The private sector is going to provide a lot of this, but huge gaps will remain. There will be gaps between the existing government programs and what the private sector will provide spontaneously. Americans are going to have a hard time dealing with this; it creates a tension between what we want from a social system—a welfare state—and what we do not want—government providing a lot more welfare benefits. I do not know how we are going to resolve the tension but it is there.

What Went Wrong?

The question now arises: What went wrong? Why has the good corporation not been as good as we thought it would be, and why did all these programs not spread as we thought they would? Bad management is one explanation—and it is correct. Well-managed companies do not have to fire employees, nor must they downsize or re-engineer. Nevertheless, almost all companies have had to do this. If bad management has existed at some time at most companies, we must ask why?

What we are discovering is what I call the corporate Peter Principle: Companies have this tendency to expand to their level of incompetence. When companies succeed, success creates the seeds of future failure. What all companies like to do is grow fast, make a lot of money, and dominate their market. They hire people; those at the top have an increasing number of employees. It is better to win than to lose, and in the United States growing is better than declining and stagnating. This view is part of our culture. People like to make a mark, and growth is one way to do that. Obviously, large profits are nice; they allow you to do all sorts of things you want to do—pay yourself and your employees well, offer good benefits, invest in the future of the company, and have the stock price rise. Companies also want to control their markets because no company wants to be the equivalent of the Kansas wheat farmer who is always a price-taker, never determines the price of wheat, and is basically a very small cog in a very large system. Companies like to have a dominant market position because it gives them some opportunity, some pricing power, and it does not leave them at the mercy of outside forces. When companies grow and attain market power, they actually succeed—and many American companies have succeeded. It is natural to congratulate themselves. Two things then happen. The first set of problems I would call the sociology of success: When companies succeed they begin to pay less attention to their own markets because they run the markets. They become slightly less attentive to questions of cost, quality, and customer satisfaction. The customers do not have too many other places to go, and the company has the best product in the market, or they would not be selling 30, 50, or 70 percent of the market. Company offices become a bit more luxurious. Fringe benefits improve slightly. Salaries get a little bit better. In unionized industries (this happened in the steel and auto industries, for example), managements buy labor peace with very expensive settlements with their unions because this makes life easier. All this is very natural. In some very extreme examples, this got out of hand; a favorite example is Bethlehem Steel during the 1970s. They had seven corporate jets—a bit much. The company refurbished some of the local golf courses in Bethlehem where the executives played golf. Bethlehem, at that point, was a paid-up member of the American business aristocracy, and that is the way it behaved.

I am not saying that this happened at all companies, but it does tend to happen. Beyond this, the marriage of business success and the ethos of the good corporation—the idea that we have to do well by our own employees, we have to protect them—creates what management consultant Judith Bardwick calls the entitlement mentality. She describes this as follows: "Under the double influence of the corporate compassion and rich treasuries, organizations stopped evaluating employees and discharging those who were not productive. They failed to hold people accountable for their performance." What I am suggesting is that success in a very subtle way breeds complacency and breeds an inattentiveness to the very minute details of competition and costs that are ultimately quite critical in determining who wins or loses in business. This undermines the economic viability of corporations and ultimately subverts their ability to fulfill the social contract of the good corporation.

Successful companies also face a second set of problems—what I call the financial problems of success. When a company succeeds and gets control of its markets and has large sales, it gets a great cash flow. So long as the markets grow very rapidly, it is in good shape because it can continue to introduce new generations of products and move into different varieties of products. There are natural ways they can diversify from the product base using the same technology. The trouble is that sooner or later almost all markets reach maturity. People have enough cars; they have enough toasters; they have enough televisions; they have enough insurance policies. Markets mature, growth slows, and then the company faces a real problem; because it has succeeded it has a large, reasonably predictable cash flow and profit stream, and yet its existing markets do not seem to require all the money the company is throwing off.

One thing the company obviously could do is just pay it out to the shareholder and say, "Look, we are selling widgets, the widget market is saturated. Maybe in ten or fifteen years there will be a great market for widgets in China, but it is not there today. We have our subsidiary in China, we are preparing for that day, but right now we do not know what to do with all this money, so we are going to give it to you the shareholders because you deserve to reap the rewards of your investment." But this essentially condemns the corporation to a period of slow growth at best, and maybe stagnation at worst. Basically, managers do not like to do this spontaneously, at least not in the United States. It is not part of the capitalist ethos; it is not part of our own culture of growing.

The company has a number of other choices, none of which is very good, all of which involve highly risky investment opportunities. First, it can continue investing in its existing markets. It can either assume that the market maturity or saturation that others say exists does not exist or, if it does exist, its product is so much better than the competition that it can gain market share. Thus, the company can continue to grow while the rest of the industry basically suffers from slow growth and maturity. The gamble succeeds. However, it might not. What happens, in this case, is overinvestment. The industry has overinvested. Returns on everybody's investment is low, and what was once a very profitable company with predictable cash flow suddenly is not so profitable, and its cash flow is reduced.

The second thing the company can do with its excess cash flow is to start a new business. It can try to find or develop new products, new services, that it thinks in a few years will be a big new industry. Obviously, this is extremely risky because (a) it may be getting into something it does not know anything about; (b) if it targets a new market that does not exist, the market may not exist because there is no demand for the product that does not yet exist; or (c) if it goes into a market that already exists, there may be entrenched competitors who are good and do not want to let the new product in.

Of course, the company can avoid all those problems by buying another company. This is diversification through acquisition. But there are problems here too. First, the price for the company probably will be high. If it is a going concern with reasonably good prospects, the only way to get it, essentially, is to pay a premium over market price. Then, the company may not know how to manage it because it is in an unfamiliar industry. Alternatively, it may be that the company may now be so diversified that corporate overhead in the mother company is high and all the line managers in the corporate subsidiaries are demoralized because they lack independence of action—they have to report to too many corporate overseers. All sorts of things can go wrong with a strategy of diversification. Many companies tried it; many failed.

To me, it seems that these two sets of problems—sociology of success and the financial problems of success—impose built-in constraints on how good management can be long-term for all companies. This is not to say that some companies will not overcome these problems for a long time or that some companies that develop these problems will not be able to refurbish themselves. But it does imply, for the system as a whole, that all companies will not be well managed all the time in the sense that we envisioned it twenty or thirty years ago and in the sense that most business schools educated their students to think was possible.

I have tried to think of companies that have violated the kind of structure I have set up. Two companies come to mind, neither major but both now very dominant in their industries in the world market, neither of which refutes this structure. One is Boeing which still, despite subsidized Airbus competition, is the dominant supplier of

commercial airjets in the world. But Boeing has never been the good
corporation, in the sense described earlier. When Boeing's markets
contracted, Boeing contracted. In 1967 Boeing's corporate-wide employment was 148,000; in 1971, it was 55,000. So Boeing, basically,
has stayed competitive by being ruthless when necessary. The other
company that is dominant worldwide in its market is Coke. But Coke
had the problem of excess cash flow and diversified with little success.
They bought Columbia Pictures but had to sell it later. They bought a
wine-making operation which did not work out. Their diversification
program apparently was not successful.

The good corporation was a great ideal but one that was unattain-
able, although the effort to attain it has had some very good social
consequences. That is my obituary for the good corporation. At the
same time, I am not saying that it is a complete jungle out there for
workers. For most middle-aged workers, and especially most white-
collar workers, we still have career jobs. In 1991 this forty-five to fifty-
four-year old group of men had been with their current employers a
median of ten years. In 1983 the similar figure was 10.3 years. The
change is slight. Statistically it may be significant, but it is not clear
whether that significance is due to demographic change—younger
people in this age group—or whether it is a result of more layoffs.
Among women workers, tenure figures of the length of time spent with
one employer is actually going up because women are becoming more
like men in their attachment to the work force. Most families still have
health insurance coverage through their employers. Pension coverage
has plateaued; it is declining slightly for men, increasing slightly for
women. The overall figure is slightly up. It has not gone down by 50
percent, so I do not think we should exaggerate the nature of the
changes that have occurred. However, our psychology and anxiety
levels have changed.

The Need to Survive

I agree entirely with the proposition that, although companies now
must be forced to act in ways considered unimaginable ten or fifteen
years ago, it does not mean that all corporate executives have suddenly
become ruthless and uncaring about their employees. This is not true
on a personal level. But even if it were, I think most executives know
that this attitude would be catastrophic for their companies. It is a
cliché but nevertheless true that, for most companies, their employees

are their most important asset. Most jobs today allow employees too much discretion for companies to alienate their employees willfully. If employees become totally demoralized or alienated from their companies, the companies will fail. I think most competent executives understand that. Aside from personal considerations, which do exist, companies, in general, are still trying to treat their employees correctly—they try to do the right thing. But that has become much more difficult than it used to be.

What clearly is going to happen, and has started already, is that there are going to be more calls for government to close the gap in the welfare system through mandated benefits and regulatory requirements of one sort or another. This is inevitable. The health-care debate is a product of this development. However, this cannot be done easily because there are very real costs to providing all these benefits.

The health-care problem is a case in point. Suppose that the government mandates universal health insurance. This is a very expensive proposition. Somehow these benefits will have to be financed, which leaves the private sector with two options. (1) Companies will reduce either other fringe benefits or salaries and wages, so the worker will pay for expanding health insurance. (2) Companies can try to recover this extra cost in higher prices. The obvious implication is that if there are too many mandated benefits and not enough cost-control, the mandates become an engine for inflation which reduces everybody's wages. (3) If overly costly mandates are imposed, in conjunction with minimum wages, some people will not be hired because it costs the company more to hire them than the company gets from the employees' work.

In Europe where they essentially have state-run systems of welfare, the evidence on these points is not reassuring. European unemployment has gone from 3 to 11 percent over the last twenty-five years. Job growth has been minimal, but what is more disturbing is that beneath this slow overall job growth, there have been almost no gains in private employment in Western Europe over the past quarter century. Three-quarters or more are gains in government employment. This obviously cannot continue forever, but it is nevertheless very discouraging. Once governments get into this trap, it is very difficult to get out. In France, the last four or five weeks, the French government attempted to reduce the minimum wage for young people only. There were riots in the streets. The government decided that, given the choice of taking an action they knew to be right and leaving office, they would stay in office. It was a modest correction, and yet the political process prevented it from happening.

I do not have any easy solutions. I will summarize by saying, first, that the situation is worse than we expected it to be; second, it is probably not as bad as we think it is; and third, we should be cautious in trying to make it better because, if we do, we might perversely make it worse.

Part II

Redefining Corporate Responsibility: The Challenge

2

The Myth of Corporate Social Responsibility: Ethics and International Business

Richard T. De George

Corporate social responsibility is neither a clear concept nor a central one for ethical business in a global economy. It is best understood as a modern-day myth, using an approach exemplified by the late French anthropologist Claude Lévi-Strauss to explain and analyze it. This does not imply that there is no such thing as corporate social responsibility. Clearly there is. The many corporate social responsibility statements, the hundreds of articles, and the numerous textbooks devoted to the topic, all testify to the presence of some reality. But the question is, What is its essence and how can we understand the phenomenon called corporate social responsibility?

Lévi-Strauss developed a theory of myths widely applicable both to ancient and contemporary myths, including much of what we call science.[1] For present purposes I shall draw from his account four salient features of myths:

1. A myth is not simply a story, but a story in all its different variations, since it may be told in a number of different ways and in a number of different versions.
2. A myth does not stand alone. It is part of a larger whole, either a package of other stories or a way of viewing reality, of which it is one part.
3. A myth is not a falsehood, as one common meaning of myth

17

maintains. A myth helps people understand, make sense of, and accept a certain phenomenon or portion of reality.
4. A myth, while not a falsehood, is not a true statement of reality either, for it hides a portion of reality, either through ignorance or through unconscious design.

The story, doctrine, or assertion of social responsibility by business and its critics is a contemporary myth in precisely this sense. It comes in a variety of forms: It is part of a larger package that involves the relationship between business and society; it captures something about the reality of that interaction, helping to make sense of it; and it hides a portion of that same reality, thus unconsciously serving certain vested interests.

Although the Myth of Corporate Social Responsibility is being exported, it does not travel well because it is part of a package that is fundamentally American. But another account counters the myth or demythologizes corporate responsibility; this account has a sounder base and has broader applicability to business on the international level than does the concept of social responsibility.

The Myth of Corporate Social Responsibility

What Is the Myth in Its Different Variations?

First, there is no uniform story or understanding of corporate social responsibility. The term became widely used in the United States only in the 1960s;[2] before that we find only occasional mention of the *social* responsibility of business.[3] Although the term's meaning remains vague and tenuous, it nevertheless gains currency after 1970.[4] In 1979 Thomas Zenisek, in an article in the *Academy of Management Review*, discusses various definitions and models of corporate social responsibility and notes that they all lack either empirical and/or theoretical support. He attempts to provide a topology but, in doing so, simply adds one more item to the confusion that he documents on the subject.[5]

There is no definitive or supposedly universal version of social responsibility. The story of social responsibility plays itself out in numerous different contexts and scenarios. We can, in Lévi-Strauss's terms, develop the different stories that were and are told about social responsibility or that embody it. All the variations together form part of the myth. Sometimes the term "social responsibility" is used, sometimes "corporate responsibility" or "corporate social responsibility." Among other terms used to express the same idea we find "social responsiveness," " social accounting," "social audit," "social conscience," "corporate social policy," and "corporate citizenship."[6]

The variant "social responsiveness," to take one example, carries with it the implication that business is responding to something that comes from society.[7] The end of the 1960s saw the rise of consumer, environmental, and social-action groups. "The military-industrial complex" became a catchphrase that grew in currency and was used to identify and attack big business in general. Business responded to this and other onslaughts that gained status and stature by being presented as social-interest attacks. Groups that had vested interests clothed their demands on business in terms that gave their demands more respectability. By calling them socially interested demands, they disguised the fact that they were often demands not of society as a whole, but of particular groups with special interests, such as themselves. Business countered by responding in a variety of ways. However, rather than saying that they responded to pressure groups either to maintain their corporate image or to preserve their share of the market, they countered by adopting the same strategy as their attackers. They clothed their answers in terms of social responsiveness or social responsibility. No one knew exactly what those terms meant, but that was unimportant. The terms indicated some concern for the social good, the general welfare, or society as a whole. The term "social responsibility" took some of the sting out of the charge that big business was part of a military-industrial complex that acted for its own benefit or for the benefit of an elite, rather than for the good of society.

We know what legal responsibility means. Corporations are governed by law. They fulfill their legal responsibilities when they do or refrain from doing what the law requires. We know what moral responsibility means. Individuals fulfill their moral responsibilities when they do or refrain from doing what morality requires. We do not know in some comparable way what corporate social responsibility means. There is no consensus on its meaning, if that meaning goes beyond legal and perhaps also moral responsibility.

When individuals or corporations do not fulfill their legal responsibilities, they are liable to state-imposed penalties. When they do not fulfill their moral responsibilities, they are liable to censure. When they do not fulfill their social responsibilities (unless these are also legal or moral), they are open to no sanctions. Firms are neither considered bad nor in any way penalized for *not* fulfilling social responsibilities. But they are praised for fulfilling them, or at least they can claim praise and lay claim to the rewards of a good reputation. Social responsibility thus turns out to be a very convenient term for business. It has little real downside in the way of penalties, and it has great upside potential.

Since no one can say definitively what social responsibility means, no one can strictly apply standards to determine if a company is socially responsible. Hence, different groups may apply different standards, none of which is binding.

The Council on Economic Priorities (CEP) exemplifies one approach to this problem. One of its publications, *Shopping for a Better World: A Quick & Easy Guide to Socially Responsible Supermarket Shopping*[8], rates companies according to their charitable giving, advancement of women, advancement of minorities, defense contracts, animal testing, social disclosure, community outreach, use of nuclear power, and impact on the environment. It also notes if the company makes cigarettes, pesticides, or beer; has misleading ads; engages in clear-cutting, catching dolphins, or union-busting, and the like; and if it bans chlorofluorocarbons (CFCs), pays 50 percent day care, makes food bank gifts, and so on. The CEP provides the information. It makes no judgments, except to decide what information to monitor and include. The shoppers are urged to make and apply their own judgments. The result is a vague notion of what it means for a company to be socially responsible.

In a 1993 *Newsweek* column entitled "R.I.P.: The Good Corporation," Robert J. Samuelson[9] lamented the demise of the good corporation, citing as the paradigm the fall from grace of IBM for, among other things, conducting its first layoffs. Using the criteria of social responsibility, it is more likely that IBM's sin in 1993 was to post the largest one-year loss of any company in history. Are employee layoffs and financial losses violations of a company's social responsibility?

A no-layoff policy is certainly an employee's ideal. But it has never been an American social policy, even if a few corporations with no such contractual agreement have followed that policy. Laying off employees in times of economic necessity is not illegal and arguably not immoral. Is it a violation of corporate social responsibility? Samuelson seems to think so, but many others disagree.

Similarly, does a company have a social responsibility to make a profit? Certainly that is why most companies are formed, and companies typically do not seek red ink. Society does not look favorably on companies that fail. But do such companies violate a social responsibility? Perhaps many people would be inclined to think that a failing company is not socially responsible. But no one can say so with certainty, because there is no way to determine what is and what is not included in social responsibility. It is not a matter of people arguing about whether or not being profitable follows or does not follow from some principle governing social responsibility. There is no principle governing social responsibility; it is a vague collection of various desiderata framed by various groups for various purposes. All the varieties are variations on the theme or, in Lévi-Strauss's terms, they are different versions of the same story. Together they make up the myth that we refer to as social responsibility.

A Myth Does Not Stand Alone

The second characteristic of a myth is that it does not stand alone. It is part of a larger set of stories into which it fits. In the United States, the set, which I shall not try to spell out in detail, is composed of a number of other myths. I have described one of them, the Myth of Amoral Business,[10] at some length in my book, *Business Ethics*. The myth of corporate social responsibility fits well with the myth of amoral business. Both have similar aims. According to the myth of amoral business, businesses are not bound by morality but by the market which, over time, will correct any social costs that business may impose on society. Either government will step in to remedy market defects and handle externalities, or competition and public reaction will eliminate what some consider unethical practices. But business itself should not be evaluated in moral terms.

The myth of corporate social responsibility complements the myth of amoral business. If the latter sounds too crass and self-serving, the myth of corporate social responsibility counters that and says that, of course, business can be held to some standards. But these standards are not strict and are matters of individual choice; they are not such that failure to live up to them is any reason for penalizing a company.

These two myths are part of a larger picture. The Myth of the Free Market is another story that both reveals and hides part of reality. The amount of government intervention, regulation, and control of business by the United States government does not square very well with any classical notion of a free market. But, again, the various versions of the free market story allow it to function successfully as a myth despite a great deal of evidence to the contrary.

Other similar myths help make up the whole; with a little thought and imagination, one can expand on them—for example, the Myth of Consumer Sovereignty, the Myth of a Level Playing Field, the Myth of Market Efficiency, the Myth of Free Competition.

The total system of myths provides the popular justification for the system. The set of beliefs makes the system acceptable. The combined strength of the myths legitimates the system, despite evidence that clearly contradicts any one of the individual myths. When contradictions occur, other versions of any particular myth can always accommodate the evidence, and the other myths supply sufficient support so the contradictions are overlooked, deemphasized, treated as exceptions or temporary aberrations, or reinterpreted to fit somewhere. Sometimes a new myth appears, a particular myth mutates, or a new version of a myth emerges to handle the contradictory evidence in some acceptable way.

Another one of the functions of myths is to make intelligible and acceptable the social practices that one inherits, with which one lives, that one rarely if ever questions, and that seem natural, eternal, and justifiable.

Yet that the myth of corporate social responsibility forms part of a larger set of social myths helps explain why it does not transfer easily to other societies. The myth is one that has developed in the United States at a particular time in response to particular social realities. It developed from a context in which other social myths were already in place, accepted, and operative, and it emerged in such a way as to mesh well with them. It cannot be ripped out of that total fabric and simply sewn as an appendage to another foreign piece of cloth. It will not fit well with most other social fabrics, will appear to be imposed, and will be appropriately viewed as foreign. In fact, this is what we find as various attempts are made to transfer the notion of social responsibility to other countries. Europeans who have had a fuller social system of worker protections than do Americans find little kinship with the concept. The same is true of the Japanese who are slowly learning what the myth means in the American context but who have no concept of it in their own society. Japanese society is one in which layoffs in large corporations are contrary to a long tradition. But the no-layoff policy is not seen as part of social responsibility, since that term simply has not functioned in Japan in any way comparable to the way it functions in the United States.

A Myth Reveals and Explains

The third aspect of a myth is that it reveals and helps to explain a certain portion of reality, and so helps to make it acceptable. What about the myth of corporate social responsibility is correct and so made it catch on? The myth is not an invention by any one person, a fabrication developed only to hide reality. It in fact captures and exposes a part of reality: that corporations and business in general are a part of society and have responsibilities. It is also a fact that to be successful, business must take into account the values and perceptions of its customers. The myth of corporate social responsibility allows corporations to acknowledge this without binding themselves to anything in particular. A company can promote itself as socially responsible if it treats the environment well, recycles, and keeps pollution to a minimum. It can promote that side of its operation even if it has practiced sexual or racial discrimination and even if, in many ways, it operates at the limits of legality.

Corporations are bound by law. This is a fact, and one can say that laws are some of the most effective ways that society has of imposing its demands and making explicit the responsibilities of corporations. If social responsibility is understood to include legal responsibility, as it usually is, then a company can claim to be socially responsible and to be a good citizen (another phrase used to convey the same message) to the extent that it keeps its nose legally clean.

For the past twelve years *Fortune* magazine has published a list of America's most admired companies. Since the list reflects the opinions of business executives, it is not surprising that profitability has typically been the number one criterion used, and the 1993 *Fortune* survey found that "roughly half of that perception can be explained by a company's financial performance over time."[11] But profitability alone is not enough to get one very high on the list. UTS, a tobacco company which was second on financial rankings, rated only ninety-fourth on the survey.

Yet no single kind of action nor set of actions defines a company as socially responsible. A part of reality that the myth captures but often does not articulate adequately is that, in addition to legal responsibility, companies have moral or ethical responsibility. They should not hurt people, an injunction that makes suspect tobacco firms, liquor companies and, in the eyes of some people, armament firms and nuclear energy companies. Hence, one's record on pollution and its control becomes an ingredient in many versions of corporate social responsibility. Moreover, corporations should help people. They should provide goods or services of high quality at a fair price, and they should provide employment, paying fair wages in decent working conditions.

Although the myth of corporate social responsibility acknowledges, to an extent, that corporations have responsibilities beyond their legal ones, it couches the acknowledgement in a way that allows corporations a good deal of leeway by conveniently blurring the distinction between moral requirements and moral ideals. Moral blame and guilt appropriately follow the violation of a moral requirement. Both are inappropriate when one falls short of moral ideals. Ideals, by definition, go beyond requirements. The myth of corporate social responsibility molds ethics on the model of the moral ideal. The myth implicitly equates moral requirements with legal requirements. It then equates its other social responsibilities with moral ideals. In this way, the myth correctly holds that fulfilling moral ideals goes beyond what is required by law and so deserves praise, while any company that falls short does not deserve blame. But that is not the whole story.

A Myth Hides a Portion of Reality

The fourth characteristic of a myth is that it hides a portion of reality, and what the myth of corporate social responsibility hides is the true nature of a corporation's moral or ethical responsibilities.

Milton Friedman was partially correct in his rejection of many of the social responsibilities that various interest groups had tried to foist on corporate America.[12] Those who claim that business has a social responsibility to rebuild the inner cities express a goal they would like fulfilled. But why does this responsibility fall on business rather than on the inhabitants of the cities or on municipal, state, and federal governments? Friedman correctly pointed out that corporate executives are not elected by the people and are thus not directly responsible to them. To expect business to do what is properly, at least in our society, the function of government is at best a questionable social responsibility and a socially risky policy. Friedman did not consider social responsibility a myth and even said that there was at least one social responsibility, namely to increase profits, admitting as well that corporations have to obey the law and to stay "within the rules of the game." What Friedman failed to acknowledge clearly and what the myth of corporate social responsibility in large part conveniently glosses over is the extent and importance of the moral or ethical responsibilities of business.

Many academic writers on social responsibility correctly see that business has ethical responsibilities. Archie Carroll was one of the first (and his text is one of the most influential) to point out this. But others have argued to the same conclusion. Corporations, he claims, have social responsibilities, which can be subdivided into economic, legal, ethical, and discretionary (sometimes called philanthropic).[13] Although this presentation reveals that business has ethical responsibilities, it hides the true nature of business. In diagram form the typical presentation is a pyramid with profit on the bottom, the base on which the other levels are built. The legal level is next, followed by the ethical, with the discretionary level at the apex. This representation hides the true status of a firm's ethical responsibilities, which are incorporated through all stages and levels. Economic responsibilities are not basic, if this means that a company must first make profits and then ask what its ethical responsibilities are. Its ethical responsibilities parallel its profit-making, and should inform and be used to evaluate the means the company employs to make its profits, the company's ends, and the profit itself. Similarly, the firm's ethical responsibilities parallel the legal and discretionary ones and should inform them.

McDonald's switched from polystyrene clamshells to paper products in packaging its Big Macs. It did so in response to heavy lobbying from a variety of groups, some of which even encouraged children to write to the corporation asking it to change. Its own studies indicated that, all things considered, using polystyrene was environmentally preferable. Nonetheless, it switched to paper products to satisfy what it considered a popular demand or a social responsibility, since doing so enhanced its image. Whether it did the ethically right thing is, at least, debatable.[14]

Social responsibilities are vague and are composed of an assortment of moral and legal responsibilities, moral ideals, and vested interests, all lumped together in a fuzzy package. The package inhibits serious consideration of the ethical responsibilities of corporations, for which they can and should be held accountable. I argued previously the difference between moral obligations and moral ideals. By trading on the ideals, the myth of corporate social responsibility deflects attention from the obligations.

For example, a no-layoff policy by most U.S. companies is a moral ideal; in general, however, they have no moral obligation not to let employees go in times of financial necessity. How they let them go is another matter. But companies that downsize, though they may become less desirable places at which to work from an employee's point of view, do not automatically act unethically by laying off employees. However, a company that dumps toxic waste into a stream, knowing that it will cause harm to people, acts unethically whether or not it is prevented by law from doing so. To equate the two kinds of actions as not socially responsible obscures an essential difference between them.

The myth of corporate social responsibility, of course, does not explicitly deny that corporations have ethical responsibilities. But it has often served to cover up or diffuse this reality.

When business schools first introduced courses in social responsibility, they followed the lead of business in replying to its critics. The rise of corporate social responsibility was not vigorously resisted by business on the whole. For the movement, the formulation of the myth served its purposes by diffusing moral attacks that could be much more demanding and damaging.

The International Scene

If we turn from the American scene to the realm of international business, we see that social responsibility has not had the same effect. I have suggested that the reason is that the myth of corporate social responsibility is part of a larger set of myths, not easily transported to other cultures and, when it is transplanted, it seldom takes root and grows.

We should concentrate next on what the myth reveals and what it hides. What it acknowledges is that corporations have responsibilities beyond those spelled out in law. What it hides, in particular, is the range and importance of the moral responsibility of corporations for their actions and failures to act. While the myth of corporate social responsibility does not transfer well, the claim of moral responsibility can and does transfer successfully across borders; morality and moral responsibility are found in all societies and form part of their fabric.

Exactly what constitutes the moral responsibility of corporations, of different kinds of corporations in different contexts, and of multinational corporations in particular, are issues that still need to be discussed and clarified.[15] But morality applies across borders, and corporations are bound by moral rules. This reality has always been accepted implicitly and is now being articulated and made explicit more and more. Just as basic moral norms must be observed to have a functioning society, so basic moral norms must be observed to have continued international trade and commercial interactions. If theft, misrepresentation, murder, and breach of contract are the rules by which people habitually operate, business in any viable sense grinds to a halt.

Can this claim about business being bound by morality be considered the Myth of Moral Business? The answer is a qualified yes. Is it any better than the myth of corporate social responsibility? The answer, again, is a qualified yes. Let me develop the qualifications in both instances.

We can understand the myth of moral business in two senses. First is a sense in which a myth of moral business is developing next to and in conjunction with the myth of corporate social responsibility, that is, part of the function of the myth of corporate social responsibility is being transferred to the myth of moral business. American business was less happy with business ethics because, potentially, applying them might demand more of companies. But business has to some extent successfully defused these effects by accepting conventional morality as the norm and playing down or ignoring critical morality.[16] What the myth of moral business acknowledges is that, to develop and maintain a favorable reputation, business must take conventional morality seriously. What the myth hides is that morality is a two-edged sword. One edge, the conventional edge, demands adherence to accepted and established principles. The other, the critical edge, holds that every action, end, goal, and principle can itself be subjected to moral scrutiny. The critical edge is the edge that some parts of the business ethics movement, which acknowledge the myth of moral business, try to hide.

The second sense of the myth of moral business is the broader sense in which morality itself can be seen as a myth that helps explain and justify certain social practices. Morality in general can be seen as a myth, just as democracy and the rule of law, and even the various parts of contemporary science, can be seen as myths insofar as they are justifiable, explanatory beliefs that form part of a system but are open to revision based on experience. Taken in this way, there is nothing objectionable to classifying morality as a myth. Business still has more to learn about morality and, undoubtedly, some of our present moral beliefs and practices hide immorality that will become apparent at a later time.

Is the myth of moral business preferable to the myth of corporate social responsibility? My affirmative answer relies on two claims. One is that the former is tied into a larger and more permanent set of beliefs, namely, those forming the moral history of humanity. In this respect, the myth of moral business has global and international roots and does not need transplanting. It simply needs articulation in places where it may not have been articulated. The second claim is that, whereas the myth of corporate social responsibility has no principled basis, the myth of moral business has. When we looked at the notion of social responsibility, it became clear there is no principle by which one can determine the content of social responsibility, hence, the many versions of social responsibility and the diffuse nature of any claims based on it. The same is not true of moral responsibility. Not only is there broad agreement on the basic moral norms, there is also considerable ethical theory, developed for over 2500 years, that provides the tools and basis for moral claims. The differences are crucial.

The Moral Responsibility of International Business

If it is difficult to say what the social responsibility of any particular American business is in the United States, because there is no principled way to determine this, it is even more difficult to say what the social responsibility of a U.S. multinational is in Germany or Japan or Saudi Arabia. Yet we can, of course, specify precisely their legal obligations in each locale. We can, in the same way, specify the moral or ethical responsibilities of all companies and the moral obligations or responsibilities of companies in given environments or contexts.

Therefore, on the international level, social responsibility is not the most useful concept; and ethical responsibility is the preferable one to stress. We should not allow the myth of corporate social responsibility to cloud the real issues or to hide the very real ethical responsibilities of multinationals. I shall illustrate this briefly by considering three aspects of the international moral responsibilities of business.[17]

Moral Norms Do Not Vary

First, while social responsibility may vary from country to country, moral norms do not. A company cannot change its moral beliefs and values as it moves from the United States to Japan, to India, or to Saudi Arabia; if it is to have any moral or ethical standards, it must adhere to these wherever it operates. If, like a chameleon, a company changes its ethics from country to country, it has no ethical standards. We can speak of a company that has defensible ethical standards that it articulates and adheres to in its operations and practices throughout the world as a company with integrity. Only by articulating the standards will those foreign nationals who make up the bulk of the

American company's employees abroad know them; only if the home company follows them will subsidiaries follow suit.

To say the company's standards must be defensible and ethical differentiates them from vague social responsibilities. All companies are morally required to do no direct intentional harm and to respect the human rights of their employees and the people with whom they interact. Thus, despite prevailing local social custom, these moral norms preclude the use of slave labor, as well as the purchase of goods from suppliers who use slave labor. Child labor often amounts to indentured labor, indistinguishable from slave labor. In such a situation, a firm with integrity cannot simply say that using child labor is the way business is done locally and close its eyes to the practices of its suppliers. To do so is to give up being a company with integrity and to engage in unethical, if perhaps not locally illegal, practices. This is much more serious than not being socially responsible.[18]

Therefore, a company with integrity asks what it is ethically required to do and fulfills those requirements. It can, of course, do more. It can seek to transform ideals into practice. No U.S. multinational company is required to operate in countries that routinely ignore child-labor laws or where it is legal to use children from the ages of eight to fourteen in their factories, nor may the multinational use suppliers who use child labor. A company with integrity must use its moral imagination if it wishes to continue using competitively priced suppliers from such countries and to refrain from exploiting children. In such situations, some U.S. companies have set up schools for the children and paid for the additional workers needed when children did not work. The variations on this theme that are ethically acceptable are many, and illustrate the importance of moral imagination.[19]

Similarly, if in a country that has lax safety requirements or lax pollution-control laws, a company operates a chemical industry in a way that endangers the workers or the local inhabitants, or pollutes the air, ground, and water, causing serious damage and illness to people, it does not act in an ethically responsible way nor does it act with integrity, even if its action is legal. The issue is not one of social responsibility. The proper standard is an ethically required one, not what local social pressures or social expectations permit. The same is true of other human rights, the environment, and sexual and racial discrimination. Companies are not free simply to follow local practice. In these issues, certain standards are morally or ethically required and can be articulated and demanded. A company with integrity has no choice but to live up to them.

These moral standards can and should be differentiated from moral ideals and other nonlegal social expectations and demands. The former are the ones that should do the most important work.

Social Expectations in Different Locales

The second aspect is that the myth of corporate social responsibility underlines the variations in social expectations that occur in different locales. Emphasis on moral or ethical standards does not deny these variations. It does not demand uniform action throughout the world, as if such action were a consequence of adhering to ethical standards. A company with integrity can and should accommodate to local customs and mores to the extent that these do not violate its ethical principles. But companies frequently view this as more of a prudent business recommendation than a moral imperative.

Any foreign corporation would diminish its chances of success if it did not learn the local customs of a host country, its way of doing business, and its expectations beyond the demands of law. Japanese firms only slowly learned that large corporations in the United States generally contribute to the charities in their local communities. Contributing to the United Fund drive is not a moral obligation, nor is it even a social obligation in the sense that it is required, yet not contributing to the community in any way tends to produce a negative image.

A company's moral responsibilities differ from these in important ways. Its moral responsibilities are not optional. Fulfilling a company's moral obligations is paramount and obligatory, whether or not it is seen as good business. Fulfilling other nonlegal social demands is not a requirement and may or may not be good business, depending on the demand, how vocally it is expressed, how much local or popular support it has, etc. Nonetheless, local conditions do give specific moral content to general moral requirements that can and should be implemented in different ways in different places.

One example is the moral requirement not to exploit workers, which means, in part, that they should be paid at least a living wage. What constitutes a living wage varies from country to country. There is no moral requirement that a firm pay mill workers in Lowell, Massachusetts, the same wages that the firm pays similar workers in Bombay, India, or vice-versa. The standards of living are very different. A living wage in Bombay would not be a living wage in Lowell. A living wage in Lowell would be extremely high pay for the typical Bombay mill worker. While morality demands that workers be paid at least a living wage, that there be no adverse racial or sexual discrimination, and that there be equal pay for equal work at any given locale, there is no moral requirement that all those doing similar work for a firm everywhere in the world be paid the same. Beyond a living wage, the local labor market determines what workers receive. The difference in wage levels is one reason that companies often relocate or seek suppliers outside their own county. This is not unethical.

In many instances in international business, moral requirements provide a much clearer guide to action than do social responsibilities, while providing the flexibility demanded by varying conditions.

Moral Responsibilities as Tougher Standards

Third, moral responsibilities, unlike social responsibilities, may require a company with integrity to operate at a higher level than is required of local firms, for a variety of reasons. Focusing on social responsibility tends to obscure this fact, and it is one that some firms would rather leave hidden.

For the U.S. company at home and abroad, we have already seen that, although a company with integrity will have and adhere to a single set of ethical principles, the implementation of the same principles in different situations may lead to differences in wages paid. They may lead to other comparable differences as well. But the situation I shall focus briefly on is one in which there appear to be two ethical standards: one for U.S. multinationals and another for indigenous firms, even though they operate in the same locale.

Assume, as is often the case, that the U.S. multinational is relatively rich and powerful and that it has the option of not operating in a particular country or locale; it is not forced to operate there in the sense that it can and already does operate successfully elsewhere. On the other hand, the local companies usually do not have this luxury; they must operate locally or not at all.

For example, consider the local companies in South Africa under apartheid. They had the option of either obeying the apartheid laws or of not operating. U.S. companies could adopt the Sullivan Principles and ignore the apartheid laws with impunity, or they could simply not operate in South Africa.[20] Were all the South African firms morally culpable? The answer is not completely clear. Small-business owners were culpable for engaging in apartheid, if they did so. But what should those people have done? If they did not run firms but went to

work for other firms, those firms would follow the apartheid laws. Was
that preferable? Or should they have refused to work for such firms?
But what was their alternative? If it was to starve, were they then
morally obliged to do so? I know of no moral theory that would
demand this extreme sacrifice. Yet they could not ethically actively
support or promote apartheid. The ethical answer people give in this
situation about the legitimate activities of local entrepreneurs may
vary. But surely the considerations for the local firms are different
from those that apply to U.S. multinationals because of the very
different circumstances.

A similar analysis applies to U.S. multinationals that may choose to
enter the Russian market, in contrast to a local entrepreneur who
wishes to engage in a business that is simultaneously encouraged by
Russian governmental policy and discouraged by local practices.[21] If
the local enterprise can only manage by resorting to bribery and paying
extortion, may these ills be tolerated? The answer, arguably, is yes,
even though in the same locale the answer for a U.S. multinational
would almost certainly be no. The U.S. multinational typically has
enormous power compared to the local firm, much-sought-after hard
currency, and available alternatives, all of which the local entrepreneur
lacks completely. If the alternative to local tolerance of passive com-
plicity in extortion is the abandonment of all local entrepreneurial
activity to those who demand extortion, is this a morally preferable
alternative? Since the answer is arguably no, there is plausible justification for what seems to be a double standard. That it is, in fact, not a
double standard becomes clear when we see that if the U.S. company
were truly in the same circumstances, what is ethically permissible for
the Russian firm would be ethically permissible for the American firm.
But their actual comparative circumstances are very different.

The notion of social responsibility does not help to clarify or resolve
these and other complicated and difficult problems which are typically
glossed over, hidden, and left beneath the surface in a social responsibility approach. By contrast, adopting and applying moral standards
and reasoning allows us to thread our way through such issues and
to see what is and what is not required, in addition to or despite
local expectations.

Although the myth of corporate social responsibility serves a certain
function in the United States, it is of limited application here and in
the international business arena. It is not about to disappear and will
undoubtedly continue to function for some time to come. Yet because
it tends to hide or obscure a company's moral obligations, there is

reason to prefer an approach that makes these obligations clear. The notion of corporate moral responsibility can fulfill the function that many people seek in attempting to impose controls on global business, to evaluate companies from different nations, and to measure the operations of any given company throughout the world.

Fulfilling its moral responsibilities is mandatory for international business. Many corporations score well by this measure, and even companies that suffer financial losses, such as IBM, continue to fulfill moral obligations. Companies can and should be held accountable to the extent that they fall short of fulfilling such responsibilities. We need not worry about whether to call firms that fulfill their moral responsibilities good or moral, any more than we worry about whether to call individuals who fulfill their moral responsibilities good or moral. Nor need we worry about the motives of companies for acting as they should. It suffices that they do so act. Encouraging them to do so throughout the world, helping them to do so, demanding that they do so, are proper roles for participant-observers in the moral community of which we are all a part. Revealing and articulating the ethical or moral reality that the myth of corporate social responsibility tends to hide is an important function of business ethics on the international level.

Notes

1. See Claude Lévi-Strauss, "The Structural Study of Myth," *Journal of American Folklore* 78 (October/December 1955): 428–44 (also available with other writings in *The Structuralists from Marx to Lévi-Strauss*, Richard T. and Fernande M. De George, eds. (Garden City: Anchor Books, 1972).

2. Among others, see William L. Kandel, "The Social Conscience in Hard Times," *Business & Society Review* 8 (Winter 1973/74): 17–20, who speaks of the "corporate responsibility movement" which he identifies as a product of the mid-1960s.

3. See Sonia Labatt, *Industry, the Environment, and Corporate Social Responsibility: A Selected and Annotated Bibliography* (Place: Council of Planning Librarians, 1990) CPL Bibliography 266: 1; and Walter F. Abbott and R. Joseph Monsen, "On the Measurement of Corporate Social Responsibility: Self-Reported Disclosures as a Method of Measuring Corporate Social Involvement," *Academy of Management Journal* 22 (September 1979): 501–515.

4. As one indication of this, the ABI/Inform database of over eight hundred academic management, marketing, and business journals lists only fifteen entries under social responsibility for 1971, compared to one hundred eighty-two for 1993.

5. See Thomas J. Zenisek, "Corporate Social Responsibility: A Conceptualization Based on Organizational Literature," *Academy of Management Review* 4 (1979): 359–368.

6. See *The Handbook of Corporate Social Responsibility: Profiles of Involvement*, compiled and edited by the Human Resources Network (Radnor, PA: Chilton Book Company, 1975): 1–12.

7. For one account of social responsiveness, see Robert W. Ackerman and Raymond A. Bauer, *Corporate Social Responsiveness: The Modern Dilemma* (Reston, VA: Reston Publishing Company, 1976); see also William C. Frederick, "Theories of Corporate Social Performance," in *Business and Society: Dimensions of Conflict and Cooperation*, S. Prakash Sethi and Cecilia M. Falbe, eds. (Lexington, Mass.: Lexington Books, 1987): 148–154.

8. See *Shopping for a Better World* (New York: Council on Economic Priorities, 1992). This edition claims over 850,000 copies sold, an advance of 150,00 over the previous edition.

9. See Robert Samuelson, "R.I P.: The Good Corporation," *Newsweek*, 5 July 1993, 41.

10. See Richard T. De George, *Business Ethics*, 3rd ed. (New York: Macmillan, 1990): especially chap. 1.

11. See Jennifer Reese, "America's Most Admired Corporations," *Fortune*, 8 February 1993, 44.

12. See Milton Friedman, "The Social Responsibility of Business Is to Increase Its Profits," *New York Times Magazine*, 13 September 1970.

13. See Archie B. Carroll, *Business and Society: Managing Corporate Social Performance* (Boston: Little, Brown and Company, 1981): 35; and Archie B. Carroll, "The Pyramid of Corporate Social Responsibility: Toward the Moral Management of Organizational Stakeholders," *Business Horizons* 34 (July–August 1991): 39–48.

14. For details of the case see *New York Times*, 1 November 1990, A1; 2 November 1990, A1; 31 December 1990, A3; and 17 April 1991, A14; "McDonald's Caves In," *Forbes*, 4 February 1991, 73–74; *Fortune*, 3 June 1991, 92; Benjamin Zycher, "Self-Flagellation Among the Capitalists," *Regulation*, 14 (Winter 1991): 25–26; and Lynn Scarlett, "Make Your Environment Dirtier— Recycle," *Wall Street Journal*, 14 January 1991, A12.

15. For two books devoted to international business ethics, see Richard T. De George, *Competing With Integrity in International Business* (New York: Oxford University Press, 1993); and Thomas Donaldson, *The Ethics of International Business* (New York: Oxford University Press, 1989).

16. See Richard T. De George, "Will Success Spoil Business Ethics?" *Business Ethics: The State of the Art*, ed. R. Edward Freeman, Oxford University Press (1991), 42–56.

17. For a fuller development, see De George, *Competing With Integrity in International Business*.

18. See "Danger: Children at Work," *Futurist* 27 (January/February 1993): 42–43; and "Slavery," *Newsweek*, 4 May 1992, 30–39.

19. See Martha Nichols, "Third-World Families at Work: Child Labor or Child Care?" *Harvard Business Review* 71 (January/February 1993): 12–23; and "Exporting Jobs and Ethics," *Fortune*, 5 October 1992, 10.

20. For details of apartheid and a list of the Sullivan Principles, see Oliver F. Williams, *The Apartheid Crisis: How We Can Do Justice in a Land of Violence* (San Francisco: Harper & Row, 1986).

21. See Richard T. De George, "International Business Ethics: Russia and Eastern Europe," *Social Responsibility: Business, Journalism, Law, Medicine* 19 (1993): 5–23.

3

Responsibility and the Virtual Corporation

Ronald M. Green

In 1978, Dr. P. Roy Vagelos, then the head of the research laboratories of Merck & Company, Inc., received a memo from a senior researcher in parasitology, Dr. William C. Campbell. The memo informed Dr. Vagelos of Campbell's hypothesis that a new Merck antiparasitic veterinary compound might be developed for human use as an effective treatment for river blindness, a disease that plagued millions in the Third World. Faced with this information, Dr. Vagelos had to decide whether and to what extent he would urge Merck to commit itself to this effort.[1]

River blindness is a disease found in the poorest regions of Africa, the Middle East, and Latin America. It is caused by the larvae of a worm carried by a tiny black fly. Individuals who are bitten by the fly face a dreadful course. The larvae embed themselves under the skin where they cause itching so severe that it drives some victims to kill themselves. Eventually, the larvae make their way up to the victim's eyes where they cause blindness. Previous drugs for combating the disease had dangerous side effects that make them inappropriate for use in mass treatment programs. Efforts to wipe out the fly had met with little success. According to a World Health Organization (WHO) survey in the late 1970s, over 340,000 people were blind as a result of the disease, and as many as 18 million people worldwide were infected with the parasite. In many villages in Africa, children believed that going blind was part of growing up.

Early in the 1970s, Merck researchers working with soil samples

37

from a golf course in Japan discovered a powerful new antiparasitic compound—ivermectin—that proved to be safe and to have astonishing efficacy against a wide range of parasites in cattle, swine, horses, and other animals. This compound became the basis of a dramatic advance in animal health treatment that by the late 1970s had established Merck's leadership and profitability in this field. It was in the course of this research that Dr. Campbell made the observation that the animal parasites against which ivermectins were effective were similar to the parasite that caused river blindness. This led him to suggest to Dr. Vagelos the possibility of developing a human formulation of the drug.

To learn whether Campbell's hypothesis had merit, Merck would have to spend millions of dollars to develop the right formulation for human use. Eventually, Merck would have to conduct field trials in some of the most remote parts of the world. Doing this would require the cooperation of WHO, a consortium of 166 member nations that often worked with private drug companies to develop drugs for Third World nations. But collaborating with WHO would not be easy. Over the years, WHO and U.S. drug companies had disagreed bitterly over such matters as WHO's international drug marketing standards. U.S. companies had also sharply criticized WHO's efforts to establish an "essential drugs list" to help poor nations spend their limited resources on the most basic, widely needed drugs.

The financial stakes involved in Dr. Vagelos's decision were even more worrisome. Developing a drug for human use might take a decade and cost the company tens of millions of dollars. If successful, there was little likelihood that this effort would prove profitable. River blindness was a disease of poor people and poor nations. It was not clear that international assistance or funding would ever be available to pay for the drug. In addition to the possibly unprofitable outlay of tens of millions of dollars and the diversion of corporate talents and energy, there were direct financial risks to the company. If the human formulation of the drug showed adverse side effects during clinical trials or field use, Merck's enormously profitable veterinary business might suffer. In the words of one Merck scientist, there was a question of "whether we should expose this fabulous commercial product to the risk of human usage."

Dr. Vagelos, originally a university researcher but by then a Merck executive (and soon to become Merck's CEO), had to decide whether to invest in research for a drug that, even if successful, might never pay for itself and that might risk one of his company's most profitable business lines. The stakes for Merck, and for victims of river blindness, were enormous.

What help can the field of business ethics bring to an executive like P. Roy Vagelos as he ponders a decision of this magnitude? A river blindness drug effort clearly has powerful ethical arguments on its side. But how are these to be integrated with Dr. Vagelos's other responsibilities as an executive of a profit-making, stock corporation? To what extent can an executive seek to alleviate human suffering if this means risking reducing the firm's profitability?

Over the years, at least two basic answers have been given to this question. One is the so-called "classical view" associated with the name of the economist Milton Friedman. The second is a broad set of views associated with the position known as "Corporate Social Responsibility." These two basic views proceed from fundamentally different moral premises. One places corporate profits to the fore; the other allows moral objectives sometimes to take priority. In what follows, I will describe briefly each of these views and develop its implications for Dr. Vagelos's decision. Next, I will propose a third view, one that offers a dramatically different perspective on the issues at stake in a business decision like this. I call this the "business excellence" perspective. Drawing on the recently developed concept of the "virtual corporation," it suggests to us that within a proper understanding of the modern business firm, ethics and profitability are not competing but mutually enhancing aspects of business decision-making.

Milton Friedman's view was bluntly expressed in his often-quoted 1970 article, "The Social Responsibility of Business Is to Increase Its Profits."[2] Early in his discussion, Friedman presents what he regards as an incontestable description of the relationship existing between all business owners, including shareholders, and the individuals they pay to manage the business:

> In a free-enterprise, private-property system a corporate executive is an employee of the owners of the business. He has direct responsibility to his employers. That responsibility is to conduct the business in accordance with their desires, which generally will be to make as much money as possible while conforming to the basic rules of the society, both those embodied in law and those embodied in ethical custom.

It follows from this basic conviction that Friedman has little room for any pursuit by corporate executives of moral or social objectives not mandated by law and unrelated to corporate profitability. On two grounds, he criticizes the notion of "corporate social responsibility," the idea that a company should pursue socially beneficial objectives for their own sake and independently of their impact on the corporate bottom line. First, he argues that such pursuits involve an unconsented diversion of shareholders' resources to purposes not their own. As such, they are a form of "taxation without representation." Second, he insists that corporate managers lack the expertise or competence to address social needs or problems beyond their business sphere. Such matters are better left to public officials who are responsible to those who elected them.

Friedman concedes that some forms of corporate social responsibility can be justified in terms of managers' primary duty to maximize shareholder wealth. For example, he admits that it may be in the "long-run interest of a corporation" to fund amenities in the communities in which it operates or to cultivate goodwill through tax-deductible charitable donations. But he would permit such actions only when they are clearly related to the corporation's own self-interest and, on balance, he would prefer that corporate executives have the courage of their convictions and resist what he regards as the unwise and ultimately dangerous pressures of social "do gooder-ism."

What would Friedman counsel Dr. Vagelos to do? At first sight, a decision to develop the river blindness drug would seem to countervene the manager's primary moral obligation to maximize shareholder wealth. There is little or no likelihood that this drug will ever turn a profit. True, a case can be made that development of the drug might burnish Merck's corporate reputation around the world, but the imponderable value of corporate "goodwill" here must be set against the real risks to the company's successful line of veterinary products. Does a manager have the right to endanger shareholder wealth in this way? The conquest of river blindness may be partial fulfillment of our ancient dream that the sick shall be healed and the blind shall see. But it may not be a dream in which a Friedmanite business executive can morally indulge.

The second position, corporate social responsibility, comes in many forms, but its basic intent is to provide a moral alternative to Friedman's classical view. The core idea is that business firms and, by extension, business managers have an affirmative moral obligation beyond their duties to shareholders and their legally mandated duties to other corporate stakeholders to improve the social environment. Few advocates of the idea of corporate social responsibility argue that a corporation must bankrupt itself or seriously erode its economic performance in the pursuit of this objective. In the words of John Boatright, "The exercise of social responsibility . . . must be consistent with the corporate objective of earning a satisfactory level of profit." Nevertheless, Boatright adds, such responsibility "implies a willingness to forego a certain measure of profit in order to achieve noneconomic ends."[3]

Various moral justifications are offered for this stance. Some maintain that the social chartering of corporations and the recognition of them as fictive legal persons implies a corresponding set of obligations to demonstrate good citizenship and social usefulness above and beyond sheer economic performance and productivity. Others maintain that the mere fact of corporate power implies the need for responsibility. Citing what he calls the "Iron Law of Responsibility," Keith Davis argues that "in the long run, those who do not use power in a manner which society considers responsible will tend to lose it."[4] Still others argue that, far from being incompetent to address social needs, as Friedman believes, corporate managers are often those with the greatest expertise in solving social problems, especially when these are related to their core business activities. Ben and Jerry's Homemade, Inc., ice cream company makes this point a centerpiece of its corporate philosophy, using the company's need for an extensive network of suppliers as a way of stimulating entrepreneurism and economic activity among otherwise neglected or impoverished social groups.[5]

Whichever justification one employs, the corporate social responsibility position would seem to support Merck's undertaking the river blindness initiative. Drawing on this perspective, Dr. Vagelos can variously justify this effort as a form of payback for society's legal concessions to business corporations, as a step needed to forestall efforts to curb the enormous power of large pharmaceutical companies, or as a reasonable expenditure of resources to address a problem fully within the company's area of expertise. Whatever the justification, however, the corporate social responsibility position, despite its striking disagreement with Friedman's recommendation for conduct, shares one basic assumption with Friedman's view: that there is a tension between a corporation's economic and moral objectives. Both perspectives agree that, short or long term, there is a real, economic price to be paid in giving moral considerations a role in corporate decision-making. They only disagree over whether managers may morally authorize the payment of this price.

In contrast to both these views, the third perspective I want to sketch refuses to accept the claim that there is a tension between business ethics and corporate economic performance. This "business excellence" perspective holds that a corporation's commitment to the needs and welfare of all its stakeholders provides the essential underpinning of economic success.

Crucial to this view is an understanding of the complexity of the internal and external environments of most business organizations today. In a world of rapidly advancing technology and constant innovation in products and services, competitive advantage increasingly lies with those companies that can stay closest to the needs of their customers, clients, and other key stakeholders. Among other things, computer technology has opened up new ways of providing highly specialized products and services, combining the advantages of mass production with custom manufacture. In all areas, more sophisticated customers with an expanded array of firms to choose from have come to expect quality and commitment with every product or service they buy. As a consequence, all firms, even those in traditional manufacturing areas, find that they are becoming service companies for which the quality of client/customer relationships is a major factor in business success.

In other areas, like pharmaceuticals, high technology firms necessarily work in the complex new environment of government-university-industry technology transfer. In this world, independent researchers, government functionaries, and corporate managers become relatively indistinguishable, often moving from one professional location to another as their careers mature.

Meeting the needs of customers, clients, and other key outside stakeholders in turn requires complex changes within the company and in its relationship to the world. Customers increasingly are involved directly in corporate decision-making, often playing an active role in determining which products and services a company should develop. "Just in time manufacture" and other new inventory procedures require close and cooperative relationships with suppliers. In some cases, these relationships involve giving suppliers a substantial role in everything from product design to the billing and payment process. Having allies in the university or government offers major competitive advantage. Quality customer service and the reliance on sophisticated technologies place a premium on employee involvement and motivation. There is little room for a disgruntled or hostile workforce in a world where employees' creativity and enthusiasm, as well as their active response to the needs of customers, constitute the company's competitive edge.

According to William H. Davidow and Michael S. Malone, these developments have begun to fashion a new type of business organization they call "the virtual corporation."[6] The virtual corporation lacks many of the features we have come to associate with business firms. Relying heavily on information and information technology, it is often dedicated to the cost-effective production of mass-customized goods (or services). Instead of maintaining strict divisions between functional areas like design, marketing, manufacturing, and finance, it puts a premium on flexible, collaborative task forces that bring together employees from various organizational levels and with a variety of skills to accomplish specific projects. It replaces the older command-and-control hierarchies of the past, which assumed that only managers could make decisions and that employees could only take orders, with an emphasis on empowerment for people at all levels. This corporation is "virtual" in the sense that its interior and exterior lines and boundaries are not fixed. The corporation exists as an ever-changing idea, whose shape is adjustable to current needs and objectives.

Davidow and Malone observe that the virtual corporation maintains an environment of teamwork, one in which employees, management, customers, suppliers, and governments all work together to achieve common goals.[7] "Within this environment, corporate ethics is not just a matter of avoiding wrongdoing, nor is it merely a philanthropic afterthought to the primary process of pursuing profit. Instead, it is an essential component in the pursuit of business success and organizational excellence. In the words of Davidow and Malone, "the virtual corporation is built upon unprecedented levels of trust. Between the company and its suppliers and customers. Between management and labor. Between senior and middle management."[8]

Davidow and Malone point to the special importance of the ethical integrity of the firm's leadership and the culture this leadership helps create. "Ultimately," they say, "it comes to this: the chief executive of a virtual corporation must be able to trust employees in the firm to make responsible decisions. Those employees must in turn trust in the vision for the corporation as devised by the CEO."[9]

Many leading companies fit this description. They are characterized by consistently good to outstanding economic performance and high employee morale. These are the companies that consistently win accolades as being among the best places to work. Merck is one such company. A review of the total process that led it to develop the drug

Mectizan against river blindness provides an extended illustration of some of the dynamics that mark the changing environment of business today.

Using the Mectizan effort as an illustration, let us explore some of the business-oriented reasons that made this investment of corporate energy not just an ethically advisable add-on to Merck's profit-making activities, but an effort that was intimately bound up with the factors that continue to contribute to Merck's business success.

Of first importance is the recognition that, like many other virtual corporations, Merck's success is a function of the dedicated commitment of its educated (and often professional) staff of managers and employees. In the end, it was Dr. Vagelos's profound understanding of the forces driving his staff that was a key factor in his eventual decision to authorize the drug development program. Dr. Vagelos strongly believed that failure to pursue Dr. Campbell's hypothesis would demoralize Merck scientists who, as a group, were committed to their work, in part because they hoped to alleviate suffering. In this instance, therefore, the moral commitments of a staff of dedicated professionals were a major factor in Merck's decision-making.

Another way of putting this is to say that there is a deep human connection between Mectizan and the successful line of veterinary products from which it sprang. The same talent, energy, and enthusiasm that produced these products created pressure within the company to develop the river blindness drug. To encourage those energies on the one hand, while stifling them on the other, is a misguided approach to managing the staff of a virtual corporation. In view of this, we can see how naive it can be to urge companies to concentrate on maximizing profit and to ignore endeavors that engage the moral imagination of key stakeholders. This wrongly assumes that the things that inspire and motivate dedicated, creative, and skilled people have no relationship to the company's financial success.

The Mectizan effort also eventually contributed to reinforcing other key stakeholder relationships connected with Merck's long-term corporate success. One is the crucial relationship with the WHO. Earlier we noted that tension and mistrust had characterized WHO's relations with many large pharmaceutical companies. Once a decision was taken at Merck to proceed with the river blindness effort, it was put in the hands of Dr. Mohammed A. Aziz, senior director of clinical research at Merck. A tropical disease expert, Dr. Aziz was a native of the region now called Bangladesh and a former WHO scientist with experience in Sierra Leone. Because of this background, Dr. Aziz knew firsthand what river blindness meant for Third World peoples.

Under his leadership, WHO was enlisted in planning and executing the complex and difficult clinical trials of the drug. Despite occasional clashes of scientific judgment and institutional cultures, a close working relationship developed over time. When the first human tests of Mectizan were undertaken at the University of Dakar, Senegal, in February 1981, Merck supplied the drug, grants-in-aid for the studies, and the resources to apply for regulatory approval; WHO provided the scientists and research facilities.

At home in a university lab, a corporate office, or in field work for an international regulatory body, Dr. Aziz exemplifies the kind of employee crucial to the success of the virtual corporation. His ability to enlist WHO's commitment to the Mectizan effort also shows how important it is for the virtual corporation to negotiate the complex world of technology transfer, a world where today's regulators are tomorrow's research collaborators. In an increasingly global environment for U.S. pharmaceutical companies, what dollar price can be placed on the solid relationships Dr. Aziz helped establish between Merck and the World Health Organization?

To complicate the picture further, we might add the array of technical specialists, research scientists, and government regulators Merck drew into the efforts of the expert committee, the group eventually empowered to oversee the worldwide distribution program for Mectizan. Once again, we see how relevant are the permeable and shifting boundaries between the virtual corporation and its external constituencies. In a world of high-technology business, it is impossible to draw lines between university research centers, corporate laboratories, and the governmental bodies whose decisions affect both. By drawing committed people together from all these sectors to work on a project valued by all, Merck was able to forge bonds of respect between itself and people who one day might be important customers, another day regulators, and a third day developers of products or technology that Merck might commercialize.

To all this, we must finally add the citizens and leaders of the Third World nations plagued by river blindness. Merck has profited enormously from the goodwill earned by its early involvement in Japan. In the 1980s, Merck gave equipment that enabled China to develop a major vaccine program, hepatitis B, a leading cause of cancer in that country. At the time of this donation, it seemed that Merck's generosity would reap benefits only in the distant future. At this moment it seems less likely that this experience soon will be repeated in the desperately poor nations plagued by river blindness. But we should keep in mind that Merck's commitment to the welfare of its larger community of stakeholders is not reducible to a quid pro quo level of business calculation. It is primarily an ethical commitment, but one that has often benefited the company. In the words of George W. Merck, son of the company's founder, "We try never to forget that medicine is for the people. It is not for the profits. The profits follow, and if we have remembered that, they have never failed to appear. The better we have remembered it, the larger they have been."[10]

This dictum epitomizes the business excellence stance. It is a stance that fundamentally rejects the need for tension between business performance and business ethics. Instead, it focuses single-mindedly on decisions that foster trust, cooperation, and value for both a business and its key stakeholders, whether these decisions are merely the fulfillment of expected daily ethical obligations or, like the Mectizan initiative, the occasionally extraordinary effort to assemble corporate expertise and resources for the accomplishment of social goals.

Like Milton Friedman, this business excellence perspective recognizes that a manager's first duty is to meet corporate objectives. But unlike Friedman, it does not see ethical commitments as a distraction from these objectives but an essential part of their pursuit. Like the social responsibility position, it sees corporations as playing an important role in addressing social needs. But unlike this perspective, it refuses to see these activities as an obligation above and beyond managers' fiscal responsibilities; it sees them as the essential part of business.

As such, this business excellence view represents a real paradigm shift. It asks us to turn away from the endless debates over whether there can be too little or too much ethics in business, to the recognition that modern business is all about ethics. Within the framework of this perspective, the only important question is which, among its many ethically necessary activities, a company finds most relevant to its business success.

Notes

1. Most of the facts regarding Dr. Vagelos and Merck's decision-making are drawn from the cases "Merck and Company, Inc. (A) (B) (C) and (D)."

These cases were adapted by Stephanie Weiss from a monograph "Merck & Co., Inc.," by David Bollier, under the supervision of Kirk O. Hanson, president of the Business Enterprise Trust. The cases are available from the Business Enterprise Trust, 204 Junipero Sierra Boulevard, Stanford, CA 94305.

2. See *New York Times Magazine*, 13 September 1970, 32–33, 122, 124, 126.

3. See John R. Boatright, *Ethics and the Conduct of Business* (Englewood Cliffs, N.J.: Prentice Hall, 1993): 386.

4. See Keith Davis and Robert L. Blomstrom, *Business and Society: Environment and Responsibility*, 3d ed. (New York: McGraw-Hill, 1975): 50.

5. See Ben & Jerry's Homemade, Inc. Annual Report to the Securities and Exchange Commission. Form 10-K. 26 December 1992; Ben & Jerry's Homemade, Inc., 1992 Annual Report to Stockholders.

6. See Ronald L. Green, *The Virtual Corporation: Structuring and Revitalizing the Corporation for the 21st Century* (New York: HarperCollins, 1992).

7. Ibid.: 8.

8. Ibid.: 183.

9. Ibid.

10. See Merck & Company (A), op. cit.

4

The New Social Contract

James E. Post

When Robert Samuelson's provocative essay, "R.I.P., The Good Corporation," appeared in *Newsweek* magazine (July 5, 1993), it expressed the concern many of us share about the continuing power and vitality of the concept of corporate social responsibility. Samuelson said it this way: "We thought all companies could marry efficiency and social responsibility. We were wrong."

Recession and corporate restructuring have produced the layoffs of several million U.S. workers from jobs in the manufacturing and service sectors. In 1993 more than six hundred thousand jobs were lost; later figures are expected to equal or exceed that number. Since 1990, the United States has experienced a net loss of more than 3 million jobs, including the higher-paying professional and white-collar jobs. Cyclical and structural changes are eroding, sometimes shattering, old ways of doing business.

Passage of the North American Free Trade Agreement (NAFTA) and the general liberalization of trade threaten more jobs in industries that will be the focus of new competition. The continued restructuring of industries such as health care that foresee tougher competition in years ahead has exacerbated the problem by encouraging mergers, anticipatory downsizing, and preemptive restructuring. For example, in March 1994, Fleet Bank, one of New England's largest regional financial institutions, announced a workforce reduction plan that will eliminate five thousand jobs. The announcement coincided with the bank's achievement of record profits.[1] Actions of this sort are common nationwide, and in other industrialized nations, taken by companies that are trying to stay afloat in the new economy.[2]

49

The biggest casualty, however, may have been the idea that "good companies" have a better-than-average chance of achieving high levels of economic and social performance. Good corporations are not guaranteed their success in this new world. Samuelson's point, in fact, is that their very virtues may make these firms vulnerable to competitive pressure from others who spend less and care less; Darwin wins, virtue loses.

Samuelson's essay is cogent, pointed, and filled with just enough facts to make it a catalytic event for scholars and practitioners who believe in the need for corporate social responsibility (CSR). Advocates of socially responsible corporate behavior have rallied around the CSR flag, arguing that either Samuelson is wrong or that the problem is temporary. Regrettably, I believe Samuelson is right and that the problem of making corporate social responsibility work in the modern global economy is indeed a huge challenge.

The American corporation, and to some extent the global corporation, has been undergoing a responsibility transformation over the course of the last fifty years. Based on research that has been under way for nearly two years,[3] I believe the evidence clearly shows that the purpose of the modern corporation, especially the large corporation, has changed considerably since the end of World War II. The result is an institution that has evolved from one whose purpose was narrow into a one with broader purpose (or multiple purposes) whose viability is now challenged.[4] Global competition has eroded the ground on which Tyrannosaurus rex-like creatures such as IBM (Samuelson's principal example) once stood. CSR advocates may wish to create a Jurassic Park, a protected enclave in which good corporations might survive, but the rest of the world needs another kind of institution that is suited to, and suitable for the modern economy. I believe it is evolving before our very eyes.

The evidence I have been studying suggests the following points:

1. The core responsibility questions—to whom and for what is the modern corporation responsible?—continue to interest thoughtful executives as well as academic scholars. But the answers have changed considerably during the second half of this century.
2. Each decade has raised fundamental questions about the purpose and contribution of the large corporation to social well-being and national progress. The question is now asked of smaller corporations as well, and we are seeing a shift in thinking about the relative value of large and small enterprises to national economic health.

3. Most importantly, a new social contract is emerging in which the responsibility of corporations to employees, in particular, is evolving to a new stage of employer-employee relations. As this new social contract becomes more clearly and widely understood, the large corporation will face the most serious challenge to its social legitimacy since the 1930s.

The Social Contract

The proper relationship between corporations and U.S. society has been at issue for decades. However, unlike other nations where capitalism itself has been the issue, the United States has more often contended with the question of what kind of capitalism do we want?[5] For the most part, that question has focused debate on corporate performance—the results of the system—rather than on structure, size, or aggregations of wealth. (There is considerable antitrust literature about these issues, but it has rarely dominated the public debate about the "terms" of capitalism's corporate contract with society.) Ideology has not dominated the discourse about the social contract between business and society; performance is the currency that counts.

Several times since the end of World War II, however, the terms of the social contract have been subjected to a searching reexamination. Following riots in American cities in the late 1960s, President Lyndon Johnson called on the business community to play an active role in redressing urban ills and help create the "Great Society." Business did respond, with job training, minority purchasing programs, and dozens of other initiatives. The Kerner Commission Report, published in 1968, still rings with the sense of urgency felt by political, business, and community leaders of the time. This was the era in which many large corporations created urban affairs departments, a corporate community-relations function, and focused their charitable donations on the needs of the community. A signal event during this era was the Committee for Economic Development's report on the social contract between business and society. CED called for a model of three concentric circles, an inner circle of responsibilities that included quality products and services, jobs, and shareholder payments; a second circle of related responsibilities for environmental protection and safe working conditions; and an outer circle of responsibilities to participate in addressing community problems such as education, urban conditions, and the arts. This concentric circle model is important because it formalized, and CED legitimized, the notion that the social contract intrinsically set out noneconomic responsibilities. The idea still lives in the minds of many executives.

The 1980s produced another reassessment of the social contract when the Business Roundtable and its membership of chief executives from America's largest corporations addressed the issues of the social contract in clearly stated terms of economic and social performance. The abiding concern of the chief executives of these very large firms may have been to deflect criticism of corporate size, per se, or to state clearly the raison d'être of focused corporate involvement in the program articulated by the new Republican president of the United States, Ronald Reagan. During the 1980 presidential campaign, Reagan talked of the need for business to provide a "social safety-net" as government support for social programs was reduced. Leaders of the business community were concerned that such an expectation would vastly exceed the capacity of the private sector. Although the Roundtable statement was the subject of intense criticism from the political right as well as from the left, it served to update the responsibility of the corporate community. The subsequent attention given to private-sector initiatives, volunteerism, and public-private partnerships was very much attributable to a redefined sense of the social contract.

A searching reexamination again seems to be in process. This time, the stimulus is neither the problems of the cities (CED's outer circle) nor the pressures for the environment, workplace safety, or consumer protection (CED's middle circle). Today, the driving force behind the reexamination of the social contract is nothing less than the widespread sense that the large corporation has failed to perform its most basic social function—to provide good jobs to a substantial portion of the American workforce. If performance matters, the impact of corporate restructuring cannot help but fuel a public reassessment of the terms of the new social contract.

The "3 R's" of Modern Management

To read the cover stories of *Fortune, Business Week,* or other leading business journals during the past few years is to see a litany of prescriptive articles on the equivalent of the 3 R's for modern managers:

- *restructure* the organization to "rightsize";
- *reengineer* the corporation's critical business processes;
- *refocus* the business on customers, quality, and costs.

Together, these ideas have become a virtual new paradigm of what corporations must be if they are to survive and be successful in the 1990s. Beneath the 3 R's, of course, lies the bedrock of economic change. Many once-in-a-generation factors are at work. Global competitors, with different mixtures of labor and capital costs, have eliminated the protection that many companies once enjoyed from having only domestic competitors with comparable cost structures. Low inflation has eliminated the pricing flexibility that once enabled companies to pass cost increases quickly on to customers. The lowering of tariffs and other trade barriers on the international front, and the deregulation of protected industries on the domestic front, have encouraged further competition in manufacturing and services.

The results often have been positive for consumers, as product quality has risen and prices have remained steady or even declined. (An exception may be Philip Morris's dramatic drop in cigarette prices, an act that may well have made it easier for teenagers to start smoking.) Prices have been under continuous competitive pressure and few industries have been able to use price increases as the quick fix to generate improved earnings.

This positive picture turns mixed, however, when the fortunes of other stakeholders are examined. Shareholders have not seen improved dividends because earnings have been under pressure. (Capital gains have occurred, but stock prices are affected by expectations of future earnings.) Cost pressures on manufacturers of durable goods, for example, have translated into the exercise of leverage against others in the value-chain of suppliers, vendors, and subcontractors. Pressures cascade throughout the economic system. The Clinton Administration brought this principle to bear on the health-care industry, setting in motion forces that have produced major restructuring of the industry even in the absence of a national health-care plan.

Among all stakeholders, the pressures are most real and frightening for employees of corporations. The 3 R's of modern management seem little other than a dressed-up version of early twentieth century Taylorism to the millions of blue-collar and white-collar employees who have lost jobs in the past decade.

The restructuring/reengineering/refocusing paradigm has at least three troubling features from the point of view of both business and society. First, it forces managers to focus on short-term results. Consultants, chief executives, and experts all have seen examples of companies going through these three processes to cut costs that may not serve the company well in the long term. There is also a herd instinct that leads competitors to emulate what others have done simply because industry analysts expect the herd to follow the leader.

The second problem is that the costs of such actions are intense and are typically absorbed in the short term. This creates maximum pain for employees who are let go, psychic hardship for those who survive, and social costs for the communities affected by closing and reductions.

The third problem, and the one most vexing to participants and observers, is the resulting imbalance. The economic benefits are often equaled or outweighed by the economic costs that must be borne by employees, communities, and others in the commercial network. The benefits, however, are often shared among a quite narrow set of beneficiaries who have no greater ethical claim to those benefits than the dispossessed.

The Emerging Management Paradigm

The shortcomings of the 3R's approach are so apparent that concerned business leaders, union officials, employees, and managers have pressed to find a new way to live with the competitive realities of the 1990s. The heart of this challenge is to harmonize the economic and social roles of the corporation during an era of profound economic change. The objective is not, as one manager put it, "to humanize the executioner," but to reinvent ways of doing business with customers, suppliers, employees, and all stakeholders who responsibly address interdependencies within the social system.

Balancing Economic and Social Roles in the Workplace

As part of the Alfred P. Sloan Foundation research project, we have interviewed the senior human-resources executive at dozens of *Fortune 500* manufacturing and service firms. During telephone interviews, we explored how each company is responding to the challenge of balancing economic and social responsibilities in the modern era. Not surprisingly, most pointed to intensified global competition as the immediate cause of their company's need for change. A few pointed to deregulation and technology changes as causal factors.

The majority of respondents framed the shifting balance between economic and social responsibilities in terms of a changing social contract with employees. Barbara Altman, my collaborator in this research, succinctly summarized the interview data this way:

> There are rich data to support the proposition that the social contract between corporations and employees, as it existed in the past, is dead!

Interviewees repeatedly spoke of the old contract as being "shattered," "broken," or "eroded"; one said, "the fabric of the employee/employer relationship has been cut out." As understood by these and other interviewees, the old social contract is characterized by the following features:

- A paternalistic system where employees are taken care of, and where employees are part of the corporate family;
- Long-term employment security;
- Employees who feel entitled to their jobs so long as they perform at an adequate level and do nothing that violates company policy;
- An entitlement mentality that has spread to include benefits, career development, and advancement over time.

What is emerging is a transition that features the following critical shifts in employer/employee relations:

- Away from the expectation of a permanent relationship to one that is temporary or transitory in nature;
- Away from an atmosphere of entitlement to one of shared responsibility;
- Away from employees being part of an organizational family to one in which people are, as one interviewee said, "just one factor in production."

What these executives see emerging is a workplace in which the social contract is quite different from that which has prevailed for much of the past three decades.

56 James E. Post

The burden of responsibility is shifting from the corporation to the employee. Life-long security will disappear, and employees will work for at least several employers in the course of a career. Employees also will bear a larger portion of financial responsibility for benefits such as health care and retirement.

Security no longer will be predicated on seniority but on performance. Pay-for-performance systems have already taken root in many of these companies, and many of the interviewees expect the phenomenon to become more widespread in the near future. There was a significant level of concern expressed that even superior performance was not enough to guarantee retention and that this was carrying things "too far." Indeed, the premise that anyone's job is secure, whatever their performance, may be the greatest casualty in the new social contract. Doubts are openly expressed as to whether a performance-based system will meet the tests of fairness and equity that have prevailed in the American workplace for decades.

With security diminished, a premium will be placed on employability. Employers and employees, therefore, are beginning to share responsibility for the continuing training, development, and broadening of an employee's ability to be flexible and adaptive. Ultimately, the social contract that seems to be evolving in these *Fortune 500* firms is based on notions of "mutual benefit," "exchange," and "self-interest." A number of interviewees expressed deep concern that "the pendulum is swinging too far" toward the economic side of relations between the corporation and employees. When employees view their relationship to the corporation only in economic terms, there is a downside for both parties. Illness, disability, and family issues inevitably touch people over time. Pay-for-performance systems that fail to recognize these realities will penalize the innocent for being normal human beings. Conversely, some respondents noted the radical shift occurring among the hard-bitten survivors of recent corporate changes: "The mentality now is, 'I'm the customer, this is a fair exchange, and I am going to do what is best for my family and my economic circumstances.' " Cynicism is certainly on the rise in many of these companies.

While these trends translate to a less humanized work environment in some companies, respondents also pointed to some counterevidence such as diversity programs, flexible hours, on-site day-care programs, and other work/family initiatives. These too are elements of the new social contract and suggest that for those people who are of value to the company, efforts will be made to accommodate the requirements of more complex family, social, and economic demands. Still, on balance, the overwhelming thrust of comments from those on the front lines of making the new social contract work in what have traditionally been our good corporations underscores the seriousness of the move away from the old social contract.

Shifting Roles in the Community

The new social contract also affects the communities in which companies do business. Most prominent is a sharpened focus on activities that serve the corporation's needs, as well as the needs of the community. This pattern has been emerging for at least a decade, but has accelerated as more rigorous internal standards are used to assess charitable contributions. One senior manager described his company's current focus this way:

> What is different is that (our company) is looking for areas of common benefit. Still, we only do things that have a bottom-line impact. There has to be a *congruence* between the social and economic. We consciously do not get involved in national efforts . . . we don't see the payback [emphasis added].

The second significant shift in community involvement relates to the beneficiaries of philanthropic contributions. Business support for the arts, for example, appears to be in decline because it fails the congruence test for many firms. On the other hand, corporate leaders appear to have bought the argument that a capable workforce is a well-educated workforce, and that to the extent that young people are not well-educated, they cannot be contributors to the national economy of the future. Recent Conference Board studies suggest that corporate contributions are being refocused to kindergarten through twelfth-grade education and away from the arts and other services.[6] Moreover, the range of education-reform initiatives has broadened to include narrow adopt-a-school programs to long-term systemic reform efforts as in Kentucky, Connecticut, and Missouri. In Louisiana, for example, Union Carbide has entered into a ten-year agreement to provide financial and human support to Lake Charles Parish school district to meet national education goals. The long-term nature of this commitment to a school district in which many of the company's employees live meets both congruence and high-priority community need criteria.

Third, companies continue to find new ways to encourage and support voluntary activities of employees in community projects. This pattern which began in the 1980s has grown in the number, variety, and range of corporate-supported voluntary programs now occurring in communities. The spate of recent earthquake, hurricane, and flood disasters has engaged companies much more deeply in the job of community rebuilding. Ironically, the success of some community economic-development efforts has led activists and experts to favor community-based, rather than company- or industry-based programs to deal with economic dislocation. The message from the most vigorous advocates is for government to stop subsidizing corporate economic strategies and instead subsidize community economic strategies.

Environmental Responsibility

The third component of the new social contract is the nearly universal commitment to address environmental effects of business activity. The steady growth of environmental law and regulation in the United States and other nations, plus the development of a global environmental -activist movement, have pressured corporations not only to adjust their operations but to rethink and recreate business strategies in ways that will protect and enhance natural resources.

The creation of global environmental policy regimes (e.g., the Montreal Protocol to protect stratospheric ozone, the biodiversity treaty, and the global climate-change agreement), plus the negotiation of environmental NAFTA side agreements and appropriate General Agreement on Tariffs and Trade (GATT) provisions all point to a global consensus that the Earth itself is a legitimate corporate stakeholder.

Corporate environmental responsibility has become a well-established part of the social contract for firms in some industries. Industries such as chemical, petroleum, pulp and paper, and mining and metals have adopted principles such as cradle-to-grave liability, resource stewardship, and sustainable use of natural resources. To be sure, some global competitors practice the principles irregularly, but the trend seems tilted in the direction of higher standards of environmental protection.

Within companies, extensive organizational-change programs are occurring. Business units are working more closely with environmental, health, and safety staffs to ensure that a company's products meet current and emerging environmental expectations. In many companies serious efforts are under way to design new generations of products (refrigerators, computers, packaging) that will meet environmental best-practice standards for recyclable materials, energy efficiency, and reduced toxins.

The nearly universal attention being given to environmental issues among manufacturing companies doing business in nations with high standards (e.g., United States, Germany) points toward an important element of what societies expect and companies provide. To the extent that many of these commitments are voluntary, they are evidence that corporate values reinforce the need the public feels for ecological responsibility.

What Is New about the New Social Contract?

The new social contract is really an evolving contract, rooted in changing relationships between the corporation, the community, people, and the natural environment. In terms of models that have emerged at other times, it seems clear that the concentric-circles model proposed by the Committee for Economic Development in the 1970s still has conceptual credibility for corporate executives who were barely beginning their careers twenty years ago. At a 1994 seminar involving seventy-five senior experts in public affairs, community affairs, and government relations, more than half endorsed the structure of the CED model. Still, when asked to describe what is different about the social contract of the 1990s, the majority responded that the inner circle (involving customers and employees) has changed the most. This group, which might have been expected to emphasize stakeholders more obviously connected with their daily political and community agendas, was very clear about the primacy of the core economic relationships.

The realities we confront daily powerfully shape the way we view the world and our place in it. In the late 1960s American cities burned, and the corporation was drawn into urban policy. In the 1980s the social safety net of government support was being recast, and the corporation was drawn into volunteerism. In the 1990s the workplace is being reshaped, industrial ecology is emerging as a vital management discipline, and the systemic relationship between the corporation and the community is being refocused in terms of economic growth.

There are reasons for a cautious optimism about the evolution of the new social contract. First, the mental and physical energies of thousands of U.S. workers are being engaged in the effort to create organizations that can function in economically and socially sustainable ways. In interviews with business chief executives, administrators in human resources, public affairs, and community relations, and general managers, usually we close by asking the respondents whether they are fundamentally optimistic or pessimistic about their company, their industry, and the United States. The results are startling: Fewer than one in ten is pessimistic about their company, their industry, or their country. In fact, most are very positive about their company's outlook over the next five years; they seem to believe the hard work of reshaping their organizations will pay off in economic and human terms. No doubt a number of psychological theories might explain this phenomenon. My sense is that these people are actually gratified to see problems addressed, old obstacles removed, and better products offered for sale.

There are also other reasons for optimism. The Clinton Administration has placed Secretary of Labor Robert Reich in the front line of the effort to transform the economy into one that is free of the rigidities associated with the old social contract. Reich's irrepressible salesmanship for education, skill improvement, and continuous retraining has gained the attention and qualified support of many in the business community. Despite its many problems, the Clinton Administration has shown hopeful signs of coordinating labor, education, and trade policies around these issues.

Perhaps the most important source of hope are the continuing efforts to *reinvent* the good corporation. Throughout this country are entrepreneurs, managers, and employees who are creating a new kind of good corporation. Two sets of ideas seem to be emerging, one from the community of large, previously successful good corporations, and the other from smaller, more entrepreneurial companies. The former include the IBMs of the business community, still filled with executives who cling to the belief that it is possible to achieve both economic and social goals. The trade-offs are more difficult, the choices more painful, but the possibility of creative leveraging still exists. Among these firms, three operating principles stand out:

- Share with everyone the realities facing the business.
- Respect people in the organization, as well as customers, suppliers, and shareholders. This reinforces the movement away from paternalism.
- Communicate more effectively with everyone about where the company is, where it is going, and how it is going to get there.

Among the smaller, more entrepreneurial firms are companies that often belong to groups like the Social Venture Network, Businesses for Social Responsibility, or Vermont Businesses for Social Responsibility. They tend to see the achievement of social and economic goals as part of a unified strategy, not separate sets of performance objectives. For example:

- Tom Chappell, president of Tom's of Maine, has written a new book, *The Soul of a Business: Managing for Profit and the Common Good* (Bantam, 1994), that makes his case for a business that has values that integrate the concerns of customers, employees, owners, the community, and the environment. The company has prospered in economic and social terms, and Chappell argues that there are no inherent reasons for the model not to be workable in larger, more complex organizations.
- Paul Hawken, California entrepreneur and co-founder of Smith & Hawken, has also written a new book, *The Ecology of Commerce* (Harper Business, 1994) that offers a comprehensive system for practices that create truly sustainable development.
- Bill Haney, a Massachusetts entrepreneur, has joined with others to form a company called Molten Metal Technology that uses a catalytic extraction process to separate toxic chemicals into their elemental components. The result is an elemental recycling technology that is being tried in chemical cleanups in the United States and abroad. This company is being built on technology and on values that respect all the company's stakeholders. These ideas, plus a well-educated and committed community of employees, investors, and advisors, have made Molten Metal Technology one of the most promising start-up firms in the entire environmental field.

These companies are not equal to the large corporations that have characterized U.S. economic prowess in the twentieth century. Still, McDonald's, Federal Express, and Microsoft were also fledgling enterprises just a few decades ago. Their success is attributable, in part, to the fit they created between emerging social values and the strategic direction in which they sought to take their businesses. There are very good reasons to believe the companies that are learning how to integrate responsibilities to customers, employees, communities, and the environment into a seamless cloth are those that will define the new social contract.

The good corporation we knew from the 1970s and 1980s may indeed be dead. The global economy may be predetermining that corporate life will become more Hobbesian ("nasty, brutish, and short") for the people involved, and more Darwinian for the institutions. That is the pessimists' view.

I believe, however, that we are seeing the good corporation being reinvented in the 1990s as we have seen it reinvented in the past. New ideas continue to emerge; new voices set forth the views. Experiments are under way.[7] The meaning of corporate responsibility continues to be redefined in the words and actions of the millions of entrepreneurs, executives, and employees who struggle with the challenge of reconciling and integrating economic and social values each day.

The good corporation, new social contract, and corporate responsibility are conceptual extensions of our need to articulate principles of conduct among people and organizations. Like "competitive advantage," "value-chain" or "corporate strategy," they are a conceptual shorthand for discussing the complex task of building social and economic success day by day, relationship by relationship.

They are concepts that matter, but what is more important is the way individuals—and the organizations they create—behave toward one another. The good corporation stood for one set of principles and ideals; its new, reinvented form will do the same for different principles. The new social contract is, in the end, a way of expressing the responsibility that each of us bears to live a life of honor, integrity, and merit in our relationships with others and in all we do.

Notes

Support for this research was provided by a grant to Boston University from the Alfred P. Sloan Foundation's Studies of the Modern Corporation research program. The views expressed are solely those of the author.

1. See the *Boston Globe*, 7 March 1994, 1; *Wall Street Journal*, 10 March 1994, A1.

2. See Thomas Friedman, "World's Big Economies Turn to the Jobs Issue," *New York Times*, 14 March 1994, D1, D6.

3. The project is entitled "The Changing Purpose of the American Corporation" and is supported by a grant from the Alfred P. Sloan Foundation's Studies of The Modern Corporation research program.

4. There is considerable disagreement as to whether the corporation has assumed more purposes (i.e., economic goals plus noneconomic goals) or whether economic and noneconomic goals are being integrated into overarch-

ing or superordinate goals. The evidence suggests that individual firms and managers adopt one or the other of these views, but not both.

5. This question remains timely as the nations of Eastern Europe struggle with the redefinition of their economies. Alan Blinder, now a member of the Council of Economic Advisors, has urged that leaders of these nations consider the performance differences between German, U.S., and Japanese forms of capitalism.

6. See Maria Buenaventura, *Corporate Contributions, 1992*, The Conference Board, Report 1054–94-RR, 1993.

7. One experiment of note is the effort of Rhino Foods, a small food producer in Vermont. When faced with a layoff decision, management found an alternative: It placed a number of its employees with other firms on a loan or "internship" basis. Rhino paid the benefits, while the firms that needed extra help to meet seasonal production peaks paid hourly wages. The creation and use of such a community network is an innovation now being tried in other parts of the United States.

5

The International Economic Order Revisited: Are We Better Off Today?

Howard F. Rosen

1994 marked the fiftieth anniversary of the Bretton Woods Conference at which the current international economic system was established. The anniversary provides an opportunity to analyze how far the world economy has come and how effective the institutions that grew from the conference have been over the last fifty years.

On the whole, the world economy has experienced considerable growth since that meeting in New Hampshire. Many nations have moved from poor to rich; most economic disasters have been limited, contained, and short-lived. Against this backdrop, however, deep pockets of poverty and economic hardship remain around the world.

The U.S. economy has experienced two important trends over this period. First, the size of the economy has grown geometrically, from about $200 billion in 1945 to almost $7 trillion in 1994. After taking inflation into account, the U.S. economy has multiplied five-fold over the last fifty years—growing at an average of 2.6 percent annually. Second, the U.S. economy has become more integrated into the world economy. In 1945 exports and imports of goods and services accounted for 7 percent of Gross National Product (GNP). By 1994 this share rose to almost 23 percent of GNP. Many other countries, both industrialized and developing, have also experienced rapid economic growth and increased integration into a single world economy. The result is that the world economy has become more interdependent, with flows of goods, money, and people occurring within and between nations at a faster pace today than in the past.

Globalization has resulted in increased competition both within the United States and around the world. New countries are producing new products and are entering new markets every day. This increased exposure to competition has led some to argue that business can no longer maintain its commitment to certain traditions and values. The theme of this conference reflects this question: given the new global economic realities, can corporations still afford to act socially responsibly while maintaining their positions in world markets? I believe the answer to this question is yes.

Those who believe the answer is no, hold that increased globalization requires international harmonization of practices, including those aimed at social responsibility, in order to remain competitive. This view is based on the argument that a firm may incur higher operating costs by abiding by regulations or practices not followed by other firms, particularly in other countries. If a firm passes on these higher costs through higher prices, holding everything else constant, it will most likely lose market share, as people switch to comparable yet cheaper products made by firms in other countries. Alternatively, a firm may choose to absorb these higher costs by reducing profits. Since prices would remain the same in this case, no change in market penetration would be expected, yet the firm may find it harder to raise capital, and its owners may be reluctant to continue operating.

The economic costs of continued commitment to "socially responsible" principles have been receiving more attention as global integration and competition have intensified. This paper sets out a model to analyze developments in the world economy over the last fifty years from an ethical perspective and looks at the impact these developments have had on the social consciousness of countries and firms.

A Model of Ethics to Evaluate Developments in the World Economy

The model separates ethical considerations into two classes: ethical behaviors and ethical outcomes. An ethical behavior is an action that conforms to some normative standard, like antidiscrimination in the workplace. An ethical outcome reflects some sense of social justice, like an equitable distribution of income. Together, they look at how one does something and the consequences of one's actions.

In some cases the distinction between behavior and outcome may be small or nonexistent, and there will usually be some cross-relationship between the two. Ethical behaviors can contribute to ethical outcomes, and ethical outcomes may require ethical behaviors. The important thing is that either one may be necessary for the other to occur, but neither is sufficient to insure the other's occurrence. An ethical outcome does not mean that there has been ethical behavior, and ethical behavior in itself will not always lead to an ethical outcome. In other words, doing good does not always result in getting good.

Ethical Behavior

Out of the ashes of World War II, the victorious powers established several institutions based on rules of behavior, agreed upon by all the members, aimed at restoring international harmony and economic prosperity. These rules were founded on three principles—multilateralism, reciprocity, and nondiscrimination. "Multilateralism" suggests decisions are taken by the group for the good of the group. "Reciprocity" basically reflects the golden rule to do unto others as you would have them do unto you. "Nondiscrimination" is the concept of a collective umbrella—those economies under the umbrella are expected to receive equal treatment from the others, which may differ from how they treat those economies not under the umbrella. The development of these institutions and international adherence to these rules set the context for an economic system based on ethical behavior.

Three major institutions established following World War II are the International Monetary Fund (IMF), the World Bank, and the General Agreement on Tariffs and Trade (GATT). (Numerous other institutions were established, including the entire network of United Nations organizations. Many of these organizations share these three principles.) The IMF sets standards for balance of payments and international financial flows, including to some extent, exchange-rate policies. The World Bank monitors development assistance and provides technical and financial project support. GATT brings together member countries to develop and agree upon rules to manage and monitor international trade and serves as a mechanism for countries to bring complaints against and seek compensation from other countries. Of these three organizations, GATT is most heavily dependent on a set of commonly agreed upon rules of behavior.

Ethical Outcomes

As mentioned above, ethical behavior alone does not necessarily lead to an outcome that is based on some sense of economic justice or fairness. For example, income distribution can be judged according to an individual's contribution to the creation of wealth, or to some equitable distribution, independent of one's contribution. This might include distributing an equal share of the additional wealth to each participant, or it may use the newfound wealth to attempt to close the gap between individuals' economic well-being. All of the industrialized countries, including the United States, have experienced considerable economic growth and wealth creation over the last fifty years. In fact, the amount of wealth created during this time is unparalleled in world history. Unfortunately, the industrialized countries have not performed as well in distributing this wealth to their citizens and improving their welfare. In fact, in some cases the distribution of income, a proxy for economic welfare, is not better but worse today than it was fifty years ago in spite of this economic growth.

One of the objectives of the victorious powers after World War II was to ensure the hard-won peace through economic prosperity. A commonly held belief was that economic growth would reduce tensions between countries and build economic bridges that would lessen the possibility of wars. Toward that end, the United States embarked on an aggressive development campaign to help restore the economies destroyed by the war. This strategy was successful, and the economies of Germany and Japan, near collapse at the end of the war, experienced rapid growth over the last fifty years. Although this model has seemed to work well in the cases of Europe and the Far East, it has been less effective in Africa, Latin America, and the Middle East.

Increased global competition is also evident in changes in international trade. The challenge of increased competition, in terms of opening up the economy to global trade, is to develop a common set of norms under which all economies can maximize their returns from trading with one another. Once there is agreement on the need for a common set of norms, the next challenge is to avoid basing these norms on the lowest common denominator. This challenge intensifies as the circle of people included in this community grows. The next challenge is to secure compliance by all parties. This has been quite difficult in the post-war period. GATT has been relatively successful in forging a common set of rules on traditional behavioral issues such as reducing tariff and nontariff barriers, but it has not been as successful in getting compliance on more sensitive issues, such as government subsidies and intellectual property rights.

The framers of the Bretton Woods system operated under the assumption that increased flows of goods and money would result in economic growth, which in turn would improve individual economic well-being. Furthermore, they held that improved economic conditions would contribute to political and social stability, thereby reinforcing the system. In spite of the good intentions of those who shaped the system by founding it on principles of fairness, the Bretton Woods system has not yielded a clearly just outcome. What resulted may not have been directly caused by the Bretton Woods system, but rather by breakdowns in national economic systems. On the other hand, the Bretton Woods system may be guilty of tolerating such an outcome.

The U.S. Economy Over the Last Fifty Years

Economic developments in the United States over the last fifty years can be divided almost equally into two periods: the period prior to 1973 and the period following 1973. During the first thirty years or so after World War II, the U.S. economy experienced strong growth, low inflation, and low unemployment. Between 1950 and 1973, output grew on average by 3.8 percent annually. This increase in economic activity was reflected in improvements in family incomes. Between 1950 and 1973, the median family income grew on average by about 3.7 percent annually (Fig. 1). The model seemed to be working: increased liberalization resulted in more economic output, thereby making individuals better off.

This apparent relationship between economic growth and improvements in family income seems to have broken down in 1973. Much happened in 1973, e.g., the oil embargo which set off inflationary pressures and contributed to a world recession, but it is still not clear why the world economy has not been able to return to higher rates of growth and lower rates of unemployment since then.

Between 1973 and 1994, the Gross Domestic Product (GDP) grew on average by 2.5 percent annually. Some economists suggest that the decline in the average growth rate may have been a response to unusually high growth rates following World War II. More importantly, the relationship between aggregate growth and individual economic well-being seems to have shattered in 1973. Over the last twenty years median family income has been stagnant in spite of moderate economic growth. In fact, the median family income in 1994 is not much different from its level in 1973, after adjusting for inflation.

Something profound apparently has taken place in the U.S. economy. Over the last two decades the economy has shown a strong

Fig. 5.1. Real GDP and Median Family Incomes.

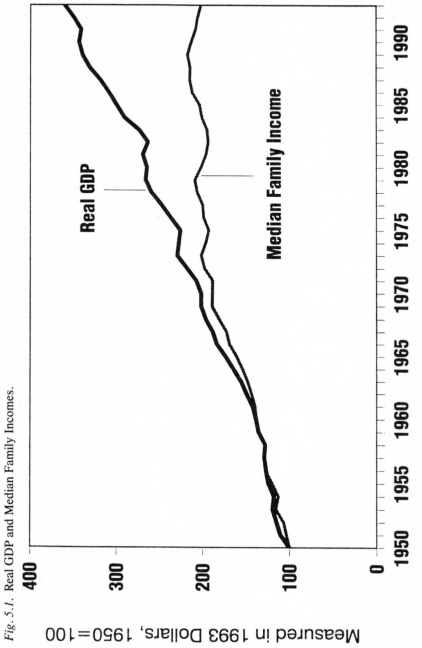

Source: Department of Commerce.

record of creating wealth, as indicated by the growth of economic output, yet individual economic welfare, measured by median family income, has not performed as well. Wealth creation alone in this economy over the last several years has not in itself resulted in improvement in individual economic welfare.

The primary mechanism for transferring the economy's aggregate wealth into improving individual welfare is through the labor market. Here also are two important developments. Employment grew at an average rate of 2 percent a year between 1974 and 1993, creating over 33 million jobs over the last twenty years (Fig. 2). At the same time, real wages fell on average by about half a percent a year, and were $0.73 per hour lower in 1993 than in 1974. The economy has experienced strong employment growth over the last two decades, stronger, in fact, than any other industrialized country. However, wages have been falling.

Real average weekly earnings in the United States, which take both wages and hours worked into account, were about $290 (in 1982 dollars) per week between 1959 and 1973. Twenty years later, by 1993, average weekly earnings have declined to about $255 (in 1982 dollars), reflecting declines in real hourly earnings and hours worked. This amounts to a $1,800 decline in annual take-home income.

Some economists have pointed to lower productivity growth during this period as an explanation for these lower wages. Economic theory suggests that workers are paid according to their marginal product, which is measured by their unit of output per hour worked, or labor productivity. Between 1950 and 1973, productivity growth averaged 2.5 percent annually. Since 1974, productivity has grown at an average annual rate of less than 1 percent, less than half the rate of the previous twenty years (Fig. 3). The slowdown in productivity growth tracks the decline in real compensation growth over the same period. Between 1950 and 1973, real compensation (wages and benefits) grew at an average annual rate of 2.75 percent. Over the last twenty years, real compensation was basically flat, growing on average by less than .5 percent per year.

In addition to the gap between the growth in productivity and increases in real compensation, there is a gap between compensation and wages. Over the last twenty years the share of benefits in total compensation has been growing due to the growth in pensions, health-care costs, and payroll taxes. Since poor productivity growth has placed downward pressure on total compensation, employers have been forced to pass some of the increased benefit costs onto workers

Average Weekly Earnings (1982 dollars)

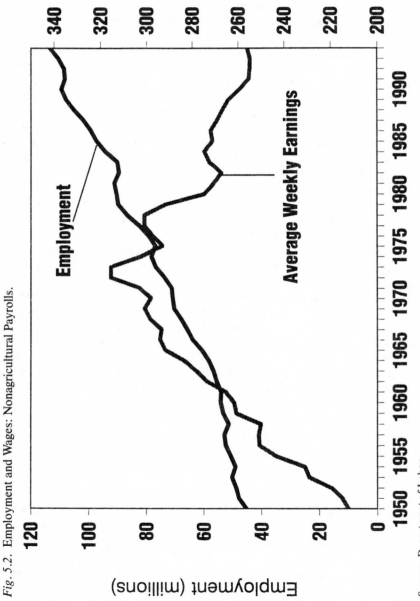

Fig. 5.2. Employment and Wages: Nonagricultural Payrolls.

Source: Department of Labor.

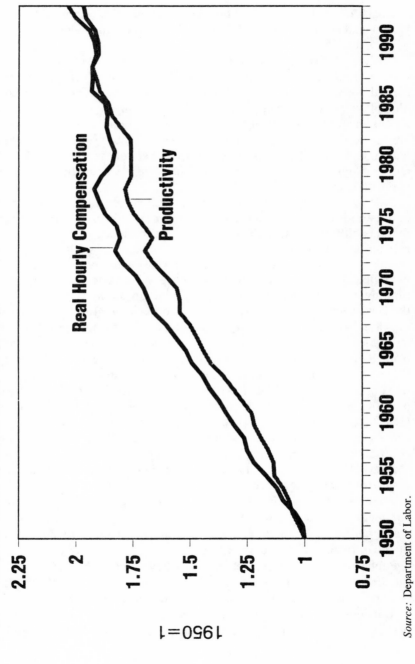

Fig. 5.3. Changes in Productivity and Real Hourly Compensation.

Source: Department of Labor.

through lower wages. Thus, the combination of lower productivity growth and rising benefit costs has resulted in reducing living standards in the United States.

Changes in the structure of the American labor market over the last twenty years help explain some of the decline in productivity growth over the same period. In 1973, over 20 million Americans were employed in manufacturing industries, constituting a quarter of total employment. Two-thirds of the workforce, or 52 million workers, were employed in the service sector. By 1993 manufacturing employment had fallen to 18 million workers, only 16 percent of the total workforce, and employment in the service sector had risen to 87 million workers, almost 80 percent of the total workforce.

Productivity growth in the service sector has traditionally been understood to be lower than in manufacturing industries. One reason for this difference is believed to be the difficulties in accurately measuring productivity in the service sector. Recent studies, employing new methodologies, suggest that service-sector productivity may in fact be higher than most analysts believe. Nonetheless, one explanation given for the decline in economy-wide productivity growth over the last twenty years has been the shift from manufacturing to service-sector jobs, from traditionally high productivity to low productivity industries. Productivity growth has two major sources. It can result from industrial restructuring, including shedding workers, assuming that output remains at least constant. Much of manufacturing productivity growth since 1973 can be traced to the decline in employment over the same period. Productivity growth at the expense of employment can produce an outcome in which incomes of some workers actually rise, while incomes for other workers fall. This outcome would contribute to a deterioration in the distribution of income.

Alternatively, productivity growth together with employment can result from increased investment in human and physical capital, improving worker skills, introducing new technologies, and modernizing equipment. Thus, one way to increase productivity growth, employment, and income simultaneously is through a strategy of improving the quantity and quality of investment.

Public investment (financed through government expenditures) is the first link in this chain. Public investment in education and training, research and development, and public infrastructure encourages private investment in job-creating, income-producing activities. In 1965 the federal government devoted 25 percent of its nondefense expenditures to public investment in these three areas (Fig. 4). Thirty years later, the share of nondefense expenditures devoted to public investment has fallen by half. As a percentage of GDP, public investment has fallen from 2.5 percent to 1.9 percent over the last twenty years, representing a decline of approximately $40 billion (Fig. 5). Private investment, after taking depreciation into account, has been relatively flat during this same period. The real estate boom in the 1980s caused a temporary increase in investment in structures. Investment in equipment, which serves as a measure of job-related investment, has been constant throughout much of the last thirty years. The lack of investment has contributed to the economy's poor performance in productivity growth. While other countries have been learning how to compete, the United States has been underinvesting in new technologies and equipment and in building workers' skills. This has narrowed the gap between the United States and the rest of the world, and has caused many U.S. industries, which traditionally dominated world markets, to face severe competition from abroad. It is as if the United States were in a race against other countries, and the United States were running in place, while others pick up momentum. This is not a good strategy for winning races or raising living standards in a competitive environment.

Public and private saving are necessary to finance investment. Low private saving rates and large fiscal deficits (public dissaving) in the United States, have significantly reduced the amount of capital available for investment. In the 1960s and 1970s the net national saving rate, private saving less government deficits, was about 8 to 9 percent of net national product (Fig. 6). Approximately three-fourths of private saving is currently financing government budget deficits, leaving less than 2 percent of net national product to invest in job-creating productive activities.

The decline in national saving also has ramifications for America's economic role in the world economy. The decline in private saving, coupled with the increase in public dissaving, has enlarged the gap between saving and investment in the United States. This gap has resulted in growing current account and merchandise trade deficits. The United States accumulated over $1 trillion in trade deficits in the 1980s and has already accumulated another half trillion dollars in the first four years of the 1990s. This pressure on the trading sector has contributed to the downward pressures on jobs and income in the economy more generally. The decline in national saving can be offset by borrowing from abroad. The United States is already the world's

Fig. 5.4. Federal Non-Defense Investment as a Percentage of Non-Defense Outlays.

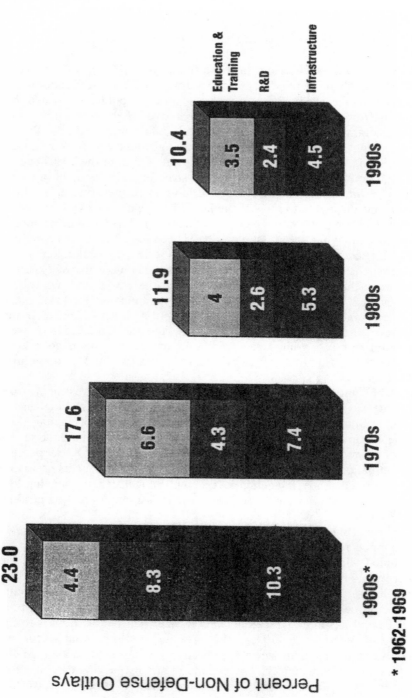

Source: Office of Management and Budget.

Fig. 5.5 Federal Non-Defense Investment as a Percentage of GDP.

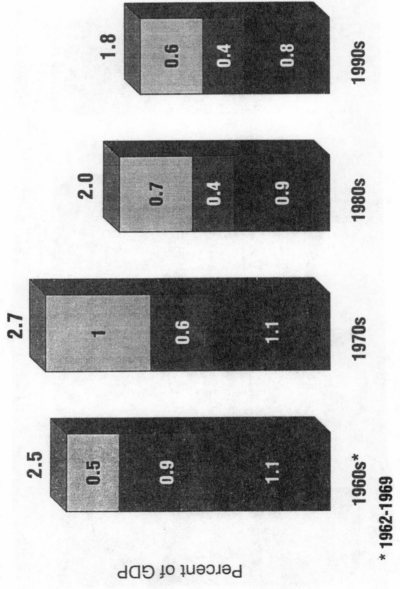

Percent of GDP

2.5
0.5
0.9
1.1
1960s*

2.7
1
0.6
1.1
1970s

2.0
0.7
0.4
0.9
1980s

1.8
0.6
0.4
0.8
1990s

* 1962-1969

Source: Office of Management and Budget.

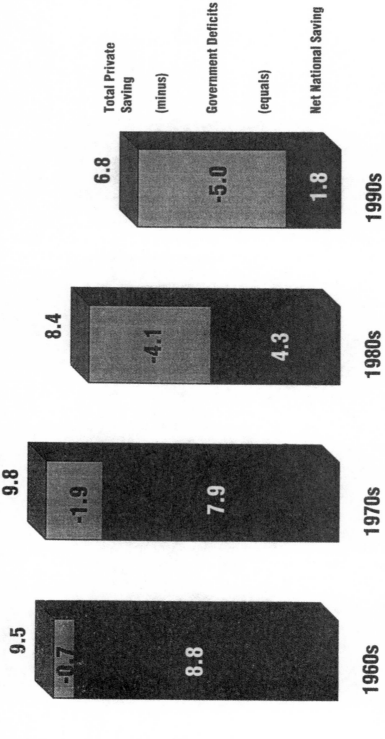

Fig. 5.6. U.S. National Savings as a Percentage of Net National Product.

Source: Department of Commerce.

Percent of Net National Product

largest debtor country and cannot prudently continue to depend on foreign capital. In addition, reliance on foreign capital reduces our control over our own economy. We should encourage the unincumbered flow of capital to where it is needed, but this should not lead to dependence on foreign capital.

The shortage of savings in the United States has contributed to the increase in public and private debt (Fig. 7). Three important developments relate to the increase in debt in the U.S. economy. First, total debt in the United States is higher today than it was fifty years ago, when the nation was financing World War II. Second, traditionally, increases in private debt were usually offset by declines in public debt, and vice versa. This rule broke down in the 1980s when there was a run-up in all three types of debt—business, government, and household. Third, in the 1990s, some reduction has occurred in the total amount of outstanding debt, but it has come primarily in business debt. This is ironic, since increased business debt can be the result of expanded private investment, which should be encouraged. These changes in saving and investment patterns over the last twenty years have contributed to a stagnation in U.S. living standards, although many would prefer to attribute this stagnation to increased competition from abroad. Clearly, increased international competition has placed more pressure on workers and business in the U.S. economy. It also appears that changes in saving and investment patterns, instead of helping resist these pressures, have actually exacerbated them.

Conclusion

The past fifty years have brought a significant increase in wealth around the world. This increase in wealth, though, has not necessarily resulted in an improvement in individual economic well-being. In the case of the United States, the world's largest economy, the economy has grown fivefold over the last fifty years, yet income for the median family has been stagnant for the past twenty years.

The U.S. economy has become more integrated into the world economy since World War II, which has been both a blessing and a curse. One the one hand, American products face more competition from abroad than ever before. However, the potential market for U.S. products has grown exponentially. Governments have assisted this process of integration by agreeing to remove barriers to trade and

Fig. 5.7. Level of Composition of U.S. Debt as a Percentage of GDP.

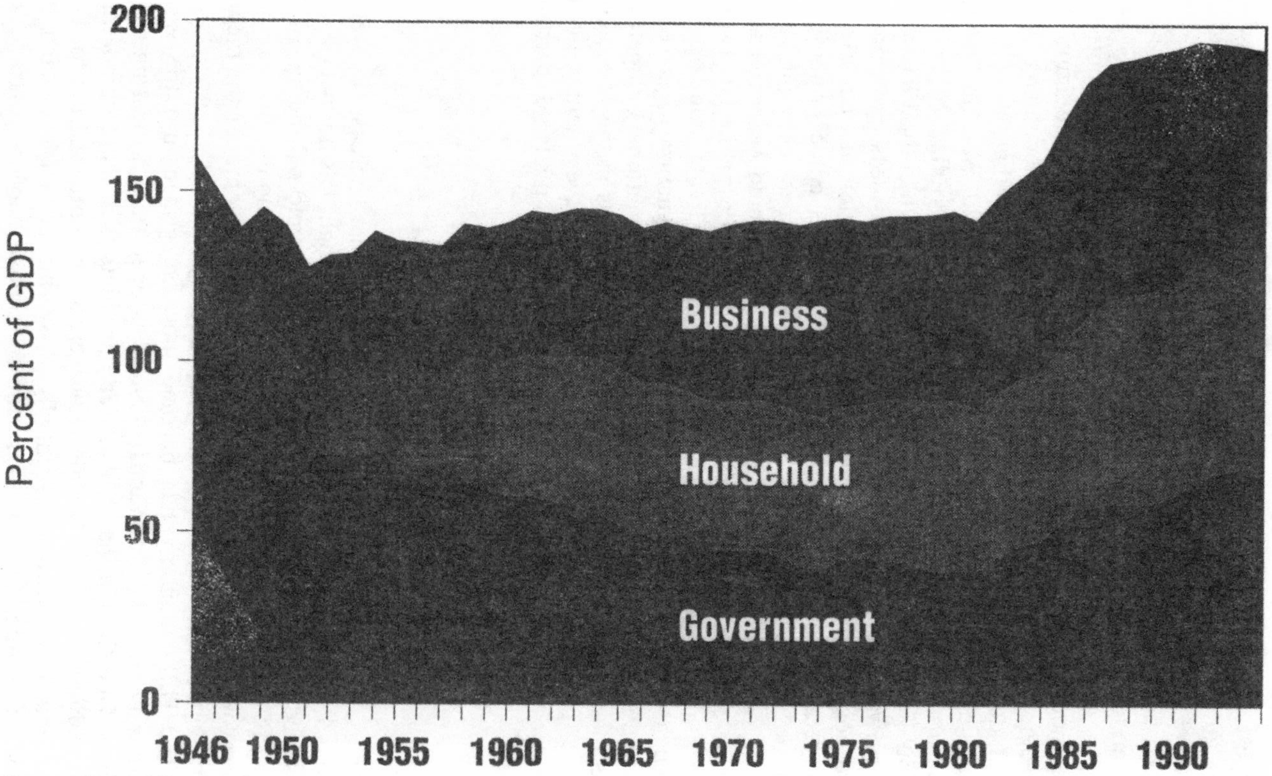

Source: Federal Reserve System.

accepting a common set of norms to regulate economic exchanges between countries.

The motivation behind encouraging more international trade in goods and services is that it should result in raising living standards for *all* the participants. Although the lack of existing statistics makes it hard to accurately measure the success in achieving this goal, evidence does suggest that this has not been the case. In spite of increased liberalization, which has resulted in an enormous creation of wealth, not all individuals benefited from these developments. This suggests that economic liberalization (an ethical behavior according to the model outlined above), although a noble goal in and of itself, may not *necessarily* result in higher living standards for all, or even most participants (an ethical outcome). In the case of the United States, shifts on economic priorities, primarily expressed in saving and investment patterns, have contributed to a gap between increased economic growth and stagnant living standards.

The difficulty in translating the economic gains from increased trade and growth into improvements in U.S. living standards has led some to suggest that firms can no longer unilaterally act socially responsibly. Although it would be preferable for all economic agents to follow similar (yet not the lowest common dominator) social practices, this condition does not seem to be a necessary one. In spite of increased globalization, firms should be able to remain socially responsible without placing their workers or home-country citizens at an economic disadvantage. But harmonization is not the only issue. Domestic economic priorities will play an important role in preserving the living standards of a nation's citizens, while enabling firms and other economic agents to continue to pursue socially responsible activities.

6

Moving from a Socially Responsible to a Socially Accountable Corporation

S. Prakash Sethi

The U.S. political debate and social psyche never seem to tire of their preoccupation with the role of the private sector—and especially the large corporation—and how it affects all aspects of our lives. In a nation where the concept of competitive markets has been elevated from a mere system of ordering economic arrangements to a high moral principle, we seem extremely reluctant to let private enterprise do what it ought to do in a market economy—what is its wont, if we would only let it go about its business. Instead, we constantly seek and expect the private corporation to be a good citizen where definitions of good corporate citizenship cover a very wide range of behavior. These definitions are constrained only by the proclivities of various stakeholders who seek a larger share of corporate resources than they could gain through market exchange. They are also informed by the imagination and persuasiveness of social reformers who would like the corporation to help alleviate society's many other problems because they believe it is the right thing to do.

The divergent nature of our expectations of a socially responsible corporation is all too apparent and manifests itself in countless confrontations between the corporation and other constituent groups. Thus, the corporation that receives public accolades for exemplary behavior in one aspect of its business is simultaneously brought into the court of public opinion and the judicial arena for morally reprehensible acts and illegal behavior in other aspects of its business.[1] While the 1980s were condemned as the decade of corporate greed, the 1990s are emerging as the decade of the heartless corporation. At the same time, we all have had our respective lists of the most admired, the most respected, the excellent, and the most desired corporations for which to work.[2]

Nowhere is this ambiguity more apparent than in the 1993 *Newsweek* article by Robert Samuelson, in which, using the trials and travails of IBM as an example, he poignantly describes the demise of the "good corporation" and the terrible loss and hurt that this demise is inflicting on hundreds of thousands of people and scores of institutions. It would seem that our previously socially responsible corporations are no longer able to provide the wages that permit a good life to their various constituencies as they go through the wrenching experience of downsizing to meet the new realities of international markets. The radical paradigm shift in our competitive environment, brought about by global competition, changing technologies, and a communication revolution, compels corporations either to alter their behavior drastically in order to adapt or risk obliteration.

This statement is not intended to disparage the notion that we should demand and expect more of corporations than what market forces would impel them to deliver. Instead, I argue that "good" business conduct cannot be examined and evaluated outside the context of prevailing competitive economic structures and inter- and intrainstitutional frameworks. To ensure this good conduct on the part of corporations, one cannot rely, solely or primarily, on the principles and motivations of their socially conscious managers. Although at the micro level, it is the conduct of the individual acting in a business context that is reflected in the adverse social impact of the business institution, this conduct is seriously circumscribed by its macrostructural context. As economic activity increases in complexity and technological orientation, it requires collective action wherein each individual and institution contributes but a tiny fraction to the whole (Sethi, 1994a). The corporation can be either good or bad depending on three factors: who is making the trade-offs, at whose expense these trade-offs are being made, and the extent of discretionary resources available to the corporation and its managers to ameliorate some of the second-order effects, i.e., externalities, of their normal business activities and to voluntarily meet nonmarket societal needs.

The paramount question for us to examine involves the circumstances, individual and contextual, that would induce business institutions and their managers to act in ways considered more socially desirable. We must ask whether there are market conditions that would define and limit the character of the good corporation, regardless of the desires of certain segments of our society for this character to remain unlimited. Finally, I argue that for the good corporation to persist and prevail, we must meet three conditions:

1. The criterion for defining the good corporation would not be confined to what the corporation does, but would include the rationale that it employs for its specific actions.
2. It would not be the magnitude of effort on the part of the good corporation that would be the determining factor, but its capacity to undertake such actions and the extent to which the corporation uses that capacity voluntarily.
3. The good corporation would be judged by the extent to which it foregoes its market power for the benefit of those stakeholders who are situated unfairly because of unequal bargaining power and leverage compared to the corporation.

It is these propositions that are the subject of our enquiry and to which we now turn our attention.

What Is a "Good Corporation"?

The archetype of Samuelson's good corporation is a financially successful and economically efficient company that would marry profit-making with social responsibility; provide stable, well-paid jobs with generous benefits; support culture and the arts; encourage employees to become involved in their communities; and be a good corporate citizen. Others have offered parallel although somewhat different visions of this idyllic corporate welfare state, in which managers combine market-competitive efficiency with enlightened stakeholder management to achieve the best of all possible worlds. For example, a recent issue of *Business and Society Review* (Fall 1993) solicited the views of a selected group of scholars, activists and government leaders on the future of Samuelson's good corporation; these views ranged widely.[3] However, most of the authors characterized the good corporation as one that does more for its workers, consumers, etc., but did not offer much of a rationale for defining and evaluating the good corporation. Professor Rosabeth Moss Kanter of Harvard Business School, in response to how one might describe Samuelson's good corporation, envisions a corporation committed to its workers, that invests in human resources through a continuous process of training and development and develops a pool of skilled workers to support planned activities of the firm. These activities are the keys to what she terms "employability security." Moving from employees to customers, Tom Chappell, president of Tom's of Maine and author of *The Soul of a Business: Managing for Profit and the Common Good*, suggests that respect for customers generates needed feedback on company products and services, and that competition should be balanced by "goodness"—defined as a demonstration of care and concern for people, nature, and the community. A contrasting perspective is offered by Doug Bandow of the Cato Institute, who points to the costs of corporate welfare; these costs, he contends, must be acknowledged and assessed against the potential benefits such welfare provides. Another contributor, United States Secretary of Labor, Robert B. Reich, emphasizes the long-term benefits of good corporate citizenship, particularly with respect to employees, over the shorter-term payoffs of downsizing strategies. *Business and Society Review*'s senior editor, Milton Moskowitz, reminds us, appropriately, that capitalist markets by definition militate against doing well simply by doing good. This brings us to our next argument.

Doing Well by Doing Good

Good ethics is good business, we are told.[4] We would not be discussing this topic if this statement were true. Business people, being rational, would need little prompting from outsiders to strive for ever-higher standards of socially responsible behavior. All empirical evidence and economic logic indicate otherwise, however. Under conditions of rising competitive intensity and an uncontrollable free-rider problem, companies cannot and will not do well. The relevant question to ask is not whether IBM is now more or less good but whether IBM has the luxury to be socially responsible if it so desired. Those who put their naive faith in the idea that corporations can do well by doing good, i.e., good ethics is always good business, are either assuming away the market advantages that these companies hold or refusing to accept history as it exists and substituting instead their perception of reality as what it ought to be.

The reality of the good corporation is quite different, as Samuelson himself readily admits. He concedes this point by bemoaning the pressure of increased global competition that compelled U.S. companies to cut back the size and scope of the corporate welfare state. Lost in this argument is the fact of management complacence and incompetence that made them fritter away the opportunities for improving efficiency and productivity during periods of prosperity. Even under the best of circumstances, the good corporation can be viewed as not all good and not good for everybody.

Consider the circumstances that made it possible for IBM to assume the mantle of the good corporation. By way of illustration, let me paint a cynical, although no less plausible, rationale for IBM's actions. I might also say that this rationale is equally generalizable to other good corporations. IBM's ability to pay higher wages and offer lifetime employment was made possible through the superior profits it could generate because of its dominant market position. Thus, while IBM took care of its employees, managers, and shareholders, it showed no such concern for the customers of its products. It was only by charging its customers relatively high prices that IBM could generate above-normal profits, i.e., nonmarket rent, which would then enable the company to reward its other stakeholders with above-market benefits. It was not the highly competitive markets that made possible IBM's gains, but the inefficient and imperfect markets that IBM helped create through its technological dominance and market power and then exploited to its own advantage. Therefore, is it any wonder that, unlike IBM's loyal workers and grateful shareholders, its abused and exploited customers would abandon ship at the first opportunity?

Clearly, it was in the best interest of IBM to maintain its nonnormal profits. It accomplished this objective by:

1. Outbidding its competition for the best talent and resources;
2. Sharing some of its above-normal profits with other segments of the community, thereby garnering public goodwill and political support for its market dominance.

The aforementioned discussion should not distract us from the fact that IBM was a benevolent employer and a good corporate citizen. It could just as easily have been an arrogant corporation that would use its market power to maximize its gain to the detriment of its various stakeholders. However, the fact remains that it is the imperfect markets and their exploitation by corporations that create opportunities for "good" corporate behavior that, in turn, is largely dissipated when markets turn sour, a situation that is presently all too apparent.

Doing Good by Doing Well

Our objective as a society, therefore, should be to create those structural conditions—economic and sociopolitical—that would induce all businesses to do good by doing well. An ancillary objective would be to create and support inter- and intrainstitutional frameworks that would encourage good corporations to become better corporations.

This premise is based on the following assertions:

1. Highly competitive markets are inimical to the creation and sustenance of the good corporation. Although competition makes business efficient, it does not make it virtuous. One could even argue that highly competitive markets provide greater opportunities for illegal and unethical behavior (Baumol 1991; Sethi 1994a). In other words, it is not possible to sustain the axiom that a company can do well by doing good.
2. Most markets become imperfect as they become large and complex, i.e., consumers and other factors of production such as labor lose their ability to bargain and compete with corporations on an equal footing.
3. Large corporations can survive only in imperfect markets. Therefore, they would take all necessary action to maintain these market imperfections so as to sustain their above-normal profits. The most logical behavior to expect from the corporation, under the circumstances, would be to do good generally when it is doing well, i.e., the economic imperative would be first, and with the societal concerns only secondary. That would largely define both the nature and extent of good corporate conduct.

Creating a Climate for Generalized Socially Responsible Behavior

In the absence of economic rationale—both at the macro and micro levels—a corporation's socially responsible behavior is in the nature of public good available to all members of society who stand to benefit from an enhancement of these values, regardless of their individual contribution to such enhancement. Unfortunately, this state of affairs creates real problems for those firms that wish to act in a socially responsible manner and thereby enhance the quality of life for the society as a whole. The economic concept is that of a "free rider." Socially responsible firms have no control over the behavior of other firms that choose not to extend themselves, but nevertheless benefit from the social values and public goodwill created by the good firms. As a result, the latter group puts inexorable pressure on the former to create more and more good deeds and receive fewer and fewer social rewards—a situation that is simply not viable. While exemplary and extraordinary altruistic individual behavior might give us our heroes, they would certainly not be the heroes that ordinary mortals could emulate in their daily, routine lives. Nor do these heroes and villains provide us with an adequate basis for structural analysis of social institutions. The emphasis in our effort, therefore, must be on those social-structural underpinnings and institutional frameworks that are necessary for improving the ethical norms of corporate behavior (Sethi 1994a).

One approach to limiting the free-rider problem would be to raise the level of overall good corporate behavior—public or free goods in the form of ethically proactive behavior—that all business firms must meet. This would be accomplished by raising public expectations and creating societal conditions to meet them. In a sense, this is nothing new. A great many business activities are already proscribed by legal statutes where such activities are perceived to be anticompetitive or contrary to public interest. Similarly, social customs and traditions may inhibit other forms of corporate behavior. The new approach, however, is prescriptive and proactive. It would then make it possible—if one assumes that most businesses do behave legally—that higher societal expectations would be met and that the problem of the free rider would be minimized.

A great deal more is possible to improve the overall moral climate for the business community as a whole, thus allowing it to behave at a higher level of socially responsible and ethically proactive behavior. This would vastly improve the total stock of social good produced by the economic system. An improved climate would also raise the level of societal expectations and corporate social performance on the part of those companies that have enjoyed above-normal profits which emanate from their exploitation of market imperfections. Religious leaders and moral philosophers have advocated some such approaches. Some sociopolitical movements in other parts of the world are leaning in the same direction. For example, in his encyclical *"Centesimus Annus,"* Pope John Paul II has outlined his vision of a just economic order with specific prescriptions for the role of property, just wages, fair profits, the value of work, distribution of wealth to help the poor and unfortunate among us, and the need for protecting the moral core of humanity.[5] Although the encyclical has been criticized in certain quarters for its selective use of history, ethnocentric bias, and fuzzy economic logic,[6] nevertheless it offers an approach to creating a more moral basis for conducting economic activity.

Philosophers and ethicists have argued also in favor of certain universal standards of corporate behavior, ones that take into account the concepts of human dignity, fairness, and equity. Although these standards may be somewhat modified to accommodate certain local, culturally based considerations, the latter cannot be used as an excuse to undermine the basic universalistic moral values and standards of human behavior.[7] Similarly, in the political arena, the International Labor Office of the United Nations as well as the European Community have advocated the creation of benchmark standards of workers' rights and a social charter involving corporations and their workers.[8]

These efforts, however, are more often flouted than adhered to by most players, including the companies and countries involved. At best, they represent a desirable ideal rather than a standard to be observed. No consensus currently exists as to the nature of more inclusive standards for the performance of market-based economic systems. There is considerable resistance to the injection of moral and ethical values in the capitalistic system which depends on individual choices and is supposedly value-neutral. Nevertheless, an improved and more comprehensive societal standard of corporate behavior—one that includes not only economic but ethical and moral values—would go a long way to making our system of market economy and private enterprise more humane and just while contributing to greater economic welfare.

From Social Responsibility to Social Accountability

The final step in our analysis has to do with the criteria that one might use in evaluating the reasonableness and adequacy of "good" in the good corporation. The approach outlined below seeks to evaluate the good corporation in terms of the extent to which it voluntarily shares its market power and resultant pecuniary gains—and thereby yields accountability for its actions and performance—with those groups who have been adversely affected by that power. Broadly speaking, imperfect markets facilitate a corporation's above-normal returns from three sources, covering three stages of interaction between the corporation and its stakeholders. These can be defined as: information imbalance, bargaining and negotiating power imbalance, and adjudication or remedy and relief power imbalance. They consist of, respectively:

- The amount and quality of information available to the two parties prior to entering into a transaction or exchange;
- The relative bargaining leverage of the opposing groups during negotiations;
- The ability of each group to seek proper adjudication of disputes and gain restitution for harm done when a transaction fails to yield desired and mutually satisfactory results.

We believe these three general principles should be pertinent to all classes of stakeholders. However, their actual application would vary because of the differing magnitude of the "stakes" involved and the comparative strength of particular stakeholders.

An attempt is made here to demonstrate that these principles would work, using the illustration of market exchange between corporations and consumers as a stakeholder group. Recall that under conditions of imperfect markets, a corporation stands to make above-normal profits through exploitation of imperfections in the marketplace. It follows, therefore, that under market conditions in which a customer is reasonably fully informed, has alternative sources of supply, can exercise independent choices, and can enforce compliance, a corporation has no obligation to protect the customer from his/her stupidity, poor judgment, or failure to forecast the future correctly. Market rewards for good judgment must also carry penalties for poor judgment and consequent loss when potentially unacceptable levels of risk are assumed carelessly. A similar logic should apply to business dealings with other groups, e.g., employees, stockholders, suppliers, and even the communities involved.[9]

Information Imbalance

Business gains from information imbalance because the lack of accurate information induces its customers to pay higher prices, accept products of lower quality, or choose different products/brands altogether. Thus, the criteria for evaluating the good corporation in this case would be:

1. The extent to which a firm provides its customers with information along the dimensions that he/she would need to make informed choices; and
2. The degree to which the firm renders the customer able to evaluate post-purchase effects in terms of his/her expectations and the producer's claims.

In one sense, there does not seem to be any dearth of information on products and services available to the consumer. Business firms alone spent over $131 billion in 1992 on total measured media in the United States, of which the top one hundred national advertisers accounted for 27.6 percent ($36.2 billion).[10] To this should be added accurate information on product labels, articles in the news media, government brochures and bulletins, and accounts of activities of consumer-based organizations.

In the logic of competitive markets, individual firms would provide customers only with the information that would encourage them to buy those companies' products. The customer is expected to learn about competitive products from other companies' advertising. However, in the real world things do not quite work out this way. In imperfect markets, firms put their major emphasis on differentiating their products and services—on the basis of both facts and perceived-illusory differences—to make it extremely difficult, if not impossible, for the consumer to make direct price-value comparisons among competing products and brands.

The information imbalance can be corrected at two levels:

The Industry

Efforts should be made to create uniform standards of product usage, labelling, and performance claims that could be compared by the customer in making buying decisions. This should be done through a cooperative effort among industry members, government agencies, and responsible consumer organizations. Multiple problems must be overcome if this approach is to work. These include the size and scope of the tasks in terms of products and brands, the cost of carrying out such a program, and the difficulty in persuading all significant stakeholders to participate in the process. Nevertheless, given a commitment on the part of industry and its important members, as well as pressure from public and private agencies, significant progress is possible in this direction. In any case, the degree of progress measured against the potential for progress would be one measure of the industry's social responsiveness and accountability.

The Firms

Companies should survey consumers regularly to assess objectively their information needs and to devise means to communicate such information to the consumer. The objective would be to provide the consumer with the information that he/she would want, in addition to the information that the firm would like the customer to have to make a pro forma purchase decision.

Secondly, where relevant, companies should maintain and regularly publish data on the volume and type of customer complaints and the nature of the companies' response to such complaints. They should disseminate information also on current research and findings that might have an adverse effect on the quality or customers' use of those products. This approach is similar to the one used by firms to provide investors with information concerning current and projected losses in a firm's financial statements. If current and potential investors of publicly held companies can demand such information to assess a firm's "quality of earnings," why should it be unreasonable for the current and potential customers to demand information on the "quality of product value" for the firm's offerings? The measure of the good corporation would be the extent to which this information is provided voluntarily and the gap between the availability of such information and its importance to the customer.

Bargaining and Negotiating Power Imbalance

Under conditions of imperfect markets, a handful of companies controls significant market share, avoids price competition, and has a great deal of influence on the nature of goods to be produced and the manner in which they are to be sold. This market dominance is reinforced further by mass advertising and the creation of customer brand loyalty based on real or spurious product attributes. Consumers, on the other hand, are largely unorganized, insufficiently informed, and lack bargaining power to deal with companies on an equitable basis.

The good corporation, therefore, will seek ways to enable consumers to gain at least part of those benefits in terms of product quality, service, and price that they would have achieved under more equal conditions in terms of information, resources, and organization. An example of such an approach would be for the companies to offer assurances as to the effective and useful life of a product, backed by independent insurance or other means to ensure that customers are getting what they believe they are buying.

Adjudication or Remedy and Relief Imbalance

The third area of restoring balance between producers and consumers has to do with adjudication of disputes and the receipt of prompt and fair settlement of their claims. Most consumers suffer from serious disadvantages in achieving this objective. Their individual claims are often small while their total impact on the company is quite large. Therefore, while the company has every incentive to fight such claims, the consumers have neither the time nor the resources to fight for equitable remedies. The two current approaches, i.e., small-claims court and class actions, are flawed from a macro perspective. In the former case, each claimant has to fight his/her dispute individually with no knowledge of the widespread nature of the problem and its resolution. The class actions are at best haphazard and end up paying more to the lawyers than to the plaintiffs.

The good corporation would institute procedures whereby affected customers could automatically receive adjudication of their disputes as well as fair settlement even when they had no knowledge of the harm done to them and had not initiated action against the offending company. The process suggested here could be termed "the internalization of class actions," wherein remedy and restitution would become an integral part of doing business and would be triggered automatically upon the occurrence of certain events.

The following example illustrates this point:

> Suppose a telephone company serves a particular area. Because of the nature of technology and usage patterns, a failure or malfunction rate of 2 percent is considered normal and has been factored into both the price of service and customers' quality expectations. Let us say that in a given period this rate has risen to 5 percent. Under normal procedures, the telephone company might be expected to make refunds, but only to those customers whose service was actually disrupted. However, we would assume that while there may not have been actual disruption of service in other cases, there was a deterioration in the overall quality of service in the area. The telephone company should refund a proportion of the service fee that it charged to all its customers in the impacted area.

Similar measures could be developed for application to other types of products and services.

Summary and Conclusions

The private sector in general and the corporate community in particular have ample scope and opportunity to become more socially involved while incorporating a higher set of ethical values in their operating norms. We have argued previously that for corporations to be good beyond the minimal legal and market-based standards, they must have above-normal profits; must stand to benefit in some way from voluntarily sharing those profits with other groups; and must be able to manage the problem of free rider. These needs notwithstanding, under conditions of imperfect markets, they certainly have the opportunity, and at least some inducement, to be socially responsible. However, ethical and social norms of corporate behavior cannot be left entirely to the personal preferences and predispositions of individual corporate managers, industry practices, fads of the moment, and the degree of successful pressure applied by community activists and other stakeholders.[11] None of these approaches is quite satisfactory and all leave a large residue of distrust and bitterness. Corporate managers seek to act in ways that would enhance their self-image and peer-group approval while protecting their vital business interests. Thus, their socially responsible behavior may deprive other businesses of critically needed resources in the economic arena because the latter could not compete on an equal basis with the superior resources of the former. In the social arena, it might also divert resources away from chronic social needs that lack glamour and are hard to tackle and, therefore, do not attract corporate interest.

Instead, an alternative approach is offered. This approach is more objective and can be applied systematically in defining the nature and extent of corporate social performance in terms of corporate activities that are voluntarily undertaken, either to ameliorate the harm done to or share gains with its various constituencies that have suffered from the exercise of market power by the corporation. This approach obviates the necessity of using subjective, disparate, and noncomparable measures of corporate social performance, given differences in financial and operating circumstances and external environments of different companies. At the same time, it is flexible enough to incorporate normative value-based standards and explicitly recognize the role of noneconomic considerations and constituencies in shaping societal expectations of corporate behavior to elicit appropriate corporate responses.

Notes

Research assistance in the preparation of this paper was provided by Ms. Linda M. Sama, a doctoral student, and is gratefully acknowledged.

1. Some of these ideas have been explored previously in an article by this author, *Journal of Business Ethics* vol. 13 (April 1994).

2. See, for example, Milton Moskowitz, Michael Katz and Robert Levering, *The 100 Best Companies to Work for in America.*

3. For a fuller exposition of these views than presented here, see "Is the Good Corporation Dead?" *Business and Society Review* 87 (Fall 1993), specifically, Bandow, Chappell, Kanter, Moskowitz, and Reich as listed in the references section of this paper.

4. Dennis P. Quinn and Thomas M. Jones, "An Agent Morality View of Business Policy," *Academy of Management Review* vol. 20 (January 1995). See also Blanchard and Peale (1988); Kotter and Heskett (1992).

5. See Pope John Paul II: Encyclical Letter *Centesimus Annus* of the Supreme Pontiff, *On the Hundredth Anniversary of Rerum Novarum* (Boston: St. Paul Books and Media, 1991). See also, Naughton and Laczniak (1993), Novak (1993), and Williams (1993).

6. See, for example, James Armstrong (1993), Green (1993), Hall and Ames (1993), Piker (1993), and Sethi and Steidlmeier (1993).

7. For a discussion of the application of universal ethics to market behavior, see, for example, Daly and Cobb (1989), De George (1993), Donaldson (1989), Etzioni (1988), Walton (1988), and Wogaman (1986). This list is by no means intended to be a comprehensive review of the related literature but, rather, serves as illustrative of parallel points of view.

8. Research on the European Community's Social Charter is vast and the reader is directed to Bercusson (1990), Curwen (1992), and Hepple (1990) for a useful introduction.

9. For example, workers should have no claim on corporate largesse or escape penalties of future layoffs when they or their representatives voluntarily enter into agreements with full knowledge of circumstances and potential for risks and rewards that might accrue.

10. Media expenditures cited here do not include unmeasured advertising spending, which comprises direct mail, promotion, co-op, couponing, catalogs, business and farm publications, and special events. The top one hundred U.S. advertisers alone spent an additional $15.3 billion in 1992 on such unmeasured nonmedia advertising, according to estimates of *Advertising Age*. All numbers

are obtained from *Advertising Age's Special Edition on the 100 Leading National Advertisers (LNA)*, 29 September 1993.

11. There is a rich body of literature that treats this subject under the rubrics of "social issues in management" and "business and society." The variety of definitions and scope of activities covered to describe what is and what is not socially responsible behavior on the part of the business community are far too numerous and contentious to be described here. There also remains the ultimate issue from the perspective of both the scholar and the practitioners: How should one link corporate social responsibility-responsiveness to corporate social performance? For an illustrative, and by no means exhaustive, set of writings, please refer to: Aram (1989); Aupperle, Carroll, and Hatfield (1985); Cadbury (1987); Carroll (1979, 1989); Epstein (1987); Frederick (1986); Freeman (1984); Gatewood and Carroll (1991); Gilbert (1989); Jones (1983); Keim (1978); Miles (1987); Sethi (1979, 1994b); Sethi and Falbe (1987); Sethi and Steidlmeier (1994); Votaw (1973); Votaw and Sethi (1973); Wartick and Cochran (1985); and Wood (1991).

Bibliography

Advertising Age, Special Edition: "100 Leading National Advertisers," 29 September 1993.

Aram, J. D. "The Paradox of Interdependent Relations in the Field of Social Issues in Management." *Academy of Management Review* 14(1989): 266–283.

Armstrong, J. "One Protestant Looks at *Centesimus Annus*," *Journal of Business Ethics* 12(12)(1993): 933–944.

Aupperle, K. E., A. B. Carroll, and J. D. Hatfield. "An Empirical Examination of the Relationship between Corporate Social Responsibility and Profitability." *Academy of Management Journal* 28(1985): 446–463.

Bandow, D. "Should We Even Bother to Mourn?" *Business and Society Review* 87(Fall 1993): 16.

Baumol, W. J. *Perfect Markets and Easy Virtue: Business Ethics and the Invisible Hand.* Cambridge, MA: Blackwell, 1991.

Bercusson, B. "The European Community's Charter of Fundamental Social Rights of Workers." *Modern Law Review* vol. 80 (September 1990): 624–642.

Blanchard, K. H., and N. V. Peale. *The Power of Ethical Management.* New York: William Morrow, 1988.

Cadbury, A. "Ethical Managers Make Their Own Rules." *Harvard Business Review* 65(5)(1987): 69–73.

Carroll, A. B. "A Three-Dimensional Conceptual Model of Corporate Social Performance." *Academy of Management Review* 4(1979): 497–505.

Carroll, A. B. *Business and Society: Ethics and Stakeholder Management.* Cincinnati, OH: South-Western Press, 1989.

Chappell, T. "The Pursuit of Goodness." *Business and Society Review* 87(Fall 1993): 17.

Curwen, P. "Social Policy in the European Community." Working paper, 1992.

Daly, H. E., and J. B. Cobb, Jr. *For the Common Good: Redirecting the Economy toward Community, the Environment, and a Sustainable Future.* Boston: Beacon Press, 1989.

De George, R. T. *Competing with Integrity in International Business.* New York: Oxford University Press, 1993.

Donaldson, T. *The Ethics of International Business.* New York: Oxford University Press, 1989.

Epstein, E. M. "The Corporate Social Policy Process: Beyond Business Ethics, Corporate Social Responsibility, and Corporate Social Responsiveness." *California Management Review* 29(3)(1987): 99–114.

Etzioni, A. *The Moral Dimension: Toward a New Economics.* New York: The Free Press, 1988.

Frederick, W. C. "Theories of Corporate Social Performance: Much Done, More to Do." Working paper, University of Pittsburgh, Graduate School of Business, 1986.

Freeman, R. E. *Strategic Management: A Stakeholder Approach.* Boston: Pitman, 1984.

Gatewood, R. D., and A. B. Carroll. "Assessment of Ethical Performance of Organization Members: A Conceptual Framework." *Academy of Management Review* 16(1991): 667–690.

Gilbert, D. R., Jr. "Business Ethics and Three Genres of Stakeholder Research." Paper presented at the Third Conference on Quality of Life, Virginia Polytechnic Institute, Blacksburg, VA, 1989.

Green, R. "*Centesimus Annus*: A Critical Jewish Perspective." *Journal of Business Ethics* 12(12)(1993): 945–954.

Hall, D. L., and R. T. Ames. "Culture and the Limits of Catholicism: A Chinese Response to *Centesimus Annus.*" *Journal of Business Ethics* 12(12)(1993): 955–963.

Hepple, B. "The Implementation of the Community Charter of Fundamental Social Rights." *Modern Law Review* vol. 80 (September 1990): 643–654.

Jones, T. M. "An Integrating Framework for Research in Business and Society: A Step toward the Elusive Paradigm?" *Academy of Management Review* 8(1983): 559–564.

Kanter, R. M. "Employability Security." *Business and Society Review* 87(Fall 1993): 11–14.

Keim, G. D. "Corporate Social Responsibility: An Assessment of the Enlightened Self-Interest Model." *Academy of Management Review* 3(1978): 32–39.

Kotter, J. P., and J. L. Heskett. *Corporate Culture and Performance.* New York: The Free Press, 1992.

LNA/Media Watch Multi-Media Service. "Ad$ Summary: January–September 1993." New York: Competitive Media Reporting, 1993.

Miles, R. A. *Managing the Corporate Social Environment*. Englewood Cliffs, NJ: Prentice-Hall, 1987.

Moskowitz, M. "In Search of the Good Corporation." *Business and Society Review* 87(Fall 1993): 11.

Moskowitz, M., M. Katz, and R. Levering. *The 100 Best Companies to Work for in America*. New York: New American Library, 1985.

Naughton, M., and G. R. Lacziniak. "A Theology of Work in the Catholic Social Tradition." *Journal of Business Ethics* 12(12)(1993): 981–994.

Novak, M. "The Creative Person." *Journal of Business Ethics* 12(12)(1993): 975–979.

Piker, S. "Theravada Buddhism and Catholicism: A Social Historical Perspective on Religious Change, with Special Reference to *Centesimus Annus*." *Journal of Business Ethics* 12(12)(1993): 965–973.

Pope John Paul II. Encyclical Letter *Centesimus Annus* of the Supreme Pontiff, *On the Hundredth Anniversary of Rerum Novarum*. Boston: St. Paul Books and Media, 1991.

Quinn, D. P., and T. M. Jones. "An Agent Morality View of Business Policy." *Academy of Management Review—Special Issue* vol. 20 (January 1995).

Reich, R. B. "Stewardship of the Future." *Business and Society Review* 87(Fall 1993): 10.

Samuelson, R. J. "R.I.P.: The Good Corporation." *Newsweek*, 5 July 1993: 41.

Sethi, S. P. "A Conceptual Framework for Environmental Analysis of Social Issues and Evaluation of Business Response Patterns." *Academy of Management Review* 4(1979): 63–74.

Sethi, S. P. "Imperfect Markets: Business Ethics as an Easy Virtue." *Journal of Business Ethics* 13(4) 1994a.

Sethi, S. P. *Multinational Corporations and the Impact of Public Advocacy on Corporate Strategy: Nestlé and the Infant Formula Controversy*. Boston: Kluwer Academic Publishers, 1994b.

Sethi, S. P., and C. M. Falbe. *Business and Society: Dimensions of Conflict and Cooperation*. Lexington, MA: Lexington Books, 1987.

Sethi, S. P., and P. Steidlmeier. "Religion's Moral Compass and a Just Economic Order: Reflections on Pope John Paul II's Encyclical *Centesimus Annus*." *Journal of Business Ethics* 12(12)(1993): 901–917.

Sethi, S. P., and P. Steidlmeier. *Up against the Corporate Wall: Modern Corporations and Social Issues of the Nineties* 6th ed. Englewood Cliffs, NJ: Prentice-Hall, 1994.

Votaw, D. "Genius becomes Rate" in D. Votaw and S. P. Sethi, eds. *The Corporate Dilemma*. Englewood Cliffs, NJ: Prentice-Hall, 1973: 11–45.

Votaw, D., and S. P. Sethi. *The Corporate Dilemma*. Englewood Cliffs, NJ: Prentice-Hall, 1973.

Walton, C. C. *The Moral Manager*. Cambridge, MA: Ballinger, 1988.

Wartick, S. L., and P. L. Cochran. "The Evolution of the Corporate Social Performance Model." *Academy of Management Review* 10(1985): 758–769.

Williams, O. "Catholic Social Teaching: A Communitarian Democratic Capitalism for the New World Order." *Journal of Business Ethics* 12(12)(1993): 919–932.

Wogaman, P. *Economics and Ethics: A Christian Inquiry*. Philadelphia: Fortress Press, 1986.

Wood, D. J. "Corporate Social Performance Revisited." *Academy of Management Review* 16(1994): 691–718.

7

Managerial Discretion: A Necessary Condition for Multinational Corporate Social Responsibility

Lee A. Tavis

This chapter addresses the dimension of social responsibility that is related to the decision-making of the individual manager or management team in allocating the resources of the enterprise within the constraints of and in collaboration with those individuals and groups affected by their decisions. Our position is that managers have a responsibility to ensure, to the extent possible, that the rights of the firm's stakeholders are preserved and their interests pursued. This will lead to economic objectives in the form of optimizing productivity and to social objectives in the form of preserving rights and pursuing interests for those stakeholders who are not adequately represented in their interactions with the firm.

The chapter focuses on the conditions necessary if resources are to be diverted from economic, corporate wealth maximization to other social needs of the firm's stakeholders. The argument is straightforward: (1) As human beings, we have fundamental rights that are essentially the same for everyone; (2) representation of these rights to the business enterprise is uneven; (3) the unevenness of the representation set against the uniformity of the rights leads to a responsibility for the individual manager or managerial team to represent those individuals associated with the enterprise whose interests are not adequately represented in the allocation of the firm's resources. We will refer to this as managerial social responsibility and as developmental responsibility when it is extended to the multinational enterprise with operations in developing countries.

If the manager is to fulfill these responsibilities, two conditions must be met. The manager or management team must have the freedom to respond to the needs of the underrepresented stakeholders. That is, the manager must have some area of discretion. Second, the manager must use that discretion to ensure that the underrepresented stakeholders enhance their position relative to the more powerful stakeholders. This paper will focus on the former, necessary condition for managerial social responsibility.

The following analysis addresses the subject based on this simple model. The first section deals with the rights-representation-responsibility framework. The second section then addresses the issue of managerial discretion applied within the neoliberal market system of the United States compared to the German social market system. The determinants of a manager's area of discretion are substantially different under these two kinds of capitalism. In the final section, we turn to the global scene.[1]

A Framework for Analysis

The business enterprise is viewed as a set of elements interacting within an organized network. The elements are those groups connected to the network through their ability to affect the network or who are affected by other elements across the network. Each enterprise network or organization is thus defined by a variety of relationships among its elements. The relationships, and thus the boundaries of the system, are determined by ownership, explicit and implicit contracts, or alliances. Individuals are represented to the firm by institutions or sets of institutions that constitute the network elements. The individuals and their representative groups are the stakeholders of the enterprise, traditionally defined as "any individual or group who can affect or is affected by the actions, decisions, policies, practices, or goals of the organization" (Freeman 1984: 25). The rights that are to be protected, as well as the way these rights are represented to the firms through the institutionalized stakeholder elements, thus become the determinants of managerial social responsibility.

Rights

Each person has basic moral guarantees as a result of his or her humanity. These human rights are universal in that they apply to everyone regardless of country or culture. They are independent in that they exist as standards whether or not they are recognized by the legal system or by other practices or institutions in society. In this tradition, Donaldson poses a set of ten fundamental international rights that comprise the moral minimum for a multinational firm (Donaldson 1989: 81).[2]

- The right to freedom of physical movement
- The right to freedom from torture
- The right to physical security
- The right to subsistence
- The right to minimal education
- The right to ownership of property
- The right to a fair trial
- The right to freedom of speech and association
- The right to nondiscriminatory treatment
- The right to political participation

In our concern over the unevenness of representation to the business enterprise, the rights to minimal education and to political participation stand out as being particularly vulnerable for corporate stakeholders.

- The right to subsistence includes some threshold level of basic human needs.
- The right to nondiscriminatory treatment can be understood as a right of access to network resources, beyond those necessary to maintain a minimum subsistence. This would be a right not to be economically exploited or marginalized.
- Minimal education is a key to the accumulation of human capital so necessary to take advantage of access to network resources.
- Political participation can be extended beyond the political process as defined by Donaldson to a general right of participation in institutional decisions that affect one's well-being.[3]

Managers are unique stakeholders in that they have direct control over the allocation of resources within the network. As a result, managers must be alert to the rights of each stakeholder in these decisions.

Representation

Within a society, each person is represented by a set of institutional arrangements. These arrangements include formalized structures and nonformalized practices that frame the interaction of one specific stakeholder element with the rest of the enterprise network.[4]

The effectiveness of an institution in representing an individual stakeholder to the enterprise network is a matter of legitimacy (how well it represents the individual stakeholder's self-interest) and of the stakeholder's power relative to the other elements in the network (Tavis 1983: 82). The institutions central to our concern over managerial areas of discretion are those that define market conditions.

Efficient markets represent well the interests of buyers. On the demand side, the access to multiple sources or potential sources with full information about each assures the buyer the best desired quality/ price combination. In this way, buyers are represented by this market. The supplier in an efficient market must meet these standards if a transaction is to take place. To the extent that markets are less than efficient, the power shifts from the demand to the supply side. For the individual enterprise, conditions in its output markets and in its input markets (where it contracts for materials, components, labor, and capital) determine the power with which those stakeholders, as elements in the system, are represented to the enterprise.

Markets do not evolve in isolation. They are enhanced and constrained by a multitude of cultural and legal factors. Governments are directly involved with enhancing market efficiency by promoting competition and information flow. Beyond that, governments constrain or subsidize market participants. They legislate protection for those who would be injured by unfettered free markets, as in child labor laws or workplace safety standards. In other cases, governments legislate the conditions through which some groups compete, for example, by providing monopoly power for labor. The criterion for efficient governmental regulation is that it must be legitimate in that it reflects the consensus of society; it must be uniformly applied, enforced, and clearly signaled to the market participants.

Responsibility

Across all societies, the violation of rights due to a lack of representation is a major problem. When the rights violated are those of the stakeholders of a business enterprise, it becomes a social problem for the firm's managers as the representatives of the network, negotiating among the various stakeholders.

Powerful stakeholders can direct the resources of the enterprise to satisfy their own selfish interests to the detriment of other, weaker stakeholders. In terms of the fundamental rights posed by Donaldson, when a stakeholder is being deprived of his or her rights, the minimum correlative duty of the manager is first to ensure that the enterprise does not participate in this deprivation and then to help protect against deprivation (Donaldson 1989: 83).

Two conditions are necessary if management is to meet these duties. First, management must have some freedom in decision-making; it must have some discretion in how resources are allocated across the system; it must have some power to lean against that of the powerful stakeholders. This is the area of managerial discretion.

The second condition is that managers use their discretion appropriately. The issue here is how managers exercise the power gained through their area of discretion. Managerial social responsibility is defined as the use of that area of discretion to allocate resources to powerless stakeholders in the face of claims by the powerful.[5]

The first concern with managerial social responsibility is thus with the power of the manager or managerial team in its role as network arbiter, resource allocator, and representative of underrepresented stakeholders. If a single stakeholder or set of stakeholder elements dominates the network, subjecting management to its dictates, there is no area of discretion within which to be socially responsible. Room for discretion is a necessary condition for managerial social responsibility.

Corporate networks are subject to economic dominance by competitive markets and the sovereign power of governments, as well as by a range of national and international institutions. Key power points that are pressuring the corporate network are the national and international product and service markets (consumers and suppliers), equity markets (shareholders), government regulation, and labor.

The most powerful stakeholders of a multinational enterprise are those located in the developed countries and the international marketplace. The weakest stakeholders would be in the less developed countries. We will start by analyzing two industrialized countries, the United States and Germany. The area of managerial discretion in the social market, "Rhineland" capitalism of Germany is bounded by a substantially different set of factors than the liberal market "Anglo-American" capitalism of the United States.

Each of these systems is affecting and affected by the European

Union. The anticipated market and regulatory structure of that Union will be considered after the comparison of the United States and Germany. Extending beyond the developed countries, we encounter the weakest stakeholders in a multinational enterprise network in the developing countries. We conclude by extending multinational managerial social responsibility to the notion of a developmental responsibility.

Two Different Market Economies

The liberal market economy of the United States differs fundamentally from the social market economy of Germany. Whereas economic interactions in the United States are competitive and adversarial, those in Germany are collaborative and relational. These countries differ in the structure of ownership and governmental regulation, as well as in the involvement of labor and communities in corporate decisions.

The United States Liberal Market Economy

Product and service markets in the United States have become more efficient in recent years. Still, few markets rival the efficiency of the U.S. financial markets. The drive of shareholder dominance has the potential to collapse the managerial area of discretion.

Shareholders as Unique Stakeholders

The shareholder dominance issue has two components. The first is a question of power exerted through large, open financial markets. The second has to do with rights of ownership in a market economy as they have evolved in philosophy and in the common law. The area of discretion for managers, opened by the inefficiency of the markets for products and services, can be closed as managers are forced by shareholders, through open markets, or through legal rights of ownership, to take every economic advantage of inefficient markets or ineffective regulation.

Market economies rely on shareholder power to force economic productivity. Owners seek to maximize their wealth in terms of share price, which, in the long run, is a function of productivity. The power of financial markets becomes critical when product markets are inefficient drivers of economic productivity. Responding to shareholder power, managers are forced to seek out and take advantage of inefficiencies in their input and output markets, thereby enhancing productivity in these markets.

In the United States, investors have the opportunity to buy or sell shares rapidly, with prices sensitive to these transitions in sophisticated financial markets. In spite of this sophistication, however, there are still problems with shareholder control. The struggle for corporate control is generally viewed as a struggle between insiders (management and/or management shareholders) and outside shareholders. The issue is one of who controls the corporate assets and how the benefits generated by those assets will be distributed.[6] The view among financial market analysts is that a substantial amount of assets is diverted to nonefficient uses. Owners and potential owners are responding.

The takeover movement of the 1980s led to a concentration of corporate ownership. The wave of mergers, acquisitions, leveraged buyouts, and basic leverage restructurings in the later years of that decade led to smaller, more concentrated equity holdings with the associated ability to coordinate among owners and impose their will directly upon management. Pressure was brought on management to enhance the earnings power of corporate assets by breaking up large conglomerates and reintroducing economic rigor into performance requirements, particularly in the form of cost reduction.

The reaction to these takeovers and restructuring was mixed. In restructured firms, managerial accountability and ownership control clearly increased, with positive earnings results (Jensen 1991). But the enhanced asset earnings of the takeover wave of the 1980s came at a high price to many: Long-term corporate strategies were often sacrificed for short-term earnings; managers were replaced and their ranks cut drastically; staffs were slashed; workers were discharged. Management attempted to change corporate charters and lobbied for laws restricting takeovers. Antitakeover statutes were passed in thirty-five states. Thus, efficiency by itself was not an important enough motivation to sustain the takeover movement.

The 1990s are becoming the decade of institutional activists. Institutions represent a large share of corporate owners who hold pension funds, insurance policies, and mutual funds. The ownership itself is widely dispersed with the broadest ownership base in the world. These institutions hold about 40 percent of all common stocks in the United States. They account for about 80 percent of all stock market transactions. Their block trading alone represents half the volume on the New

York Stock Exchange. Many institutional investors in the United States own a substantial percentage of individual corporations.

In years past, institutional investors exercised their judgment by buying or selling shares. Recently, a growing number of institutions endorse a strategy of "relationship investing" in which a two-way dialogue is encouraged. Investors concentrate on communicating their analysis and objectives to corporate boards and managers. At the same time, investors seek information about long-term strategic plans (Pound 1993: 33). Investors are exerting an informed voice, rather than exiting, with the intent of maintaining a longer-term working relationship.

Other institutional activism is being exerted through nonexecutive members of the board of directors. These outside directors have instigated top management changes in firms such as General Motors, IBM, and Westinghouse (Lohr 1993). Still, this new institutional activism is limited to the very large firms (Mieher 1993).

The important point in financial market control is to note that, even with the incredible sophistication of the United States financial markets, managers still have substantial discretion, due to the limited ability of shareholders to impose their will on management.

The discussion about philosophical or legal ownership rights focuses on the fiduciary responsibility of the manager as agent to the owner as principal. In a rigid adherence, this fiduciary relationship subjects managers to the economic, wealth-maximizing preferences of owners. Legal fiduciary responsibility is a fundamental tenet of corporate law. In the early decades of this century, it was illegal for the directors to consider the interests of any stakeholders other than those of shareholders. The 1919 case of *Dodge v. Ford* has become famous for its philosophical discussion of the corporate role in society at that time. Henry Ford wanted to retain earnings for expansion and to lower the price of the automobiles for social altruistic reasons. The courts told Mr. Ford that the purpose of a business was for the profit of the stockholders and that "if he wanted to pursue a particular eleemosynary policy he should do it with his own money, not with other people's" (Hanks 1991: 89).

Recent state statutes portend a major change in legal stockholder rights.[7] The antitakeover laws of the late 1980s have broad ramifications for the exclusivity of corporate shareholders. While their main purpose was to prevent or impede unfriendly takeovers, these statutes broke the lock on legal responsibility to shareholders and made it legally acceptable for directors to represent other stakeholders in their decisions.

Antitakeover statutes vary among the states. Many have adopted packages of takeover protection. Some of these statutes regulate the exercise of voting rights by the acquiring investor. Others require a waiting period during which the acquiring investor cannot in any way combine with the target. Fair price statutes eliminate two-tiered tender offers.

One kind of statute promises to be critically important for the exclusivity of shareholder rights. Twenty-three states have passed statutes that allow directors to consider nonmonetary factors in judging tender offers. "Nonmonetary factors which boards of directors may consider include the interest of the company, its subsidiaries and shareholders; the interests of employees, creditors, customers, and suppliers; and the interests of the local, state, and national communities" (Wagner and Kaplan 1990: 26). Legal analysts view these state stakeholder statutes with alarm as fundamentally changing corporate governance (Hanks 1991).

As we end the century, shareholders have lost the kind of legal claim on directors and officers that they had in its beginning—directors and officers likewise no longer have the kind of legal responsibility to shareholders. The legal fiduciary responsibility to shareholders as unique stakeholders is much less constraining on the managerial area of discretion than it was even a decade ago.

Governmental Regulatory Agencies

In the United States, myriad federal and state agencies administer and to a substantial extent determine the regulation of business enterprises. In creating these agencies, the Congress or state legislature delegates power to nonelected agencies, typically within broad guidelines. In many cases these agencies are authorized to make rules that have the force of law and to adjudicate these rules. Administratively, these agencies do much of the day-to-day work of the government (Dunfee et al. 1989).

One set of governmental agencies strives to enhance the efficiency of the market through enforcing competitive structures and enhancing information flows. For the United States product markets, there are agencies such as the antitrust division of the Department of Justice concerned with industrial sector competition. The Federal Trade Commission attempts to ensure truth in advertising. For financial markets, the United States has the Controller of the Currency and state banking commissions working to enhance competition in banking. The Securities and Exchange Commission focuses on the accuracy of the information provided to financial markets. These agencies support the marketplace drive for productivity.

At the same time, other agencies attempt to constrain the activity of market participants. Regulatory agencies intended to protect market participants from the workings of unfettered markets include: the Department of Labor, the Occupational Safety and Health Administration, the National Labor Relations Board, the Equal Employment Opportunity Commission, the Consumer Product Safety Commission, and the Food and Drug Administration. These agencies provide the boundaries that management encounters in its drive to productivity.

At the federal level, some important agencies such as the Federal Reserve Board, the Securities and Exchange Commission, the Federal Trade Commission, and the Interstate Commerce Commission are structured independently of the executive branch. While the executive branch can still exert substantial pressure, it does not control these agencies.

A large body of literature contends that regulation in the United States is not very efficient. It is charged that regulatory agencies do little to enhance market efficiency and, over time, come to be dominated by those they are regulating (Posner 1974). To the extent that these charges are true, governmental regulation does not provide the kind of effective constraints necessary to crisply bound the area of discretion for the managers of U.S. enterprise.

Thus, in the United States we find that the financial markets, in spite of their efficiency, struggle to impose their wealth-maximizing objectives on management; the basis for legally imposing shareholder objectives has been seriously eroded through state anti-takeover statutes; governmental agencies do not meet the criteria for effective regulation. Managers thus have a substantial area of discretion within which they may use the freedom to allocate corporate resources to serve objectives they choose.

The Germany Social Market Economy

Managerial discretion in the United States as outlined above is different from that in other capitalistic systems. Since the feasible region of managerial decision-making depends upon markets, regulation, and other institutions in a society, it is specific to the national structure and power relationships of these institutions. The systems in many continental European countries, for example, are identified as social market economies or "Rhineland" capitalism, as distinct from the liberal market economies or "Anglo-American" capitalism of the United States and the United Kingdom. The social market economy of Germany is the prototype of Rhineland capitalism. Differences in both the role of the government, and the structure of corporate governance change the area of managerial discretion.

The Regulatory Framework

In Germany, the regulatory framework is termed "Ordnungspolitik." Regulation under this concept is very specific. It grows out of the corporatist form of German government in which the "social partners" (government, employer, and employee associations) work out a social contract and then reflect it in the legal structure of institutional interactions. These regulations reflect what observers have called a sense of organic unity in Germany (Hodges and Woolcock 1993: 337). In this approach, the duties of the governmental agency are carefully specified in the law, as are the requirements for the firms being regulated. Once the regulation is in place, governmental intervention that does not fit clearly within the guidelines is not allowed. Compared to regulation in the Anglo-American model, German regulators are seen more as auditors whose purpose is to ensure conformance to a set of clearly stated legislated requirements.

Germany's regulatory bodies are politically independent. A recent example of this independence is the determination of its Central Bank to control German inflation. The bank remained true to its charter to maintain price stability and refused to lower interest rates in spite of substantial pressure from the German government and an open outcry across Europe.

This is in contrast to the United States where the government is continually monitoring and changing policies based on its interpretation of the public interest and intervening through its agencies to ensure that the public interest is served. Within the broad mandate legislated to regulatory agencies and their rule-making powers, there is ample room to accommodate changing policies without new legislation. Even when agencies are not part of the executive branch, these policymakers have substantial influence (Dunfee et al. 1989: 1091–1119). In Germany, state intervention to achieve these short-term political objectives is limited.

The collaborative nature of the German economy is clearly evident in the governing structure of corporations. German industrial democracy is based on coresponsibility. As described by Albert: "In Germany, all parties are invited to participate in company decision-making: Shareholders, employees, executives, and trade unions alike cooperate in a variety of ways to achieve a unique form of joint management" (Albert 1993: 110). There are two boards in all German firms of over two thousand employees: a supervisory board and a board of directors. The supervisory board is the senior body with the assignment to oversee the activities of the board of directors. Representation on the boards is divided equally between owners and employees, although the chairman is always a shareholder representative. The board of directors is a management board. Worker rights are also legislated in the form of works councils. It is mandated that management interact with the council in a broad range of decisions such as layoffs, schedules, and work patterns.[8]

Thus, in Germany, the social consensus between government, labor, and business exists all the way from the shop floor to the national government. In fact, the consensus is very much a bottoms-up, decentralized phenomenon.

Industrial/Financial Structures

Typical of Germany is collaboration within industrial/financial clusters. These clusters are built around the German universal banks that conduct the full range of financial activities, from commercial lending to the underwriting of security issues to institutional investing. Banks have substantial ownership in German enterprises. Banks hold shares on their own account and as trustee investors. Deutsche Bank, for example, is reputed to hold at least 10 percent of over eighty German companies. Eighty-six percent of German companies listed on the stock exchange have a single shareholder of 25 percent or more (Waller 1993). Members of the bank management board represent the bank as owner and trustee on the corporate supervisory boards. Often, a bank's equity portfolio will be concentrated in a specific industrial sector, in which case the bank is at the center of strategy for the sector as well as for the company. The industrial members of the cluster also have their position as shareholders in the bank.

The German model is, thus, very different from the open market for corporate control of Anglo-American capitalism. Unfriendly takeovers are a rarity, since outsiders find it impossible to penetrate the density of these webs.

Systemic Productivity

Historically, the German system has successfully competed in global markets. The emphasis on *Exportmodell Deutschland* has made industrial adaptation to changing structures of global competition an agreed priority among the social partners, in order to maintain and enhance export capacity. This policy of continuous consultation and adaptation has produced informal coalitions or "modernisation cartels" to deal with sectors in decline (with the banks, rather than government, playing a primary coordinating role), the promotion of knowledge-based industries, and government-sponsored research and development policy that emphasized continuous improvement of both product and process technology (Hodges and Woolcock 1993: 337).

At the plant level, productivity enhancement has been supported by the involvement, commitment, and skill of the German worker. At the enterprise level, German worker participation is regulated. Their membership on the senior governing board (the Supervisory Board) includes them in the discussion of strategies and policies. On the shop floor, works councils are an integral component in determining work procedures, changes in operations, and other job-defining tasks, as well as dismissals and labor protection.

Worker involvement has led to flexibility in the production process. In Germany, jobs are broadly defined, and workers share in the various activities of the process. This is in contrast to the United States, where labor unions have pursued rule-based regimes that tie labor rights to narrowly defined jobs. In these regimes, there is a rigidity to changing job descriptions that leads to tensions as labor tries to protect specific jobs and employers attempt to dismantle the resulting rigid structure (Thelen 1991).

Backing up this worker skill and production flexibility on the plant floor is an efficient technical training program. These programs, again part of German regulation, are tightly integrated community/corporate efforts. The programs include formal technical instruction provided by the local community, combined with on-the-job training in local industry. Both community and corporation tailor their programs to fit the other through close collaboration. Thus, German workers have every opportunity to retrain as the demands of the marketplace change (Essmuller 1992).

Managers of American enterprises are pursuing many of these same worker policies as a means of enhancing corporate flexibility and competitiveness. Policies stressed throughout this volume include the building of a committed team through employee participation in the United States and Papua, New Guinea (Sullivan, this volume) and the notion of employee participation and expanding skills across families of jobs, or "broad banding" (Fox, this volume). In some cases, training involved very formal procedures as well as on-the-job efforts (Galvin, this volume). Post notes that this participation and empowerment involves a new social contract in our society (Post, this volume).

These programs are motivated by productivity enhancement. They differ from the German system in that United States' programs are initiated by management within the individual enterprise, not by federal or state regulation. Where applied, they are generating enthusiasm and seem to work well. Still, training is a critical component of both systems. Again, in the United States, these tend to be firm-specific corporate training programs and are seldom integrated with community efforts. Firm-by-firm programs, however, will never achieve the broad application of the German systemic regulation. Still, the existence of a union shop can be a source of substantial tension in the United States as unions attempt to protect individual jobs.

The greatest difference in these two attempts to motivate workers and maximize productivity is in dealing with worker redundancy. This is an integral part of the program in the United States where the present managerial assumption is that workers will no longer spend their whole career at the same company. The broad basing of skills and the training efforts are undertaken with the expectation that they will enhance the ability of the worker to change jobs within the company or to find other employment in the event of redundancy.

Challenges to Consensus

The social consensus of Germany is being challenged by three factors: reunification, guest workers, and the intensity of international competition. German reunification presented a critical test for social consensus. The two Germanys had lived apart for almost half a century. Setting the East Germany's ostmark at a par with the deutsche mark overvalued East German pay scales in spite of the country's substantially lower productivity. Wages in the former East Germany are now higher than in the United States, Japan, or the United Kingdom. Since unification, Germany has invested heavily in employment creation, training, and unemployment compensation schemes for East German workers. While the huge unanticipated economic cost continues as a challenge, Hodges and Woolcock conclude, "Reports of the demise of the German social market economy are, however, exaggerated. The degree of social solidarity that has been maintained (despite the speed and the massive resource requirements of the [reunification] process) indicates that Germany continues to exhibit 'a sense of organic unity, a commitment to action in the national interest which transcends the interests of individuals or particular groups' " (Hodges and Woolcock 1993: 337).

A second challenge to German social consensus has been the large number of guest workers. This challenge has been confronted in a different manner. Foreign workers, welcomed into Germany in the postwar boom years to fill unskilled jobs at the bottom ranks of the industrial economy, now find themselves redundant with the availability of workers from eastern Germany and the recession. Seeking permanence through German citizenship can be difficult and expensive,[9] and many foreign workers attempt to maintain their own ethnicity by resisting integration into the German society. There has been a massive inflow of asylum seekers[10] that the government has tried to stem. Recession, unification, immigration, and segregation have contributed to the numerous instances of violence against guest workers over the past three years. These workers are not an integral part of German social consensus.

In spite of past success, there is a question of the extent to which the German system can survive the current intensity of international competition. German firms are taking actions that break the tight fabric of their clusters. The collaboration of Daimler-Benz and Deutsche Bank, one of the strongest in Germany, is being scrutinized. Deutsche Bank has held a major position (now 28 percent ownership) of the Daimler industrial group since 1926. To be listed on the New York Stock Exchange, Daimler is publicly disclosing more information than is required in Germany, and members of both the Deutsche and Daimler boards have suggested the bank should reduce its holdings (Riley 1993, Waller 1993). The chief executive of the bank, who has traditionally been the chairman of the Daimler supervisory board, may step down from that position (Betts 1994).

The most serious challenge to the German economy is the cost of labor compared to that in competing countries. Associated with the German legislated worker participation has been the ability of German labor and the consensus process to push up wages and labor perquisites. German workers are the highest paid and most secure in the world. Labor costs, including the share of social security contributions paid by employers, are now higher in Germany than in any other industrial country (Koelle 1993), labor costs that are not currently offset by productivity. For example, in Britain, labor costs are 60 percent of those in Germany but productivity is 70 percent (Hodges and Woolcock 1993: 338). The cost of skilled labor in the Czech Republic is one-sixth of that in neighboring Bavaria (Hoffman, Kamm, Frederick, and Petry 1994: 35).

> Even Chancellor Kohl has been highly critical of worker benefits. Chancellor Helmut Kohl is calling on the nation to change its way of thinking. On October 21, he urged industry to "break rusted molds, become more innovative and learn how to take risks." Mr. Kohl told Germans they will have "to change attitudes, work harder and demand less from employers and the public trough. Six weeks vacation plus 12 national holidays and an average 37.5 hours a week working time have eroded Germany's competitiveness," he said. "We can't secure the future by organizing our country as a collective leisure park," Mr. Kohl said in his policy statement. "In all areas of our economy, we have to take the necessary steps for fundamental change" (Roth 1993).

These are strong words from the chancellor. Kohl's challenge is, however, to the agreements within the system, not to the system itself. Kohl is calling for a new social consensus, not a dismantling of the consensus process.

A number of firms such as BMW and VW are investing abroad to access cheaper labor. These actions replace domestic production for export with foreign production and extend the stakeholders in these enterprise networks well beyond those joined together in the German consensus system.

> Pointing to the large number of German companies shifting production abroad to escape high domestic costs, Mr. Ludolf von Wartenberg, general manager of the Federation of German Industry says, "Companies are moving away from a 'made in Germany,' toward a 'designed in Germany' concept. German industry will regain competitiveness," he says. But he admits doubts on how German society will cope with the strain (Marsh, March 1994: 8). The movement of production facilities abroad reflects a judgment by a number of German firms that future productivity will not overtake the high cost of German labor. They may be premature.

Analysts of the German economic future argue that Germany will not be able to compete due to its high labor costs and constraints on downsizing. Given the broad base of the German regulated system and the experience with worker-involved productivity enhancement, it is likely that productivity will catch up as international competitive pressures and the close proximity of cheap, skilled labor in central European countries constrain wage hikes. Worker flexibility within plants and across industries will enhance the efficient production of high-technology products produced by skill-demanding industrial processes. This may be one of the reasons German executives are far more optimistic that Europe will maintain its role in global economic competition than are those in the United Kingdom (Marsh, February 1994: 10). It is the low-technology, low-skilled production that will relocate to lower-cost regions outside Germany (Hoffman, Kamm, Frederick, and Petry 1994: 38).

The most immediate challenge in the current economic cycle is how to deal with redundancies. In the long term, as Germany presses through the necessary restructuring and the current recession, and as productivity increases against constant wages, the redundancy issue will decrease. Germany will undoubtedly need to return to guest workers for the unskilled labor pool, although the estimate of half a million foreign workers per year is probably high (Wright 1993). Overall, I do not share the grim future of other analysts. (For example, see Albert 1993 or Marsh, 24 February 1994.)

Comparative Managerial Discretion and Social Responsibility

Comparing these two forms of capitalism, the managerial area of discretion can be described as substantially smaller for the German manager than for his or her U.S. counterpart. The greater participation across the German system means that resources are allocated collaboratively among the stakeholders. Managers have little individual decision-making freedom. To the extent that responsibility is a function of freedom to respond, we must conclude that managerial social responsibility is less in Germany than in the United States.

If we were to extend our level of analysis from the micro level of managerial social responsibility to the meso level of the corporation and further to corporations as a group participating with government and labor at the macro regional and national levels, our conclusion would be different (Enderle 1991). German business is an integral component of the social consensus at the national level through the

Federation of German Employers Associations and the Federal Association of German Industry, and regionally through Chambers of Trade and Industry (Erd 1992: 127). In this process, as one of the three parties to the consensus, corporations have a substantial area of discretion and therefore a substantial responsibility.

Could we also say that social needs of the corporate stakeholders are better served in Germany? There are two answers. Stakeholders represented through the corporatist government, the interactions within the industrial/banking clusters, the supervisory boards, or through the works councils are effectively represented by these institutions. In terms of fundamental rights, German stakeholders are assured of subsistence, access, education, and participation. This is particularly the case for German workers compared to those in the United States. Thus, social needs for the Germans are well met while the micro managerial responsibility, and credit, for these needs is minimal. There is one exception. Guest workers are not adequately represented to the firm or in the system. Ironically, the German managers have limited areas of discretion within which they can act to support non-German workers.

The areas of discretion will change as these two systems drift toward each other. The United States is showing some signs of collaboration in the management emphasis on job flexibility and training, in the slowly emerging trend of relationship investing, and the legal flexibility to consider nonshareholder stakeholders in corporate decision-making. Still, a drift is not a movement. Alternatively, Germany's response to increasing competition may well move her substantially closer to the Anglo-American model.

Managerial Discretion and Developmental Responsibility in the Global Society

These national systems unfold into the global economy in three steps. The first includes the Anglo side of Anglo-American capitalism joining with the continental Rhineland capitalism in the European Union. The second is the intense trade and investment interaction among the industrialized countries. Finally, for the global impact, developing countries are a central part of the analysis, particularly when our concern is with exploitation and marginalization.

The European Union

The drift of Rhineland and Anglo-American capitalism is reflected in the European Union. The Union has progressed far more than most of us anticipated thirty years ago. Much of the single-market regulation is now in place, and cross border constraints have largely disappeared, although there is still national resistance and slow implementation in areas such as subsidies, liberalizing state-owned monopolies, and opening public contracts to free competition. The political Union and its political bodies wield increasing power.

Elements of both systems are included in the structure of the Union. Although the final balance is still a judgment call, the influence of liberal market capitalism is far greater than the size of Britain, compared to the continental countries, would suggest. Three features of the Union are particularly relevant: the structure of regulation, competition policy, and the social chapter.

Regulation reflects the multicultural makeup of the Union and the difficulty with which national members relinquish political control. In the Union, regulation is based upon mutual recognition of national rules where "an economic agent operating under one nation's rules is allowed to operate in all member states, subject to certain minimum essential regulations to safeguard public welfare and security" (Hodges and Woolcock 1993: 331). The regulations that are legislated by the Union will thus necessarily have broad bounds, allowing ample room for national control of the business enterprise. When legislated, the Union regulations, although minimal, will contain the kind of specificity typical of the German system, rather than the politically influenced policy of U.S. regulatory agencies.

The power to prevent restrictive business practices is firmly in the hands of the Union. In the case of competition regulation, the Union now has a preemptive right to rule on large-scale mergers and take-overs (Leonard 1992: 100).

Still, within this union structure is ample room for regulatory arbitrage as countries act to minimize labor costs and regulations. Some observers forcefully argue that this will lead to a triumph of Anglo-American capitalism in the Union. Britain, with her relatively unregulated labor markets and modest corporate social overhead costs, is attracting substantial foreign investment by multinationals seeking a production site within the Union. The Community's social charter, and now the Union's social chapter, is an attempt to equalize these variations. Eleven of the twelve heads of community governments signed the charter in 1989. Britain abstained on the grounds that it would reverse her government's labor policy. At this point, the eleven may enact the forty-seven pieces of legislation in the charter's accompanying Social Action program while excepting the U.K. from these provisions (Leonard 1992: 146). The tension between the U.K. and European social affairs ministers continues to mount over this issue. The future of this chapter is tied to the long-term economic success of Germany as discussed earlier and the other continental Rhineland capital countries. To the extent they can compete, the exclusion of Britain becomes less of an issue.

The Industrial Country Triad

Externally, the Union is part of an intense trade and investment interaction among industrialized countries. Ohmae describes this interaction as approaching his ideal international marketing system (Ohmae 1990). Turner and Hodges call it supercompetition: "The world is faced with an intensity of competition which is completely unprecedented. The globalization of competition is forcing companies all around the world to reassess their strategies and restructure their operations" (Turner and Hodges 1992: 2). The General Agreement on Tariffs and Trade (GATT) will accelerate the process of competition within and beyond the industrialized countries. It will increasingly limit what governments can do to regulate business not only through tariffs and quotas but also internally through subsidies and technical standards.

The triad countries (Europe, North America, Japan) dominate world trade, accounting for three-fifths of global imports of manufacturers and two-thirds of exports. Multinational corporations dominate the size and pattern of these trade flows. Intraenterprise transactions among the affiliates that are part of a multinational network account for more than one-fourth of total world trade. Three-fourths of foreign direct investment flows take place within the triad.

The nature of competition among the multinational corporations maneuvering for position in the triad is changing. Industry today is technology-driven. Given the high cost of technology, the complexity of its individual components, the rapidity with which it is outmoded, and the related compression of product life cycles, even the large multinationals can afford neither the massive commitment of financial and human resources nor the strategic risk of cutting-edge technology. Product life-cycles, for example, have been reduced from spans of around fifteen years just two decades ago to as short as two-to-three years (Kline 1988).

Advances in production techniques allow manufacturing firms to keep pace. In computer-aided manufacturing, the combination of re-programmable numerically controlled machines with robotics and automated materials handling systems provides a capability for flexible automation as machines and processes can quickly be reprogrammed (Parthasarthy and Sethi 1992). This capability allows producers remarkably flexibility to change products, volume, machine loadings, production sequences, and processes in a short time at costs that are competitive or lower than with mass production. Cutting-edge technology is now linking computer-aided design and computer-aided manufacturing into computer-integrated manufacturing facilities (*New Approaches to Best-Practice Manufacturing* 1990: 31). Most firms can no longer survive through the mass production of standard commodities.

Corporate organizational structures are shifting with the change in the market, product technology, and production processes. Centralized control is giving way to coordination. Suppliers are becoming partners. Firms are entering into equity joint ventures or nonequity strategic alliances as a means of tapping into technological networks and global production facilities where, due to the short product life cycles, the results of the technology are introduced into the three markets simultaneously.

Global Competition and Developmental Responsibility

When developing countries are included in the analysis, the nature of competition, regulatory effectiveness, and stakeholder power balances changes substantially. Multinational corporations are active in developing countries. Whereas 92 percent are based in industrialized countries, 55 percent of the affiliates are in developing countries. While 97 percent of foreign direct investment originates in the developed world, 35 percent of it flows to the developing world. In trade, multinationals account for a significant amount of developing-country exports (*World Development Report* 1993).

In the developing countries, we encounter market failure due to the inefficiency of domestic markets and governmental failure in the form of confused national regulation and limits on power, compounded by a lack of international regulatory bodies (Tavis 1988). These failures are in sharp contrast to the efficient financial markets, the relatively efficient product and service markets, and the effective regulation of the developed countries as outlined above.

Differences in market efficiency and regulatory effectiveness exacerbate the stakeholder power imbalances facing the manager of the multinational enterprise. Affluence and power reside among the industrialized-country stakeholders and their international markets. The area of discretion for the managers of multinational enterprises with activities in developed and developing countries is subject to a more complex set of determinants as the enterprise network directly links stakeholders possessed of such uneven representation. The managerial social responsibility to represent the underrepresented stakeholder becomes a developmental responsibility.

The manager of a multinational enterprise owned and headquartered in the United States, finds some area of discretion within our national constraints imposed by the financial markets, product and service markets, labor, and government regulatory agencies. On the developing-country side, the constraints allow for a wide area of discretion.

Developing countries across the world are rushing headlong to domestic deregulation and an opening of their markets to international trade in products and services as well as to foreign portfolio and direct investment. The World Bank index of trade openness of developing countries has moved from 1.5 in 1978 to 2.4 on a 5-point scale of totally open markets (*World Investment Report* 1992: 13).

This opening is a result of government failure in the import substitution strategies of Latin American countries and the collapse of the command economies in Eastern Europe and the former Soviet Union. Institutionally, the World Bank and International Monetary Fund are exerting great pressure for deregulation. When developing-country markets and investment are deregulated, governments relinquish much of their power to buffer their citizens from the pressures of the international marketplace.

The collision between the relatively efficient international markets and inefficient domestic markets has not been kind to developing-country peoples. It is severe in the former command economies. Their problem is one of learning how to regulate a market, not one of deregulation. The idealized regulations legislated in these countries often do not fit their unique needs nor are the backup court systems in place. Privatization is taking place in crassly inefficient financial markets. The history of government failure in these countries is being replaced with a good deal of market failure. On balance, the stakeholders and potential stakeholders in these countries are not well represented.

The weak manager will allow the power of industrial-country stakeholders to flow through the network and exploit those in the developing countries, denying them their rights. The strong manager operating within an effectively organized network will use his discretionary power to take advantage of the less-than-absolute power among industrial-country stakeholders, and channel resources to developing-country stakeholders beyond those needed to optimize productivity.

In the long term, the manager will work to aid the developing country stakeholders in representing their own interests to the enterprise network. This task is more difficult today than yesterday. To the extent that governments have abrogated their regulatory control to the international marketplace, the multinational manager can no longer work with a potentially powerful governmental regulatory ally to empower the unrepresented developing-country stakeholders (Tavis and Glade 1988).

Conclusion

The argument of this paper is that managerial social responsibility is primarily dependent upon the freedom of management to divert resources from activities that advance the firm's productivity as a means of enhancing shareholder wealth, to applications that benefit or empower stakeholders who are disadvantaged by the wealth-enhancing allocation pattern. The focus is on the decision-maker's area of discretion as defined by national and international economic and governmental constraints. The framework was applied in the national institutional structures of the United States and Germany and then unfolded through the European Union to the interactions among the developed countries and further to the global system.

Managerial areas of discretion are clearly diminished by the current unprecedented supercompetition. They are not, however, eliminated. Within the United States, as a parent country, shareholders are less dominant than before, and governmental regulation is more fluid than in Europe. For operations within the developed-country triad, constraints are more limiting than in the United States. In Germany, as an example of Rhineland continental capitalism, managerial decisions are made in regulated participation with owners, workers, and communities. Stakeholder needs are well served, but management has little independent decision freedom. Japan, although not covered in this paper, has many of the characteristics of Rhineland capitalism (Albert 1993; Turner and Hodges 1992). Competitive pressures are essentially the same across the triad.

When multinational activities are expanded into developing countries, however, the local constraints on the area of discretion fall away. The danger, of course, is that the area opened through the lack of developing-country constraints will be closed on the other side by the power of industrialized-country stakeholders. This is the challenge for the developmentally responsible manager.

Notes

1. This chapter is drawn from a book by Lee A. Tavis forthcoming in 1996 from the Notre Dame Press. It will be Volume V in the series, "Multinational Managers and Developing Country Concerns."

2. This discussion of rights is based on an earlier presentation. See Tavis 1994.

3. This broader participative definition is in line with Shue's original work on basic rights upon which Donaldson relies for his determination of fundamental rights (Shue 1980: 71). Tied to this general right, however, are the constraints necessary to assure organizational efficiency.

4. Institutions include formalized structures such as labor unions, chambers of industries, governmental regulatory agencies, or organized activist groups such as the Interfaith Center on Corporate Responsibility. The notion of institutional arrangements also extends beyond these organizations to include nonformalized practices. A market, for example, is a complex of formal structures and informal practices.

> The institutional arrangements of interest in our framework are those formal structures and informal practices that frame the interaction between a specific stakeholder element in the enterprise network with the rest of the network. This is the microequivalent of the macro concept described by De George as "background institutions." "The plethora of laws, governmental regulation, customs, unions, consumer and environmental groups, and popular pressures, demands, and expectations." (De George 1993: 26). See also Pettit 1992 and Thelen and Steinmo 1992.

5. The term "managerial social responsibility" is selected in an attempt to keep our focus on managerial decision-making, and to avoid the many, diverse definitions of corporate social responsibility.

6. There are two theories of financial market control currently being tested.

The first is the free cash-flow theory. This theory focuses on mature companies with few new investment opportunities in their own industry. These companies generate substantial cash flows from their previously committed assets. The management, however, does not search for new opportunities, but reinvests these free cash flows into less-than-optimal investments in the mature industry.

A related, but different, theory focuses on cash compensation. This theory is limited to the distribution of benefits from the firm. Insiders (shareholders or managers) use their control to divert cash flows from dividends to insiders as private benefits of control. These cash flows can flow as prerequisites for managers or inside owners or in the form of special treatment for other corporations in which the insider has a special interest.

7. I am indebted to Karen Miller for pointing out the potential impact of these state statutes.

8. Germany has a dual system of labor representation in which workers are represented by unions and works councils. This system is precisely defined by law as with all German regulation. Sixteen unions are organized into the German Federation of Trade Unions which represent workers in the national social consensus with government and owners. On the shop floor, while a worker is generally a member of the union and votes for the works council, the role of each is defined in the regulatory law. While unions representing workers at the regional and national levels are present on the shop floor, it is the works councils that represent worker interests at the plant level. The works councils are the organizations involved in decisions. Their representation on the supervisory board assures a voice in decisions such as working hours, vacations, social amenities, vocational training, hirings, and transfers. Management must consult with the works council itself in decisions such as manpower planning, dismissals, work procedures, or operation changes (Erd 1992: 121–122).

9. Under a German law passed in 1913, citizenship is a blood right rather than a birth right ("Citizenship" 1993: 45). Third- or fourth-generation ethnic Germans can obtain citizenship upon demand through an extended process of proving their ethnicity.

For foreign workers, application is bureaucratically complex, time-consuming, and costly ("German Law" 1993). About two hundred thousand guest workers and their children out of some six million guest workers have obtained citizenship since the mid-1970s ("Citizenship" 1993: 45). About one-third of the guest workers are Turkish. An added limitation for them is that they must give up their Turkish citizenship and property rights in their homeland if they are granted citizenship in Europe since Turkey does not allow dual citizenship. Cash grants are offered to foreign workers to return home.

10. The flow of asylum seekers into Germany has been cut in half from the 1992 flood of four hundred thirty thousand with the exclusion of economic refugees who are not suffering political persecution at home (Wright 1993).

Bibliography

Albert, Michel. *Capitalism Against Capitalism*. London: Whurr Publishers, 1993.

Baumol, William J., with Sue Anne Batey Blackman. *Perfect Markets and Easy Virtue: Business Ethics and the Invisible Hand*. Mitsui Lectures in Economics. Cambridge, Mass: Blackwell, 1991.

Betts, Paul. "Daimler-Benz Head Likely To Be Airbus Chairman," *Financial Times*, 28 February 1994, 1.

"Citizenship: One of Us, or One of Them?" *The Economist*, 31 July 1993, 45.

De George, Richard T. *Business Ethics*, 3rd ed. New York: Macmillan, 1990.

De George, Richard T. *Competing with Integrity in International Business*. New York: Oxford University Press, 1993.

Donaldson, Thomas. *The Ethics of International Business*. New York: Oxford University Press, 1989.

Dunfee, Thomas W., Frank F. Gibson, John D. Blackburn, Douglas Whitman, F. William McCarty, and Bartley A. Brennan. *Modern Business Law*, 2nd ed. New York: Random House, 1989.

Enderle, Georges. "Business Ethics and Market Failure," in *Market Morality and Company Size*. Brian Harvey, Henk Van Luijk, and Guido Corbetta, eds. Boston: Kluwer Academic Publisher, 1991: 67–85.

Erd, Rainer. "Labour Relations" in *The Times Guide to Germany: Doing Business with Europe's New Giant*. Susan Stern, ed. London: Times Books/HarperCollins, 1992.

Essmüller, Ilka. "Education and Training" in *The Times Guide to Germany: Doing Business with Europe's New Giant*. Susan Stern, ed. London: Times Books/HarperCollins, 1992.

Freeman, R. Edward. *Strategic Management: A Stakeholder Approach*. Boston: Pitman Press, 1984.

Friedman, Milton. *Capitalism and Freedom*. Chicago: University of Chicago Press, 1962.

"German Law Won't End Immigration Problems," editorial. *New York Times*, 9 January 1993, 22.

Gold, Michael, ed. *The Social Dimension: Employment Policy in the European Community*. London: The Macmillan Press Ltd., 1993.

Hanks, James J., Jr. "Playing with Fire: Nonshareholder Constituency Statutes in the 1990s." *Stetson Law Review* 21(1)(1991): 97–120.

Hodges, Michael, and Stephen Woolcock. "Atlantic Capitalism versus Rhine Capitalism in the European Community." *West European Politics* 16(3)(1993): 329–344.

Hoffman, W. Michael, Judith Kamm, Robert Frederick, and Edward Petry Jr., eds. *Emerging Global Business Ethics*. Westport, Conn.: Quorum Books 1994.

Industry and Development: Global Report 1993/94. Vienna, Austria: United Nations Industrial Development Organization, 1993.

Jensen, Michael C. "Corporate Control and the Politics of Finance." *Journal of Applied Corporate Finance* 4(Summer 1991): 13–33.

Kamm, Henry. "In Europe's Upheaval, Doors Close to Foreigners," *New York Times*, 10 February 1993, 1.

Kline, John M. "Advantages of International Regulation: The Case for a Flexible, Pluralistic Framework" in *International Regulation: New Rules in a Changing World Order*. Carol C. Adelman, ed. San Francisco: Institute for Contemporary Studies, 1988.

Koelle, Hans Martin. "Germany Needs to Take Its Medicine." *Wall Street Journal Europe*, 7 December 1993, 10.

Leonard, Dick. *The Economist Guide to the European Community: The Original and Definitive Guide to All Aspects of the EC*. Avon, England: The Bath Press, 1992.

Lohr, Steve. "Big Business in Turmoil," *New York Times*, 28 January 1993, A1.

Marsh, David. "Balance of Economic Power Begins to Shift," *Financial Times*, 9 March 1994, 8.

Marsh, David. "Can Europe Compete? An Elusive Corporate Consensus," *Financial Times*, 24 February 1994, 10.

Mieher, Stuart. "Weak Force, Shareholder Activism, Despite Hoopla, Leaves Most CEOs Unscathed," *Wall Street Journal*, 24 May 1993, A1.

New Approaches to Best-Practice Manufacturing: The Role of Transnational Corporations and Implications for Developing Countries. United Nations Centre on Transnational Corporations, Series A, Number 12. New York: United Nations, October 1990.

Ohmae, Kenichi. *The Borderless World: Power and Strategy in an International Economy*. New York: HarperCollins, 1990.

Parthasarthy, Raghavan, and S. Prakash Sethi. "The Impact of Flexible Automation on Business Strategy and Organizational Structure." *Academy of Management Review* 17 (January 1992): 86–111.

Pettit, Philip. "Institutions" in *Encyclopedia of Ethics, Volume I, A–K*. Lawrence C. Becker, ed. New York: Garland Publishing, Inc., 1992.

Porter, Michael. *The Competitive Advantage of Nations*. New York: The Free Press, 1990.

Posner, R. A. "Theories of Economic Regulation." *Bell Journal of Economics and Management Science* 5(2)(1974): 335–358.

Pound, John. "Creating Relationships Between Corporations and Institutional Investors: An Introduction." *Journal of Applied Corporate Finance* 6(2)(1993): 32–34.

Riley, Barry. "Feeling of Betrayal in Corporate Germany." *Financial Times*, 22 September 1993, 27.

Roth, Terence. "Germany Shows Signs of Being Pulled Apart by Economic Changes." *Wall Street Journal*, 29 October 1993, 1.

Shue, Henry. *Basic Rights*. Princeton: Princeton University Press, 1980.

Stern, Susan, ed. *The Times Guide to Germany: Doing Business with Europe's New Giant: A Comprehensive Handbook*. London: Times Books 1992.

"A Survey of Corporate Governance." *The Economist*, 29 January 1994.

Tavis, Lee A. "Bifurcated Development and Multinational Corporate Responsibility," in *Emerging Global Business Ethics*. Michael W. Hoffman, Judith Kamm, Robert Frederick, and Edward Petry Jr., eds. Westport, Conn.: Quorum Books, 1994.

Tavis, Lee A., ed. *Multinational Managers and Host Government Interactions*. Notre Dame: University of Notre Dame Press, 1988.

Tavis, Lee A. "Stewardship Across National Borders," in *Stewardship: The Corporation and the Individual*. T. R. Martin, ed. New York: K.C.G. Productions, Inc., 1983.

Tavis, Lee A. and William P. Glade. "Implications for Corporate Strategies," in *Multinational Managers and Host Government Interactions*. Lee A. Tavis, ed. Notre Dame: University of Notre Dame Press, 1988.

Thelen, Kathleen. *Union of Parts: Labor Politics in Postwar Germany*. Ithaca, New York: Cornell University Press, 1991.

Thelen, Kathleen and Sven Steinmo. "Historical Institutionalism in Comparative Politics," in *Structuring Politics: Historical Institutionalism in Comparative Analysis*. Sven Steinmo, Kathleen Thelen, and Frank Longstreth, eds. New York: Cambridge University Press, 1992.

Turner, Louis, and Michael Hodges. *Global Shakeout*. London: Century Business, 1992.

Wagner, Michael K. L. and Amy R. Kaplan. "State Anti-Takeover Legislation: Necessary Protection or Rationalization of Entrenchment." *Insights: The Corporate & Securities Law Advisor* 4(2)(1990): 26.

Waller, David. "A Shock to the System," *Financial Times*, 6 August 1993.

World Development Report 1993: Investing in Health. New York: Oxford University Press, 1993.

World Investment Report 1992: Transnational Corporations as Engines of Growth. New York: United Nations, 1992.

Wright, Frank. "Nation Seeks Asylum from Wave of Refugees: Open-Door Policy Got Out of Control," *Star Tribune* (Berlin, Germany), 13 December 1993, 11A.

8

The Socially Responsible Corporation: Responsible to Whom and for What?

Marina v.N. Whitman

In December 1983 I was privileged to participate in a symposium on Catholic Social Teaching and the U.S. Economy at Notre Dame. The symposium was convened by Professor Houck and Father Williams at the request of the National Conference of Catholic Bishops, which was preparing a pastoral letter on that subject.

Looking back over the published volume that resulted from those discussions (Houck and Williams 1984), I was startled to realize how similar the issues we discussed in 1984 are to the ones we are wrestling with today. The context of the discussion has changed in at least one surprising way, however. In 1983 much of the discussion, as well as the manifest concern of the U.S. bishops, was centered on the question of whether corporations had too much power. Today, if one takes Samuelson's article as the point of departure, the concern seems to be more with corporations' having too little power or, at least, with some of the negative aspects of the erosion of power suffered by large, traditional corporations in today's global economy:

> The idea of the "good corporation" assumed that superior American management could easily blend two roles: the company as a fierce economic competitor, and the company as a welfare state for its workers. There seemed to be no conflict. Stable jobs and ample fringe benefits would make workers loyal, and loyal workers would make companies prosper.[1]

129

Background: Multiple Stakeholders and Rising Expectations

In his article, Samuelson focused on one particular aspect of corporate "social responsibility"—the relationship between a company and its employees, current and former. Social responsibility, however, is much broader and more complex. The concept of corporate social responsibility has as many facets as there are stakeholders, that is, individuals or groups who feel they are affected in some significant way by the actions of a corporation and therefore should have some say in what it does or does not do. Among the most important of these stakeholder groups, for any corporation, are customers, stockholders, employees and retirees, labor unions (these last two groups are by no means identical, although they overlap on many issues), suppliers, communities, and government legislators and regulators at every level, who at least purport to represent the interests of society at large.

Given the number and variety of stakeholder groups, tensions and conflicts among their demands are inevitable, and corporations are required constantly to make difficult and frequently painful trade-offs in responding to the diverse goals of often divergent interests. Some of these trade-offs are technical; the examples here are from the auto industry, with which I happen to be most familiar, but they have counterparts in every sphere of economic activity.

Among the societal expectations confronting the auto industry in the 1980s—and today—were those for greater fuel efficiency, increased safety, and reduced emissions into the environment. But no technological magic bullet can avoid trade-offs among these goals, and between them and the demands of customers for affordability, comfort, convenience, performance, and so forth; companies must satisfy these demands to be successful and viable. Increases in governmental safety and emissions requirements add structure and hardware to a vehicle that reduce its fuel efficiency; significant increases in fuel efficiency—in the absence of a new technological breakthrough—require either downsizing of vehicles which, *ceteris paribus,* reduces passenger protection in an accident, or the use of premium materials which increase costs and reduce affordability. Alternatively, an engine's fuel efficiency can be increased by reducing its performance—the length of time required for acceleration—but that is likely to make the customer unhappy.

Similarly, the current substitutes for the ozone-depleting substances in air conditioners, now progressively banned under the Montreal Protocol, are not only less destructive but also less efficient than their predecessors, meaning that new automobile air conditioners will be larger and heavier and occupants sometimes uncomfortably warmer than they used to be. One measure of a company's success is how creative it is in finding new ways to resolve specific trade-offs—that is what technological progress is all about—but the class of problems they represent will not go away.

Broadening beyond the technical realm, corporations confront a variety of sociopolitical tensions among different stakeholder groups. One such set of issues that has been commanding considerable public attention in recent years is associated with environmental concerns. Where these concerns take the form of pressure for modifying particular product characteristics, the tension is likely to be with the desires of customers, even though the concerned voters and demanding customers may often be the same people acting in different capacities. When they take the form of pressure to restrict particular processes or types of economic activity, workers whose livelihoods appear threatened are likely to be a major opposing force, as in the ongoing controversy about the preservation of the spotted owl and restrictions on logging in the Northwest.

Even more fundamental is the issue of the rights of stockholders versus those of workers as claimants on a firm's "surplus" revenues. At one extreme is the "stockholder as king" view best articulated by Milton Friedman in his famous statement: "Few trends could so thoroughly undermine the very foundations of our free society as the acceptance by corporate officials of a social responsibility other than to make as much money for their stockholders as possible" (Friedman 1962, 133). If a corporation takes on social responsibilities that go beyond pursuit of its own long-term interests, he argues, its management is arrogating to itself the right to make decisions that properly belongs to the stockholders.

At the other extreme is the view, more often associated with the Japanese than with the U.S. perspective, that it is the workers who are the primary claimants on a firm's residual surplus. Witness, for example, a recent statement, quoted in the *New York Times,* by a young official of the Japanese Ministry of Trade and Industry (MITI). He was discussing arguments his ministry was having with the Americans about getting rid of an elaborate regulatory and certification process everyone agrees gets in the way of open access to the Japanese marketplace for foreign products and of the freedom of Japanese consumers to choose such products. He readily agreed that the present process cries out for simplification. "But," he said, "we have to think about the livelihood of the people involved in those activities. That is the difference with us. We are concerned with those people.''

The statements just cited represent two opposing extremes in the current discourse on the nature of corporate social responsibility. But the tensions they reflect so starkly are inherent in many of the decisions facing the modern corporation and are reflected as well in the legislative and regulatory environments within which it functions.

As this brief discussion of the multiplicity of demands confronting the U.S. corporation of the 1990s suggests, these institutions have been the subject of constantly rising expectations over the half-century since the end of World War II. As noted by Post elsewhere in this volume, "The result is an institution that has evolved from narrow purpose roots into a broader purpose (or multipurpose) institution whose viability is now challenged.''

On one side are the societal demands, articulated by governments and the voters to whom they are ultimately answerable, as well as by a variety of nongovernmental interest groups, that corporations exercise two types of social responsibility, categorized by Sethi in his paper in this volume: "(a) to ameliorate some of the second-order effects, i.e., externalities, of their normal business activities; and (b) to voluntarily meet nonmarket societal needs." Among the types of social responsibilities that fall into one or the other of these categories are those relating to consumer safety, environmental friendliness, promotion of workplace diversity, mandated benefits for workers—such as pensions, family leave, or shutdown notification—community responsibilities, and many more.

At the same time, corporations must strive to satisfy the continually increasing private demands of their customers, actual or potential, for quality, style, comfort, convenience, leading-edge technology, and affordability, among other attributes. The pace at which these demands accelerate, in fact, has been intensified by the rising affluence and increasing sophistication of consumers and the ever-growing breadth and intensity of competition on the part of business to satisfy them.

Social Responsibility, Competition, and Market Power

With this background of multiple and often conflicting stakeholder interests and ever-rising expectations, let us return to the "people" aspects of corporate social responsibility that Samuelson emphasized. These relationships are indeed affected by the pressures of global competition and technological change but not, I believe, in quite the way that Samuelson seems to imply:

> The spread of the "good corporation" was supposed to provide stable jobs and generous fringe benefits—health insurance and pensions—for more and more Americans. Instead, the process is sliding into reverse. As companies strive to stay competitive, they are shedding workers, encouraging early retirement and cutting fringe benefits.[2]

To put it bluntly, Samuelson's concerns, at least in the abbreviated form in which they come to us, appear to reflect some confusion between social responsibility and oligopoly, that is, market power. Or perhaps it is not confusion at all, but simply an association of the two, an association that Sethi's paper spells out more explicitly: "The fact remains that it is imperfect markets and their exploitation by corporations that create opportunities for 'good' corporate behavior."

Certainly the corporations cited by Samuelson as examples all possessed substantial market power. The surprise, and the associated ethical conundrum, arise because the economic rents, or above-market-level profits, associated with oligopoly turn out to have become embedded in some unexpected places. They are conventionally associated in the public mind with high executive pay and lavish perquisites, as well as with organizational inefficiencies—often including redundant layers of management—and high overhead costs. But that is not by any means the whole story.

Clearly, rank-and-file workers have shared in these economic rents. Average hourly earnings of workers in the automobile industry, for example, are some 45 percent higher than the average for all private employment and 35 percent higher than the average for manufacturing employment (*Statistical Abstract of the United States* 1993). These premiums are persistent; they have not declined over the past decade, despite all the trials and tribulations of the automobile industry in the United States and the widespread job losses that have resulted.

Much less obvious are some of the other repositories of economic rents. These include the willingness of oligopolistic firms to acquiesce in overly generous (to the taxing jurisdictions) calculations of their tax obligations, commitments that, in today's cost-conscious environment, are frequently being reduced through difficult negotiations or successful court challenges. Such processes are particularly painful in cases where a single plant or firm or industry accounts for a substantial portion of a community's tax revenues.

Among the other beneficiaries of economic rents are heavy charitable involvements by corporations and their frequent willingness to subsidize research whose results will redound to the benefit not primarily of the sponsoring entity but of an entire industry, including the sponsor's competitors, or perhaps to the broader society at large. When AT&T was a regulated monopoly, some of the most dramatic research results to emerge from its famed Bell Laboratories were of no direct benefit to the company or even its industry but represented basic scientific advances capturable by the entire society. Today, Bell Labs' efforts are not only downsized but also much more narrowly focused on projects that are likely to yield some direct benefit to AT&T.

Similarly, when General Motors' leading market position seemed reasonably secure, its Technical Center was the scene of a number of research projects, such as the development of improved crash dummies, that yielded no competitive advantage to the company because their benefits were immediately appropriable by the industry or the society as a whole. Today, with its share of U.S. sales down from more than half to about a third and struggling to get its North American business back above break-even point, GM is much less inclined to tolerate free-riding on its research. Instead, the costs of projects like the search for breakthroughs in fuel-efficiency or recyclability, whose benefits cannot be translated to the bottom line, are being shared through industry-wide consortia or, in some cases, industry-government partnerships. However, almost certainly, in some cases that type of research is simply not occurring at all, at least not on its previous scale.

Given that the economic rents associated with oligopoly were so widely distributed, it is hardly surprising that their elimination through intensified competition is a painful process, painful not only for the stockholders and managements of the corporations involved but for their workers and communities as well and, in some respects, for the broader society of which they are a part. But, before we wax too nostalgic for past glories, it is worth remembering that a high degree of market power has its less beneficial aspects as well.

Most obvious, perhaps, is that oligopolistic firms tend to have higher costs, as well as higher accounting profits, and charge higher prices to consumers than would prevail in a more competitive environment. One need only compare air fares in the fiercely competitive U.S. airline industry with those of its regulated-oligopoly (or monopoly) European counterparts to recognize that, despite all the complaints, the competition bred by deregulation has had a democratizing effect on American air travel. Similarly, the lively competition that characterizes the computer industry, together with rapid technological advance, has produced an astonishingly rapid decline in prices as well as an exponential increase in the power of its products. Indeed, the pace of technological change is itself likely to benefit from competition; without its relentless pressure, firms in oligopolistic industries may not always be motivated to remain on the technological leading edge.[3]

Finally, U.S. society has been characterized ever since its beginnings by concern and skepticism regarding "excessive" concentrations of power. From the *Federalist Papers* onward, the American legal and regulatory framework has been designed to minimize such concentrations. As regards the private sector, it is the desire to limit market power that, perhaps more than anything else, sets the American style of capitalism apart from its European and Japanese counterparts.

Such concerns about the power of oligopolistic firms are reflected at two levels. One is the fear that such large traditional firms tend to be characterized by a paternalism that erodes the autonomy of both workers and managers. Writing in 1956 during the heyday of the good corporation, Samuelson takes as a benchmark, William H. Whyte who immortalized this view in *The Organization Man* (p. 404):

> The organization man . . . must *fight* The Organization . . . for the demands for his surrender are constant and powerful, and the more he has come to like the life of the organization the more difficult does he find it to resist these demands, or even to recognize them. . . . The peace of mind offered by organization remains a surrender, and no less so for being offered in benevolence.

At the macroeconomic, as opposed to the individual, level, our society has long been apprehensive about the arrogance of power, including economic power. This deep-seated apprehension is reflected in a famous misquote attributed to C. E. Wilson, chairman of General Motors and nominee for Secretary of Defense, to the effect that "What's good for General Motors is good for the country." What Wilson actually said, in response to a query about whether he saw a potential conflict of interest between the GM chairmanship he was just leaving and the cabinet position for which he had been nominated, was "What was good for the country was good for General Motors," which conveys a quite different emphasis. But the fact that the erroneous version has persisted for more than forty years in the face of numerous efforts to set the record straight provides a kind of Rorschach test of

American attitudes toward large, powerful corporations, an attitude reflected succinctly in President Eisenhower's long-remembered warning about the dangers of the "military-industrial complex."

Indeed, in their heyday, corporations like those alluded to by Samuelson were constantly under threat of antitrust initiatives aimed at sharply reducing the degree of market power they possessed. AT&T actually was broken into eight pieces (AT&T and the seven Baby Bells) as a result of legal action, while the structure and behavior of GM were significantly modified by the constant threat of such action, and IBM was subject to a formal legal challenge whose resolution stretched over more than a decade. As late as 1986, the author of a book about the latter case could write with a straight face:

- In 1985 IBM was the most profitable company in the world. It earned almost $6.6 billion in profit on over $50 billion in revenues, more than Exxon, more than General Motors, more than any other company.
- IBM continues to dominate the computer business and is well on its way to dominating everything that is connected to and/or operates with these computers.
- IBM faces no significant domestic or foreign competition that could threaten this dominance. It has such overwhelming political, financial, and technological power that what competition it faces exists at its sufferance.
- The antitrust laws, designed to police just such unequal competition, are of little use. The Reagan Administration gives its actions a clean bill of health. It is perilous to trust a single company with such power. (DeLamarter 1986, xiv–xv, xviii.)

This quotation conveys dramatically the attitude, however misguided, of many Americans, toward the exemplar of the good corporation before its fall.

We see that negative as well as positive attributes are associated with the traditional good corporation. Beyond this observation, some advantages of intensified global competition are worth noting. One is the widened range of choice, in terms of price, quality, and types of goods, now available to consumers in this country and around the world. A second is that this relatively wide-open global competition is the vehicle by which some formerly poor countries have grown rich, and many more appear to be starting the climb up the ladder. First came Japan, whose rise from war-devastated poverty to conspicuous affluence in the space of a few decades was fueled by its successes in global competition. Then came the Four Asian Tigers—Hong Kong, Korea, Singapore, and Taiwan—following in Japan's footsteps, whose rise has been equally remarkable, although they have yet to achieve the income levels at the top of the ladder. Now, countries such as Brazil, Malaysia, Mexico, and others are moving into middle-income status by virtue of their active participation in the global marketplace.

Finally, global competition makes the intimate link between profits and jobs very clear. Academics and social critics too often tend to talk as though the two were mutually exclusive alternatives or even antithetical to one another, and governments have attempted repeatedly to preserve the latter in firms or industries where there is no realistic hope of maintaining or restoring the former, sometimes because of the actions of those same governments. The pressures of global competition lay bare the fallacies involved and drive home the point that plentiful good jobs and healthy profits are in reality not adversaries but partners.

Organizational Structure and the Information Revolution

In describing the changing fortunes of the large, traditional corporation, Samuelson mentions not only global competition but also technological change. Indeed, the latter may be an even more potent agent of change than the former. It is not simply that automation makes possible productivity increases that, while they lay the only durable foundation for long-term increases in income and living standards, also produce significant job dislocations in the short term. That situation has been with us for a very long time; we are today replicating in the manufacturing sector a process that resulted in a drop in U.S. agriculture's share of employment from 36 percent in 1900 to less than 3 percent today, while our agricultural output steadily increased.

The novel factor today is the impact that the most dramatic aspect of technological change, the information revolution, is having on the organizational structure of U.S. business. Because modern information technology makes communication, and therefore coordination, easier, American firms are becoming smaller and more tightly focused, and rely more heavily on outsourcing for many aspects of their operations. Internally, they are becoming less hierarchical, with flatter organizational structures and fewer layers of management. The downsizing of large, traditional corporations is not simply a matter of getting rid of redundant "fat" under the pressure of global competition. It is also a function of changes in organizational structure made possible, indeed, inevitable, by the availability of powerful new information technology.[4]

These changes tie back to the trade-offs between paternalism and individual autonomy mentioned earlier. The flattening of management layers and the shift from hierarchical to more participatory management styles is bestowing more responsibility and opportunities to take the initiative on workers at every level. We are moving away from the concept of cradle-to-grave loyalty in both directions to a much more transactional concept, in which loyalty is defined in terms of mutual respect and support for however long the relationship lasts.[5]

An anecdote from my GM days illustrates the latter shift. A year or so after I arrived at GM my immediate deputy, who had done a superb job of supporting me through my initiation into the corporation, accepted an attractive career opportunity from one of GM's major suppliers which GM, to my regret, was unable to come anywhere near matching. Accepting the inevitable, I gave him a farewell party at which I expressed my gratitude for his outstanding performance before a substantial gathering of our coworkers. Imagine my surprise when I found myself being criticized, not once but repeatedly, for thus recognizing the contributions of a "traitor" who was voluntarily leaving the corporation.

By the time I myself left GM, a little more than a decade later, we were all gaining weight from the plethora of farewell parties being given for departing colleagues. Far from objecting, in many cases the company was offering substantial incentives for people at every level to take such a step.

Problems and Pressures

Does all this mean that there is nothing to worry about? To do so would be to ignore the very real problems, both transitional and ongoing, associated with the changes just described.

The nature of the transitional problems is as simple to summarize as the ramifications are difficult and complex: the social costs of job dislocations to individuals, families, and the communities in which they live are very real. This is true even, and perhaps most, when the long-term benefits of these same changes, in the form of increased productivity, output, income, and living standards, is greatest. The appropriate solution, though, is not to attempt to avoid or retard the adjustment process, however strongly those who are affected negatively and the politicians who represent them press for it, because such a course is inevitably costly and ultimately self-defeating. Rather, we must find effective ways to cushion the shock for those adversely affected, to avoid creating "throwaway people" without, at the same time, throwing sand under the wheels of change.

Our concern must be greatest for those who conducted their lives under one set of rules only to find, late in the day, that the rules have changed. To use an analogy from a different area of relationships, consider the moral complexities of the view, increasingly adduced by judges in divorce cases, that alimony is an outmoded concept with no place in modern society. This seems both fair and appropriate in the case, for example, of two thirty-five-year-old MBAs who decide to part ways after a decade or less of marriage. But what about the woman of fifty-five or so who played by the old rules—staying home and allowing her professional skills to obsolesce while she supervised the household and raised the children and her husband provided the family income—who suddenly finds that her marriage is over, and she is financially as well as emotionally on her own?

The situation of a middle-aged worker who started working right out of high school under the old rules—I give you loyalty and you give me job security followed by a good pension—and now finds himself downsized out of a job is not dissimilar. An implicit contract between employer and employee, based not on job tenure but on job skills, on a mutual respect and support between employer and employee with no expectation on either side that the relationship will necessarily last forever, is great for younger people who start out with that set of assumptions. But the same contract is hard on the person in midlife or beyond who finds himself playing under a new set of ground rules.

The challenge is to find ways of being fair to such a person without reducing the flexibility of labor markets that is one of the great strengths of the U.S. economy. As we move through this period of transition from old to new rules, that flexibility should be based, not on personal insecurity, but on a new basis for security, defined not in terms of job tenure but in terms of embodied skills that translate into "employability security" (Kanter 1993) even when jobs and employers change.

First among the ongoing, as opposed to the transitional, problems associated with the new economic environment is that pressures to perform in the face of intense competition can increase the likelihood of ethical corner-cutting (Baumol 1991). Second, there is a well-documented inverse relationship between job turnover and on-the-job training that could have negative implications for the quality of a nation's labor force (OECD 1993). Third, global economic integration increases pressures for harmonizing rules and regulations and standards among countries in ways that may work against the differing preferences and priorities of their citizenries. These pressures arise because, as economic activities increasingly span the globe, tensions created by differences in legal structures or customary ethical strictures are inevitably exacerbated.

In the case of the United States, these tensions are heightened by a moral universalism that has characterized our nation since its beginnings and that is a frequent cause of irritation and resentment abroad. The globalization of production and competition has allowed these tendencies to manifest themselves in new ways. Should this country, for example, use trade sanctions to impose its own views of proper behavior toward the environment or toward labor rights on countries whose own views of these issues differ from ours? In certain cases such as banning imports of harmful products or the products of processes that, although conducted beyond our borders, cause environmental damage to our own air or water, these sanctions are legitimized by every country's right to protect its own citizens. However, in other instances such as the banning of products produced by slave labor, appeal to a universal code of morality is likely to be widely accepted.

But what about banning imports of goods produced under processes we find offensive even though they do not have a direct impact on us? When the United States banned imports of Mexican tuna caught in dolphin-killing nets, an international tribunal weighed American sensibilities against Mexican fishermen's jobs and ruled in favor of the latter. Similarly, most of us find it entirely appropriate that a rich country like ours should define "child labor" as relating to people under sixteen or even eighteen. But does this give us a moral right to restrict imports produced by such teenagers in countries where the average age at which children go to work is twelve or thirteen, because the alternative is often starvation? Moving from the ambiguous to the absurd, what about Ross Perot's proposal, during the height of the NAFTA debate, that the United States impose a "social tariff" on imports from poorer countries to compensate for any difference in their wage levels and our own?

The close linkage between global economic integration and the exacerbation of these kinds of friction was highlighted at the signing in Morocco in April 1993 of the agreement that signaled the completion of the Uruguay Round of multilateral trade negotiations. At American insistence and after much wrangling, the final communiqué made reference to the need to incorporate guidelines on the environment and on labor rights into the agenda of the newly created World Trade Organization. Almost unanimously, the developing nations among the signatories gave public vent to their anger and irritation at what they regarded as either moral imperialism or disguised protectionism or both, on the part of the United States.

One last continuing problem associated with the current economic environment is the increase in income inequality, particularly in the gap between the incomes of high-skilled and low-skilled workers, which has been occurring not only in the United States but in other industrialized nations as well. A number of studies suggest that increased global competition is a relatively small factor in this growing inequality, while rapid technological change favoring skilled labor looms much larger, but the issue remains an open and controversial one among economists. Whatever the cause, the situation poses significant ethical as well as political and social challenges. Nor is it clear what measures can best alleviate the situation, although more effective schooling and training of non-college-bound students and perhaps some form of wage subsidies, at least on a temporary basis, for the least-skilled workers, are among the more likely possibilities.

The New Rules of the Game: Guidelines for Firms

What do the ethical pitfalls outlined above suggest about new rules for defining corporate social responsibility in a globalized environment? The following list, by no means comprehensive, provides some suggestions, first for firms and then for governments.

First, a major responsibility of the chief executive of any firm must be to make clear, by example and precept, the ethical guidelines by which the firm operates and to make sure they are disseminated, understood, and followed in every part and at every level in the organization. A major responsibility of the board of directors must be to make certain that the chief executive performs this function effectively and continuously.

Second, systems must be in place to ensure an effective linkage between pay and performance at every level in the organization. The weakening of this link for top executives during the 1980s created tremendous frustration and loss of morale and led, among other things, to the passage of a law imposing limits on the deductibility of executive compensation that exceeds one million dollars annually.

The results of this legislation so far have been mixed and, as is so often the case, different from what its authors had anticipated. There has been, to my knowledge, no instance in which an executive's effective compensation has been reduced as a result of the new rule. In fact, it has been suggested that, as a result of the discussion and publicity surrounding this law, a million dollars has become effectively a floor for the compensation of chief executives of large publicly held corporations.

At the same time, however, because preserving deductibility of compensation over a million dollars requires a stockholder-approved plan that ties such compensation to the company's performance, corporations have been forced to lay out such plans explicitly in proxy statements and to think more carefully about how these should be designed. Many companies were doing this already, and for some others it remains primarily window-dressing. But it has brought about greater transparency and more thought and discussion regarding the whole issue of executive compensation.

For employees at all levels below the very top, as layers of management are reduced and the space between the rungs on the promotion ladder widens, pay should increasingly be tied to an individual's breadth of skills rather than to her or his standing in the corporate hierarchy. That is, pay should be much less tightly tied to promotion than in the past, as organizations move away from hierarchical and toward participatory styles of leadership that demand initiative and responsibility from all workers, regardless of job title.

Third, in addition to encouraging the upgrading of skills by directly assisting and rewarding their acquisition, firms could push the public sector to provide more effective and relevant education by demanding well-trained entrants into the labor force. This need for better primary and secondary education is something to which companies pay enormous lip service, but many do not reflect it in their hiring practices. Relatively few companies, for example, make a serious effort to look at and evaluate the academic performance of new hires who are not college graduates, although such efforts may be increasing. One of the things we have learned from the hiring practices of Japanese "transplant" firms in the United States is how much emphasis they put on screening and evaluating the work-related skills of potential employees, and how great the payoff is in terms of productivity and product quality. More to the point in the present context, such behavior should have significant payoff in terms of insuring employees' "employability security" as well.

Fourth, a firm's commitment to the new style of employer-employee relations must be genuine. In some instances, early efforts in this direction, such as "quality circles" and similar experiments, foundered on the shoals of worker mistrust when the promised sharing of information and decision-making power did not in fact materialize. One important aspect of such a new relationship is creating a link between the contingent pay received by executives, for example, in the form of bonuses or stock options, and whatever form of profit-sharing is included in the compensation of nonexecutive employees. The formulas and triggering performance criteria need not be identical, but there does need to be some logical and easily understood link between the two.

The role of labor unions is one major conundrum confronting the evolution to a new type of social contract between firms and their employees. So far, this evolution has been accompanied by a steady decline in the proportion of workers who belong to unions, particularly in the private sector, and a concomitant decline in unions' power.

Those who applaud this trend point out that U.S. unions have become increasingly rigid and bureaucratic. They note that, particularly in such formerly oligopolistic industries as steel and auto, unions' efforts to preserve the far-above-average compensation that reflected their share of economic rents when those rents no longer existed, accelerated the declining competitiveness and rapid fall in employment in these industries. Because this union rigidity is incompatible with the flexibility required in today's highly competitive and fast-changing environment, they conclude, American unions remain healthy only in the public sector and in a few highly regulated industries where monopoly is essentially unchallenged. In contrast, the more widespread unionization of workers in Europe is associated with high structural unemployment and a lack of job-creation in the private sector.

The lessons of history suggest that healthy unions have represented an important source of worker protection and countervailing power in democratic societies. It is hard to believe these needs have lessened in a world where the global mobility of capital and technology has increased far more than that of labor which crosses national and even local boundaries far less readily. What, then, is the answer?

It seems clear that the changing nature of firms needs to be accompanied by a change in the nature of unions. This involves a shift on both sides from the traditional adversarial relationship to a far more cooperative one, a recognition by managers that workers represent assets rather than costs and a recognition by unions that a shared responsibility for increasing productivity and competitiveness is the only viable foundation for increased wages and benefits. Even more difficult, but probably essential, will be unions' acceptance of a growing substitution of "employability security" for the traditional concept of job security. Some of the more far-sighted companies and unions have recognized and begun to wrestle creatively with these issues, but the evolution of U.S. labor unions into organizations that protect workers without rigidifying labor markets remains a major challenge.[6]

Finally, corporations in the United States need to move beyond the definition of competitiveness and continuous improvement in terms of downsizing and shedding workers to a definition in terms of building (by investing in human and physical capital), pioneering and innovating, according to business analyst Michael Porter. Such a shift may be starting already. There is no question that many firms were too fat and had too many people, but eliminating redundancy is to some extent a once-over matter, and some companies are beginning to recognize that they may be trimming past fat into muscle and bone. Wall Street's infatuation with "getting leaner and meaner" is bound to fade, particularly as firms learn from experience to distinguish between downsizing that is strategic and that which is not.

The New Rules: Guidelines for Governments

Corporations do not set the ground rules for their own behavior in a vacuum. Observers of all political stripes agree that one function of government is to set the rules or the framework of law within which firms and markets operate and that define the structure for ethical behavior, however strongly they disagree on what the specific nature of those rules should be.

What steps, then, should governments take to set an appropriate and effective framework or structure for socially responsible behavior on the part of corporations? Here is my own list of some guidelines that are particularly relevant to the issue with which we are wrestling.

First, it is critical that government avoid the always-strong temptation to protect and preserve market power for its firms through trade
barriers or regulatory requirements that restrict competition in product
or labor markets. Contrary to widespread belief, government actions
create or enhance oligopoly power far more frequently than they limit
or restrict it.

Second, government should resist political pressure to threaten or
use actual trade sanctions to force other countries to "harmonize"
their labor, environmental, and other laws to match those of the United
States. Such pressures engender hostility, particularly on the part of
developing nations, toward American moral imperialism and suspected
or actual cryptoprotectionism.[7] Indeed, the benefits of international
trade and investment are generally enhanced rather than reduced by
diversity among the participants. Also, trade restrictions are much
more likely to hamper than to foster the progress of the targeted
countries in the desired direction, since poverty is far more likely
than perversity to underlie their failure to conform to our standards
of behavior.

Recent history should alleviate fears about the likelihood of an
international regulatory "race for the bottom" via competition in
loosening regulatory restrictions on corporate behavior. Increasing
global integration has, on the whole, been accompanied by a strength-
ening rather than a loosening of developing nations' laws and regulations in the sensitive areas just mentioned. Certainly international
agreements can play a role in such issues: "Where nations actually
agree on basic standards, international agreements can make such
standards more credible domestically and reduce the opportunity costs
of imposing them alone" (Lawrence 1994). But with the exception of
rogue countries whose behavior is universally regarded as unacceptable, both the effectiveness of such agreements and the good faith of
their signatories might be enhanced if trade sanctions were avoided.
Possible alternatives might include financial or technical assistance to
developing countries to help them conform to the standards and/or
labeling of goods (e.g., tuna fish) whose production processes violated
the agreed standards (Lawrence 1994).

Third, a governmental role in improving the school-to-work transition for non-college-bound students is probably the most effective
contribution that government can make toward narrowing the growing
gap in incomes between skilled and unskilled workers. But one must
be aware of inappropriate models; recent research (Heckman *et al.*
1994) suggests that simply emulating the much-vaunted German

apprenticeship system may not prove effective in preparing our youth for the workplace of the future. Given our ignorance on what measures are likely to be most effective, it would behoove government to encourage educational experimentation and alternatives to monopoly in public education.[8] In light of mounting evidence that training and learning are becoming lifelong processes, support for such institutions as community colleges and for public-private partnerships directed toward such ongoing processes is likely to have a high payoff.

In addition, government must constantly look for ways to alleviate the social cost of adjustment to structural change without creating the rigidities in labor markets against which Samuelson warns. To enhance the portability of labor markets, one step would be to encourage the ongoing shift from defined-benefit to defined-contribution pension plans. Another would be to avoid measures in health-care reform that link either coverage or payment obligations to particular categories of employers or a person's employment status.

Finally, the evolution of new labor-market arrangements will benefit from continuing experimentation of the sort that normally occurs in the private sector, provided government resists its inclination toward premature or excessive regulation. We should, however, note that some countries in Western Europe that imposed tight restrictions on labor markets in the name of job preservation or worker protection are now starting to loosen such restrictions. This is because the rigidities that accompany the welfare-state approach have been associated increasingly with persistently high unemployment rates, a low rate of new job creation, and a high proportion of long-term unemployed.

Finally, I must underline the importance of continuously searching for ways to move the traditionally adversarial relationship between government regulators and private business in the United States toward a cooperative approach to resolving social issues. Such an approach will foster solutions that are economically efficient and responsive to the dislocation and disruption that change can cause for some of those people caught up in it.

What, then, can we conclude from this analysis? Unquestionably, the U.S. economy is undergoing a period of very rapid transition which is a product of both global economic integration and the technological and organizational changes associated with the information revolution. Transition is always painful, and we need to alleviate the pain for those who are hardest hit. But at the same time, we must avoid the twin dangers of sentimentalizing the past and trying to hold down the costs of change by throwing sand in its wheels. The common task we face is not to say farewell to the good corporation, but to help reinvent it in a form suitable for the twenty-first century.

Notes

1. See Robert J. Samuelson, "R.I.P.: The Good Corporation," *Newsweek*, 5 July 1993.

2. Samuelson, "R.I.P."

3. There is no contradiction between this statement and the fact that technological innovation is a time-honored way for a corporation to create or preserve market power.

4. For further discussion of this phenomenon, see Whitman 1994, and the *Fortune* article quoted there: "Welcome to the Revolution," 13 December 1993.

5. See, for example, "What Companies and Employees Owe One Another," *Fortune*, 13 June 1994.

6. See "Why America Needs Unions but Not the Kind It Has Now," *Business Week*, 23 May 1994, and the 1994 Report of the Commission on the Future of Worker-Management Relations.

7. Although some general language regarding environmental protection is incorporated into both the North American Free Trade Agreement (NAFTA) and the Final Agreement of the GATT Uruguay Round, it was not accomplished without considerable wrangling. Mexico agreed to sign much more detailed "side agreements" covering environmental and labor issues as the price of approval of the NAFTA by the U.S. Congress, while the latter issues were put on the agenda for future discussion at the insistence of the United States at the time the latest GATT agreement was signed.

8. Among the possibilities currently being tried are a variety of voucher schemes and so-called charter schools. The latter are financed with public funds and are open to all students but, at least in some states that have authorized them, charter schools are allowed to experiment with educational methods and structures outside the restrictions imposed by local school boards and teachers' unions.

Bibliography

Baumol, William J. *Perfect Markets and Easy Virtue: Business Ethics and the Invisible Hand*. Cambridge, MA: Blackwell, 1991.

DeLamarter, Richard T. *Big Blue: IBM's Use and Abuse of Power*. New York: Dodd, Mead, 1986.

Friedman, Milton. *Capitalism and Freedom*. Chicago: University of Chicago Press, 1962.

Heckman, James J., Rebecca L. Roselius and Jeffrey A. Smith. "U.S. Educa-
    tion and Training Policy: A Re-evaluation of the Underlying Assumptions
    Behind the 'New Consensus'." Paper presented at Conference on Job
    Change and Federal Labor Policies, American Enterprise Institute, Washing-
    ton, D.C., 7 March 1994.
Houck, John W. and Oliver F. Williams, editors. *Catholic Social Teaching and
    the U.S. Economy.* Washington, D.C.: University Press of America, 1984.
Kanter, Rosabeth M. "Employability Security." *Business and Society Review*
    87 (Fall 1993): 11–14.
Lawrence, Robert Z. "Labour Market Performance and Standards in the
    OECD: The Concern About Globalisation." Paper presented at the Informal
    Policy Dialogue meeting on Globalisation and Regionalisation, OECD Head-
    quarters, Paris, 28–29 April 1994.
Organization for Economic Cooperation and Development (OECD), 1993.
    "Enterprise Tenure, Labor Turnover and Staff Training." *OECD Employ-
    ment Outlook,* July, 119–155.
U.S. Department of Commerce, Bureau of the Census, 1993. *Statistical
    Abstract of the United States 1993.* Washington D.C.: U.S. Government
    Printing Office.
Whitman, Marina v.N. "Flexible Markets, Flexible Firms." *The American
    Enterprise,* May/June 1994: 26–37.
Whyte, William H. *The Organization Man.* Garden City, N.Y.: Doubleday,
    1956.

Part III

Religious Perspectives on Corporate Social Responsibility

9

Accountability in a Global Economy

J. Philip Wogaman

The major thesis of this paper can be stated simply: the free market mechanism, for all its benefits in other respects, is unable to set and preserve adequate standards of corporate ethics. That simple fact poses an enormous challenge to everybody who cares about business ethics in a rapidly changing global economy. In this chapter I wish to explore this thesis and its ramifications in broad structural terms. I am not a professional economist, but my academic work as a Christian ethicist has been enriched by a number of practical experiences with global companies facing real moral dilemmas—most notably with corporations marketing infant-formula products in Third World settings.[1]

Business Ethics and the Market Mechanism

A revival of interest in business ethics during the past twelve years has coincided with widespread ideological commitments to the free-market mechanism. After half a century as whipping boy for ideologies of welfare-state and mixed economy, free market ideologies—even in their more extreme laissez-faire form—returned with vigor in the political triumphs of Ronald Reagan in the United States and Margaret Thatcher in the United Kingdom. Their return produced corresponding effects in the politics of many other countries. The unexpectedly sudden collapse of the Soviet empire—including the Soviet Union itself—and many of its socialist economic institutions gave profound

new impetus to the view that the market mechanism is both economically and ethically the highest form of economic organization, thus
reversing much of the conventional wisdom of the previous half-
century. Business ethics was not, of course, invented during this
period. But it too gained new vigor, as expressed in a burgeoning
literature, more academic courses and chairs in business schools or
departments, and even in the appointment of ethics consultants to
major corporations. Although this correspondence between historical
political forces and new developments in business ethics may or may
not be more than accidental, those who are serious about business
ethics must nevertheless take into account political and economic
developments and the ideological spirit of the times.

As articulated by its contemporary theorists, the market mechanism
promises extraordinary economic benefits.[2] This mechanism:

1. Best assures that what is actually wanted is to know what will be
   produced and in the quantities that will best approximate
   demand;
2. Best preserves freedom for individual decision-making in employment and consumption;
3. Best guarantees the continued existence and prosperity of enterprises that are responding efficiently to the market and the
   replacement of inefficient and unresponsive enterprises.

The market system thus represents the most creative, productive,
dynamic organization of economic life. By comparison, previous economic systems (such as feudalism) were less dynamic and less efficient, and socialist alternatives are wasteful, inefficient, and often
prone to corruption. The claim can even be made that the market
mechanism is, in the long term, even more egalitarian in its actual
consequences,[3] although contemporary theorists usually are content
to argue that the mechanism best guarantees that people will get what
they deserve.

My purpose in this chapter is not to confirm or refute the main
points in the ideology.[4] Rather, I am most interested in one aspect of
the theory: the claim that competition in the free-market system
rewards efficiency and penalizes inefficiency. Absent external interfer-
ence and other variables, enterprises capable of producing and marketing essentially the same goods or services at lower prices than their
competitors will win increasingly large shares of the market and
ultimately drive those competitors out of the market altogether. No-

body will want to buy essentially identical goods or services for higher prices; the less efficient competitors either will have to become more efficient or produce something else. The market rewards efficiency and punishes inefficiency, sometimes ruthlessly. In theory this is very simple and, in actual practice, it is scarcely less so. The point is that, other things being equal, anything that decreases the cost of producing or selling goods and services similar to those of one's competitors will be rewarded by the market mechanism; anything that increases those costs will be punished. The rewards and punishments are not conferred by external authorities or moral laws but by economic forces themselves. It is economic efficiency that is rewarded, not moral efficiency. The mechanism is neither moral nor immoral; it is simply the demonstrable working of the market when the market is left to its own devices.

This is the environment in which business ethics must function in the absence of other external constraints. Business leaders are asked to take full account of moral objectives in their decision-making: to be honest, to pay fair wages, to avoid damage to the environment, to reinforce higher standards of community culture in advertising, and to provide external benefits to the communities in which they operate—in short, to be responsible corporate citizens in every possible way. Under some circumstances each of these objectives can also be good, competitive business practice. It often pays in business relationships to be known as honest and dependable. Fair wages and working conditions can contribute to a more stable and loyal workforce. Environmental pollution can diminish a corporate image, possibly lowering sales. In spite of the occasional correlation of "good ethics" with "good business," it seems absurd to believe such a correlation always or even usually occurs. Wages, working conditions, environmental protection, and community betterment impose costs. These are costs that either raise the price of goods and services or lower the margin of profit. What could be more obvious, if the competitive market does what the market is alleged to do?

The realities of the market notwithstanding, business ethics is sometimes approached as if ethical standards in business were determined by the character and decisions of the businessperson. But if good behavior is penalized by market forces and bad behavior is rewarded, are there not clear limits to what even the best-intentioned businessperson can do? In some market situations, a kind of Gresham's Law of morality may even be in effect,[5] with low standards of morality driving out high standards. Elmer W. Johnson, formerly of General Motors, makes that point:

> While GM management can exercise a considerable degree of discretion in attending to its responsibilities in areas involving important social interests, this autonomy is not without limits. The competitive market system very promptly penalizes and ultimately bankrupts the firm that would go very far in promoting social goals at the expense of private profit. Thus, when there are important social interests that the market fails to protect, even with the application of long-term enlightened corporate self-interest, management may have an obligation to support efficient government intervention or to cooperate with church and other groups to advance particular social reforms.[6]

From this, we might expect that a businessperson would have greatest maneuvering room in a market that is less rather than more competitive. It might be more difficult to express one's conscience freely, say, in retail sales or used car sales rather than in a highly monopolistic situation such as that enjoyed some years ago by the Xerox and IBM corporations.

The U.S. airline industry is a case in point. Prior to deregulation, airfares and routes were more or less fixed, and competition centered more on the small touches of service. Occasionally, the existence of a particular airline was at risk, but the giants of the industry, such as TWA, United, and American, were quite stable. After deregulation, the appearance of cost-cutting operations like New York Air, Air Florida, and People Express, each of which had nonunion workforces with lower wages, placed severe pressures on the established airlines' labor policies. My point is neither to defend nor criticize the actual labor policies of the newer airlines (though I would critique them), but only to note that the highly competitive new situation placed severe constraints on what the established airlines could do. Even the most highly motivated corporate leader in the airline industry would confront severe, market-imposed limits on the freedom to act in accordance with his or her standards of business ethics.

Yet another illustration can be drawn from the years prior to unionization of farm workers, when they also were not covered by federal minimum wage requirements. This meant that a single farmer was virtually powerless to pay decent wages. The price of farm commodities already reflected the extremely low wages prevailing throughout agriculture in the United States. By providing substantial, even decent wage increases for farmworkers, no farmer would have been able to market farm produce anywhere near market rates, which would have forced either bankruptcy or reduced the farmer's own income below the already-depressed levels. The market set limits on what could be done to improve the condition of farmworkers.

In principle, then, it is naive to regard business ethics, as practiced by individual businesspeople, as a sufficient guarantee of moral standards in a free-market situation. Different markets afford different degrees of latitude for "ethical" behavior. But wherever such behavior imposes costs, the free market is a deterrent. The point was well illustrated in Milton Friedman's cryptic comment on corporate social responsibility that "few trends would so thoroughly undermine the very foundations of our free society as the acceptance by corporate officials of a social responsibility other than to make as much money for their stockholders as they possibly can."[7]

External Constraints on the Free Market

Sometimes the most obvious realities are the ones most easily overlooked. Business ethics, to be effective, depend very much upon the unwritten rules that govern business competition. When all competitors are forced, either by law, custom, or other social constraint, to abide by the same standards of moral behavior, then immoral behavior is penalized, not rewarded. The highly principled business leader, therefore, is not at a disadvantage in competing against the least principled, and the moral version of Gresham's Law can be set aside.

This is an obvious point, easily assumed but just as easily forgotten. I know of no free-market theorist, other than out-and-out anarchist writers, who would countenance total freedom in competition. Contracts should be enforceable, as should property rights. Limits should be placed upon acceptable forms of advertising. Criminal threats should not be tolerated. Bribery of governmental officials should be prohibited. Child labor should be prohibited or tightly regulated. Slavery should be forbidden. Views on these unwritten rules vary widely, but even the most hard-bitten economic competitors and the theorists most enamored by the freedom of the market would absolutely insist upon some general constraints by which all economic actors must abide. In large measure, these constraints should be governed by the moral attitudes of the community.

It is true that the best operative constraints are sometimes those imposed by cultural attitudes and customs. It is equally true that few laws can be effective if they are not supported by cultural attitudes and customs. For example, the American experiment with Prohibition had the force of law (eliminating beverage alcohol from the market), but it lacked sufficient sociocultural support to be effective, and a brisk illegal market developed. On the other hand, customary racial segregation in the American South defined many commercial relationships until the Civil Rights Act of 1964 rendered much of this market behavior illegal. By that time, the conscience of the community was sufficiently stricken by the immorality of racial discrimination that many, if not most, businesses were willing to acquiesce to the new law. The relationships between law and culture can be complex; my point is that either or both can have the effect of redefining the boundaries of acceptable market behavior. But a single market competitor is rarely capable of doing that by itself. Thus, ethical business practices alone are inadequate as a support for the moral behavior of even the most conscientious businessperson in a competitive market in which bad ethics are rewarded and good ethics penalized.

Governmental Regulation

Recognizing this fact, twentieth-century governments have played a much more activist role not only in defining and enforcing market constraints but also in including activist supports for fair-labor practices, environmental protection, social welfare, and other policies directly or indirectly limiting the freedom of the market. Those whose economic interests are most affected have resisted such policies, usually in the name of the principle of economic freedom. But since absolutizing that principle is inconsistent with the objectives of business ethics, it is a legitimate test of the good faith of those espousing business ethics as to whether they are willing to accept—even to advocate—necessary regulation of the market to ensure that bad ethics will not be rewarded by the disciplines of the market.

Where the market corresponds to a political community, the means are usually at hand to translate community perceptions of moral good into appropriate legal regulation. That may be particularly true of a large, substantially self-sufficient nation like the United States, despite the limited ability of government to control market activity in this country. The problem is much more difficult in smaller and less affluent countries that are disproportionately dependent upon international trade and capital. Regulations can be adopted and laws passed, but in reality, outside economic forces cannot be so easily controlled. The sometimes-alarmist literature on multinational corporations, dating from the mid-1970s,[8] often understated the contributions of such enterprises while overstating their evils. But that literature clearly was correct in noting the power of such corporations and the difficulty of any one country (especially a small one) in bringing them under regulatory control. Even the United States has difficulty in enforcing standards of ethical behavior in the wider global environment. One illustration leaps to mind: the Foreign Corrupt Practices Act. That law, adopted on the wave of genuine concern about business ethics, prohibited American businesses from offering bribes to officials of foreign governments. It would be difficult to ascertain the extent of actual compliance with this law. However, in the absence of similar constraints upon European and Japanese firms, it is easy to see who had competitive advantage in foreign markets where corrupt public officials were prepared to accept bribes.[9]

Even under ideal circumstances, it is not so easy for governments to establish and enforce rules of conduct to govern markets. It is virtually impossible for the government of one country to deal effectively with activities beyond its own borders.

Insufficiency of Nongovernmental Accountability Movements

Even more difficult, however, is for nongovernmental organizations and movements to set the ground rules. Consumer movements, labor unions, and environmental organizations have attempted to influence standards of behavior in international economic markets, all with indifferent success. The farm-labor movement of the early 1970s had some success with corporations that marketed products in countries where consumer boycotts could be mounted effectively among sympathetic workers. One incident illustrates both the possibilities and limitations. In early 1972 the Farm Workers' Organization (of Cesar Chavez) sought to secure union contracts with orange growers in Florida. It was successful in negotiating a contract with Minute Maid, a subsidiary of the Coca-Cola Company, by threatening a world-wide boycott of Coca-Cola. The threat was entirely credible, the soft drink product being popular with a mass public in many countries. The union was not successful with independent Florida-based citrus-growing corporations not similarly vulnerable. This meant, of course, that Minute Maid was placed at a competitive disadvantage and that its contract could not be as generous, from a moral standpoint, as it needed to be.

The most celebrated business ethics case along these lines was the Nestlé boycott of the 1970s and 1980s.[10] An international boycott of Nestlé products was commenced by a coalition of nongovernmental organizations in 1977, in response to evidence that the Swiss-based company was using high-pressure and deceptive marketing techniques to sell breast milk substitutes (infant formula) to Third World mothers who, for health and economic reasons, should have been breast-feeding their infants. It seemed a particularly vivid illustration of irresponsible behavior by a giant multinational corporation. The boycott was undeniably effective, particularly in the United States where sales of several Nestlé products were affected and the overall corporate image widely stigmatized. Partly in response to the Nestlé situation, the World Health Organization (WHO) was led to adopt a voluntary code of marketing guidelines for the infant-formula industry. The WHO Code, although not binding, became the benchmark against which companies that were manufacturing formula were held accountable by the movement. The boycott, however, was directed solely against Nestlé, and that company reached an agreement with movement leaders in early 1984, committing the company to abide by the WHO Code. On the whole, the company has abided by its commitments. But in several instances, Nestlé's restraint simply provided an opportunity for its competitors to increase their market share by continuing to use the questionable marketing strategies.[11] Clearly, high ethical standards in the international infant-formula market could not be maintained simply by targeting one company, even less by appealing to the conscience of individual corporate executives of Nestlé or any other company.

In the long term, the boycott movement probably did effect major changes in Third World countries by most companies, partly by influencing WHO to adopt its marketing code and partly by stimulating a number of countries to take steps to regulate that market within their own borders. Nevertheless, this movement could not have been so successful without mobilizing enormous energies of social activists in North America and Europe and focusing them upon one target. It is difficult to imagine similar energy being brought to bear upon many industries and markets simultaneously. Corporate ethical problems continue throughout the world in many industries, and it remains to be seen whether the standards set by the infant-formula industry will be maintained and improved over the long term in the absence of continued pressure of the same magnitude. In any event, it is hard to see how international nongovernmental movements could hope, by themselves, to establish and maintain adequate rules to govern the international free market.

Underlying Problems

Why is it so difficult to establish adequate guidelines to govern the free market in the new global economy? I wish to cite four interlocking problems.

First and foremost is the reality that there is no global political/legal regime corresponding to the global economic community. The latter exceeds the bounds of any nation-state. Thus, while many countries have established laws and precedents to restrain unethical practices, they can no longer control their own economies; the dominant forces are increasingly global, not national. There are undeniable advantages in the new global economy, not least being the ability of transnational corporations to maneuver the factors of production efficiently, overriding national borders and locating the comparative advantage of different parts of the world with greater precision. But the new situation also offers new opportunities for unethical practices that cannot so easily be restrained.

The second, related point is that nationalism in the contemporary world is largely a divisive force. National sovereignty also has undeniable advantages such as the preservation of cultural heritages and the protection of nations from potential large-scale tyrannies. Nevertheless, the nation-state system inhibits the development of adequate regulatory frameworks on a scale corresponding to actual markets. Thus, abuses can go unchecked and responsible behavior can be penalized.

Third, the vast economic disparities between First and Third World societies invite abuses, particularly where higher ethical standards are accompanied by higher costs. For example, the exploitation of the Amazon basin has been identified by environmental organizations as a potential ecological disaster. But seen in purely economic terms, especially in the short term, the Amazon basin is an important source of jobs and foreign exchange for Brazil. To Brazil and other countries in similar situations, high environmental standards can appear to be a luxury they cannot afford. The great gap between the rich and poor countries also creates temptations and opportunities for corruption. In some situations bribes can be a fully accepted and even necessary, though still dishonest, portion of the income of those in decision-making positions.

Fourth, great differences of culture remain, including definitions of moral values, within the global community. What is unacceptable, even outrageous, in one cultural setting may be quite acceptable in others. One person's bribe may be another's gratuity, one society's injustice to women may be another's recognition of the order of nature. This is not to say that all cultural values are simply relative; it does mean that universal agreement upon acceptable standards is seldom easy, even when mechanisms of implementation are at hand.

These interrelated problems do not mean that progress cannot be made toward greater ethical accountability in the free market. If that were so, we should also have to abandon any hope for business ethics in any form. They do mean that the global economic environment is complex, and progress requires patience and creativity.

The Post-Cold War Global Environment

While the new global economic situation may pose great difficulties for business ethics, it may also offer new possibilities. I wish to mention three.

First, a freer trading environment, overall, carries with it the problems we have been considering insofar as the new international markets lack accepted ground rules. But regional free-trade areas such as the European Union (EU) and North American Free Trade Agreement (NAFTA), however imperfect, do embody market restraints that support broader social objectives. Success on this level can lead to better global systems of accountability. Moreover, free trade often has strengthened national economies, indirectly and in the long term better enabling weaker nations to control economic life within their own borders. Asian countries such as the Republic of Korea, Taiwan, Singapore, and Malaysia illustrate the point. It remains to be seen whether Mexico, through NAFTA, will provide a good Latin American example. It also remains to be seen whether free trade can have this effect throughout the Third World. In general, poor countries that are unable to exploit fully their own comparative advantage in a global economy are limited to their own inadequate resources. Most countries can achieve subsistence on this basis at some level; few can develop levels of well-being much beyond that level.

From the Third World perspective, the problem is how to gain the advantages of a freer world market while minimizing international exploitation (or neoimperialism) and internal corruption? Few countries can be expected to achieve this by themselves.

Second, the end of the Cold War, besides its undoubted political blessings, promises greater freedom from some of the distortions in global economics. In the polarized world of the past forty years, both the United States and the Soviet Union cultivated many client states, paying whatever price seemed necessary to ensure the continued loyalty of political leaders and economic institutions. Thus, there were enormous pressures to overlook corruption not only as expressed in a multitude of simple venalities but also in the deep distortions of economic life resulting from over-arming numerous countries and even assisting elites to keep a lid on restive populations. Elite groups in many countries acquired artificial leverage on the policies, including economic policies, of the United States and the Soviet Union. Sometimes that may have contributed to useful foreign aid. More often, one suspects, the effect of the Cold War relationships between the superpowers and their client states obstructed healthy economic development and internal social justice.

Of course, now that the Cold War is essentially over, there is a danger that the rich nations will feel free to ignore the poor. In a free-trade environment, small, weak nations in Africa or Latin America may appear to have little to offer. One wonders how, in this new global environment, business leadership can be stimulated to assist the developments of neglected parts of the world. What, for example, can be done about Bangladesh or Bolivia or Tanzania, none of which has substantial assets to offer in international trade?

Third, the end of the Cold War has brought in an era of new possibilities for collective security in a new world order. That is not purely, or even primarily, an economic matter, but it has important economic ramifications. Insofar as the world moves beyond political-military isolationism, it will be forging political institutions with economic possibilities.

We have identified the importance of some agency, external to the free market, to help establish and maintain the ground rules in such a way that ethical behavior in business is rewarded and not penalized. We have noted also that no global regime corresponds to the realities of global economics. If the world is moving toward a universal economic order, there is no regulatory government at that level to help ensure that business activity will support and not undermine broader community values. The achievement of such governing institutions is fraught with difficulties and dangers and will require much patience. But the growing recognition throughout the world that we have need for collective security can move us further in the direction of an international legal framework to govern economics.

Movement toward Accountability

What can accountability mean in this changing global climate? Clearly, it cannot simply mean that individual businesspeople become more ethical, important as that will always be. Individuals always have some latitude to make better or worse decisions, but the disciplines of the market sharply restrict that latitude, especially in the markets where it is most needed.

Clearly, also, nongovernmental organizations and movements (including religious groups) cannot provide a sufficient framework to support high ethical standards. Such organizations and movements are necessarily selective in their targets, and their attention span can be limited. Once a particular objective appears to have been gained, activist groups tend to lose their zeal or move on to some other cause. The major value of corporate-responsibility efforts may, in fact, be more cultural than institutional. While the institutional mechanisms are usually ineffective, activist movements can help change the cultural values of the wider community. That can help, both by making business leaders more sensitive to moral issues and by changing the perceptions of the wider public.

There is room for collaborative agreement on the rules among enterprises within a given industry. There is a built-in problem, however, in agreements among competitors whose collaborative impulses are limited by their corporate interest in besting the competition. I suspect that such agreements, when reached, tend more often to be against rather than for good business ethics. There is the further problem in the United States of antitrust laws under which any collaborative agreements among competitors are automatically suspect before the law. All of these points can be illustrated by the difficulties within the infant-formula industry to arrive at collaborative arrangements in support of the World Health Code. Collaboration around 1980–81 was designed more to defeat the then-proposed code. An industry-wide arrangement in the early 1990s for monitoring the marketing practices of the various infant-formula companies was, in my opinion, more cosmetic than real.[12] Industry-wide agreements, where legal, can play a role, but they are hardly a sufficient mechanism of accountability.

We come back to government. Government is the one institution capable of reflecting the wishes of the entire society and bringing sanctions to bear upon unacceptable behavior. There is a remarkable ecumenical consensus of support for such a role by the state. The great papal encyclicals, from *Rerum Novarum* to the present, make that clear. *Centesimus Annus* affirms the relative autonomy and freedom of the market, but then makes this point:

> The State, however, has the task of determining the juridical framework within which economic affairs are to be conducted, and thus of safeguarding the prerequisites of a free economy, which presumes a certain equality between the parties, such that one party would not be so powerful as practically to reduce the other to subservience.[13]

That encyclical, explicitly following *Rerum Novarum,* thus insists that "society and the State must ensure wage levels adequate for the maintenance of the worker and his family."[14] It can be argued that neither encyclical fully solved the problem of how to relate the market mechanism to a family-maintenance theory of the just wage, but both are clear in affirming the importance of a juridical order governing free markets for these and other ends required by moral principle. Since its inception, the World Council of Churches also articulated a conception of social responsibility in which the free market cannot be the last word:

> Man is created and called to be a free being, responsible to God and his neighbor. Any tendencies in State and society depriving man of the possibility of acting responsibly are a denial of God's intention for man and His work of salvation. A responsible society is one where freedom is the freedom of men who acknowledge responsibility to justice and public order, and where those who hold political authority or economic power are responsible for its exercise to God and the people whose welfare is affected by it. Man must never be made a mere means for political or economic ends. Man is not made for the State but the State for man. Man is not made for production, but production for man. . . . It is required that economic justice and provision of equality of opportunity be established for all the members of society.[15]

Recent ecumenical literature has emphasized the criterion of "participation" in judging the moral acceptability of both government and economic life. Ultimately, government alone can be the institutional expression of an entire society, focusing its authority and power upon other institutions to assure their relative freedom and their accountability to values considered important within the society.

Our problem is: No institutions of government are effective on the global level. Some would say there is no society either at that level. But despite the deep rifts and fragmentations of humankind, and the divisive, competing nationalisms, there really is an emerging global community. That is certainly true in economic life, which is our principal concern in this paper. In his encyclical *Pacem in Terris,* Pope John XXIII called attention to the lack of an international legal order in one memorable paragraph:

> Today the universal common good presents us with problems which are worldwide in their dimensions; problems, therefore, which cannot be solved *except by a public authority with power, organization and means co-extensive with these problems, and with a worldwide sphere of activity.* Consequently the moral order itself demands the establishment of some such general form of public authority.[16]

This, then, is the objective problem: There is an emerging global free market of great significance. The demands of business ethics in that market are limited to the extent that market forces reward bad behavior and penalize responsible behavior. For enterprises to be held accountable in such an environment there is need for global forms of regulation, but currently no institutional regime is capable of meeting this need.

Moving toward Global Accountability

It is beyond the scope of this paper (or the wisdom of its author) to supply definitive answers to this problem. I do wish to make a few observations about serious movement toward a structure of accountability.

The first is directed toward morally sensitive business leaders themselves. A serious test of the good faith of those who wish to act responsibly is their willingness to advocate and work for morally adequate regulations governing markets. Those who insist upon the adequacy of purely personal expressions of goodwill either have not absorbed the plain meaning of the discipline of the market, or they have sentimentalized the meaning of moral responsibility. Some business leaders such as Elmer Johnson grasp the point.

Second, the regional free-trade zones such as the EU and NAFTA can proceed with further refinements of the social responsibility provisions in the existing agreements. The effect of this is to regularize the laws of the participating countries so that corporations crossing international lines will be required to comply with the same ground rules in every country. Moreover, competition among the countries themselves can, by agreement, be conducted within agreed guidelines. This will not be easy, particularly as it affects wages and worker benefits in both high- and low-wage countries (as in the present deep contrast between the United States and Mexico). Successful regional regimes of economic accountability can be helpful models on the global level.

Third, the handful of dominant countries (including the Group of Seven, Russia, increasingly China, and even India) can do much to set responsible guidelines for the whole world through their dominant role in the General Agreement on Tariffs and Trade (GATT) negotiations, the International Monetary Fund (IMF), the World Bank, and other global economic entities. Insofar as these economic powers ignore the Third World or see the world primarily through the lens of their own national economic interests, they will not move the world toward greater moral responsibility. But a fairly small number of enlightened national leaders, supported by a perceptive public and morally sensitive business leaders, can make a major difference in this new, post-Cold War environment.

Fourth, the United Nations, playing a more modest role throughout the Cold War era, at last may be in a position to provide a more serious institutional framework for global economic as well as political cooperation. The UN has always been more than a center for rhetoric-posturing, as charged by its critics, but the large number of smaller nations must be challenged to see in new ways that their representatives' words and actions in that arena can have important consequences only insofar as they, too, are committed to a global conception of the common good.

Finally, the Christian churches, alongside other world religions, are already global institutions, uniting people of different nations, languages, and cultures in common conceptions of the good and in worldwide communities of mutual accountability. Churches need to be advocates everywhere, not only of good business ethics as such but of a sufficient number of institutions to guarantee that, in the global marketplace, good ethics will be rewarded and bad ethics penalized. The temptation of churches is to sentimentalize their mission too much, preferring hands-on ministry to the poor and marginalized, which is sometimes a substitute for advocacy of broader institutional solutions. But I also hope the churches will never abandon their ministries of direct service. I hope they will not let that be a substitute for broader systems of accountability.

Notes

1. From 1980 to 1984 I chaired a task force commissioned by the General Conference of the United Methodist Church to negotiate with four global corporations, seeking termination of marketing practices deemed injurious to the health of Third World children. The corporations were the Nestlé Company, American Home Products, Ross-Abbott Laboratories, and Bristol-Myers. From 1982 to 1991 I served on the Nestlé Infant Formula Audit Commission. The latter commission, chaired by former U.S. Senator and Secretary of State Edmund S. Muskie, was charged by the Nestlé Company to monitor and audit its marketing practices, independently, to ensure their conformity with the World Health Organization's Code of Marketing of Infant Formula Products. Both these activities involved detailed exposure to business decision-making in this field and investigative activities in a number of Third World countries.

2. See, for example, Milton Friedman, *Capitalism and Freedom* (Chicago: University of Chicago Press, 1962); Michael Novak, *The Spirit of Democratic Capitalism* (New York: Simon and Schuster, 1982); George Gilder, *Wealth and Poverty* (New York: Basic Books, 1981). Friedman and Novak accept the desirability of some regulation and modification of the pure market system such as antitrust legislation and some welfare transfer payments. Gilder is more inclined to trust the market mechanism entirely for such things.

3. See, for example, Joseph A. Schumpeter, *Capitalism, Socialism and Democracy,* 3rd ed. (New York: Harper and Row, 1950): 67.

4. I have explored the claims in greater detail in *The Great Economic Debate: An Ethical Analysis* (Philadelphia: Westminster Press, 1977), *Economics and Ethics: A Christian Inquiry* (Philadelphia: Fortress Press, 1986), and other writings. While I have found value consistently in the market mechanism, I have rejected the maximum claims as efforts to translate Christian ethics into economic practice.

5. According to Gresham's Law in economics, "bad money drives out good."

6. Elmer W. Johnson, "How Corporations Balance Economic and Social Concerns," *Business and Society Review* 54 (Summer 1985): 13.

7. Milton Friedman, *Capitalism and Freedom*: 133.

8. See especially Richard J. Barnet and Ronald E. Muller, *Global Reach: The Power of the Multinational Corporations* (New York: Simon and Schuster, 1974), the most frequently quoted title in this literature, and a recent "sequel" of sorts, Richard J. Barnet and John Cavanagh, *Global Dreams: Imperial Corporations and the New World Order* (New York: Simon and Schuster, 1994). The former volume explores the ability of multinational corporations to evade regulation and taxation while dominating countries having less overall power and wealth than the individual corporations themselves. The latter volume chronicles the expanding influence of such corporations and the corresponding shrinkage of the power and influence of governments. Neither volume sees much positive benefit to the multinational corporations nor much hope for our ability to bring them into greater accountability.

9. A friend who was in the business of brokering coal once related difficulties he had encountered in contracting for the delivery of American coal to utilities in, respectively, a Latin American and an Asian setting. In the Latin American country, an influential legislator who was in a position to influence the awarding of contracts set himself up as broker for his country's public utility and required payment of 1 percent of the gross amount of the contract as his fee. Since this piece of extortion was a "fee" it could be treated as exempt from the U.S. Corrupt Practices Act. My friend did not go along with this arrangement and lost the contract to European competitors. In the Asian country, my friend was delayed for weeks during which time he failed to take the hint that substantial payments to government officials were expected. When the requirement was made unmistakably clear, he again refused to offer these bribes and, once more, the contract was awarded to others.

10. The most definitive study of the Nestlé boycott is S. Prakash Sethi, *Multinational Corporations and the Impact of Public Advocacy on Corporate Strategy: Nestlé and the Infant Formula Controversy* (Boston, Dordrecht, London: Kluwer Academic Publishers, 1994). Among other studies, note Jean-Claude Buffle, *Dossier N. Comme Nestlé* (Paris: Editions Alain Moreau, 1986). My observations about this case are based largely upon personal involvement as chair of the United Methodist Infant Formula Task Force, which was charged by the United Methodist Church with negotiating with Nestlé and three U.S. infant-formula marketing corporations and as a member of the Nestlé Infant Formula Audit Commission, chaired by Edmund S. Muskie, which was charged by Nestlé with identifying unethical marketing practices within the company itself for a period of nine years.

11. That was most evident in the distribution of sample formula supplies to new mothers in maternity hospitals. While engaged in field monitoring of Nestlé in several Third World countries for the Muskie Commission, I visited maternity hospitals to which Nestlé no longer provided free supplies of the product, thus creating a vacuum that other companies promptly filled. This created predictable bitterness in the affected countries among Nestlé managers who pressured the central corporate headquarters to relax the guidelines.

12. An International Association of Infant Food Manufacturers (IFM) was organized in 1990, with a principal objective of regularizing market activity in compliance with the WHO Code. But the compliance staff was limited to a single "ombudsman" with limited authority and funding.

13. Pope John Paul II, *Centesimus Annus*, 15, *Origins* 21, No. 1 (16 May 1991). The Pope is supporting views he attributes to *Rerum Novarum*.

14. *Centesimus Annus*.

15. Report of Section III, "The Church and the Disorder of Society." First Assembly of the World Council of Churches, Amsterdam, 1948. Typical of the times, the document uses generic male language when all humanity is intended.

16. Pope John XXIII, *Pacem in Terris,* in Michael Walsh and Brian Davies, eds., *Proclaiming Justice and Peace: Documents from John XXIII to John Paul II* (Mystic, Conn.: Twenty-third Publications, 1984), par. 137. Emphasis supplied.

10

Evolution of Corporate Social Responsibility: Educating Stakeholders and Virtuous Entrepreneurs

Gerald F. Cavanagh

This conference challenges us to understand corporate social responsibility better in a global economy. Business has been affected profoundly by the need to do business in the world market, and in this chapter we will examine two models of corporate social responsibility that take this need into account. The model of twenty-five years ago was simple and straightforward, and was a reaction to changing public expectations and poor publicity. Companies then sought to improve their reputations by attempting to demonstrate to the public that they were socially responsible.

A more recently developed model of corporate social responsibility retains most elements of the earlier model. In addition to efficiency and basic responsibilities, it adds: teamwork, cooperation, personal development, and honesty with customers. Some firms are attempting now to be "caring organizations."

Corporate Responsibility Twenty-five Years Ago

During the 1970s many large U.S. firms were in the forefront of corporate social responsibility activities. IBM, Xerox, and General Motors provided year-long, fully paid leaves for selected employees to do such good works as teaching in an inner-city high school or helping

169

in a social-service agency.[1] These initiatives made both the firms and the individuals involved models of socially responsible behavior. It also provided valuable public relations stories for these and similar firms.

IBM and a few other corporations then had an effective no-layoff policy; as highly successful and growing firms, they could afford such a policy. Both the fully paid leave and the no-layoff policies were expensive and thus did not last into the 1990s.[2] In the 1970s Control Data Corporation (CDC) was an innovator in manufacturing and selling electronic equipment. Its founder and chief executive officer, William C. Norris, was a leader in the business community and spoke and wrote widely, urging social responsibility for business. CDC itself set up several plants to employ the urban poor in Minneapolis and Washington, D.C., and they designed and distributed software to teach marketable skills to poor people and prisoners. CDC was a leader in socially responsible actions.[3] When the company lost money in the mid-1980s, Norris was forced out, and many of these activities ceased.

Image Advertising and Self-Seeking Behavior

Image advertising was a more focused means used in the 1970s to change public perceptions of a firm.[4] Dow Chemical is one corporation that successfully has engaged in image advertising. Dow was criticized for its production of napalm, a petroleum jelly that sticks to the skin and burns, and thus kills people. It was used by the U.S. military in Vietnam, and sometimes burned civilians. The television images brought protests, so Dow then ran corporate-image and public-service television advertisements to improve their image. These advertisements continue today to tell us effectively about the good things that Dow and chemicals do for society.

Mobil pioneered paid opinion editorials in leading newspapers, which they hoped would influence public opinion. General Motors and Atlantic Richfield, among others, organized and distributed comprehensive social reports and even ran conferences for community leaders and academics in which they showcased their own socially responsible activities. General Motors has published a detailed social report every year since 1971.[5] In 1973 GM sponsored a comprehensive exhibit and invited community leaders from around the United States to demonstrate what they were doing about pollution control, auto mileage and safety, diversity of workforce, and the like. All of GM's top executives were present.

There was considerable discussion during this period on how to measure the effects of corporate social programs and of social audits. The large accounting firms were the vanguard of this planning and discussion, undoubtedly foreseeing new markets for their skills.[6]

Social activists criticized these efforts as being self-serving. Image advertising and social reports did benefit firms, but they remained just as socially irresponsible. However, such public service advertisements and social audits raised the expectations of the public with regard to business in general and to the specific firm in particular. This is an indirect, though perhaps unintended, benefit to society as a whole; it also indirectly places additional social responsibility demands on the firm in the long term.

During the 1970s, however, socially irresponsible corporate behavior was equally common. Some firms received much attention because of their lack of social responsibility. International Telephone & Telegraph and Gulf & Western, and their respective CEOs, Harold Geneen and Charles Bluhdorn, were widely known for their self-serving behavior. ITT paid millions of dollars of bribes to American and foreign government officials to look after the interests of ITT.[7] Bluhdorn used company assets to enhance his personal wealth.[8]

Cases of such behavior multiplied during the 1980s, the Reagan years. General Dynamics, the second-largest defense contractor in the United States, was twice suspended from further contracts by the Navy because of allegations of "pervasive" misconduct. Many General Dynamics executives were indicted. A former executive vice president in charge of the electric boat division, under indictment himself for taking $2.7 million in kickbacks, testified that his division of General Dynamics overcharged the government $843 million. During this period executives of GE, Litton, Northrup, Raytheon, Hughes, and Teledyne were convicted of kickbacks. Yet during the 1980s, most of these firms continued to obtain U.S. government contracts, in spite of kickbacks, bribes, convictions, and fines on individuals and the firms.[9]

During this decade many other businesspeople contributed to this me-first atmosphere; a large number were later convicted and spent time in prison. Paul Thayer, CEO of LTV, served nineteen months in federal prison for his role in an insider-trading scheme. Fourteen other top executives were similarly convicted. This was the decade of hostile takeovers, greenmail, golden parachutes, political-action committees, bribery, and greed. Thirty-nine federally appointed officials resigned or were indicted for accepting bribes, misappropriation of assets, and a general lack of responsibility.[10] For many people, these highly publicized cases in effect seemed to institutionalize and even legitimize self-serving behavior.

Transition

Many of the problems of this earlier period, such as environmental pollution and underemployment of women and minorities, have been addressed by most companies. Through voluntary actions and government pressure, changes have taken place and become institutionalized. Some large businesses now make billions of dollars cleaning up the environment. However, since the market system, acting by itself, encourages pollution, government regulation was required before environmental cleanup could become profitable in the marketplace.

Today, businesses hire and promote many more minorities and women. In the 1970s some firms began releasing figures to the public on the number of minorities and women they employed and what positions they held within the firm. Large companies have been required to provide this information (the EEO-1 Form) to the federal government for decades, but revealing it to the public is voluntary. The statistics show that firms now hire many more women and minorities than they did twenty-five years ago and that they have greater responsibilities within the firm. These early pressures enabled corporations to clean up their actions and policies.

A transition in corporate ethics from such easily identified and measured behaviors to activities more integrated into the fabric of the firm occurred in the late 1980s. This transition was chronicled in 1988 by a study of corporate ethics commissioned by the Business Roundtable. Since the Roundtable is composed of the chief executive officers of the largest U.S. corporations, it had good access to information.[11]

The report of the Business Roundtable found common elements in the firms with good records of ethical conduct, including corporate responsibility:

1. Commitment, leadership, and the example of top management;
2. A belief in the importance of clarity of expression of ethical

intentions—a clear tradition of ethical behavior and, most commonly, a written code of ethics;
3. Procedures for implementation of the policies;
4. The involvement and commitment of personnel at all levels;
5. A system of measurement of results.[12]

The elements do not surprise us; they are the steps one finds in the formulation and implementation of any important policy.

Integration of Social Responsibility into Fabric of Firm

The global marketplace has brought sudden and dramatic changes in the world view of and in methods of operating for U.S. business. The challenge of producing and selling products in other countries has focused management's attention on understanding other countries and their cultures. In addition to expanding the horizons of executives, it has also brought a demand for greater efficiencies; to compete where wage rates are lower requires U.S. firms to become even more innovative. Ultimately, of course, the consumer benefits worldwide.

Efforts to make firms more competitive contain reorganization strategies such as "total quality management"[13] and "the horizontal organization" or "reengineering the corporation." Many recent initiatives are designed to increase efficiency and thus cut costs. They can also ultimately work to the benefit of most parties: the individual within the firm, the firm itself, and society as a whole. Let us examine some of these initiatives.

Current efforts to make firms more efficient contain some common elements. Most try to encourage:

1. Cooperation, teamwork and trust among all employees;[14]
2. Respect for people, which, in turn, demands investment in the individual employee (or colleague) in training and development;
3. Honesty with all stakeholders, especially customers, to build customer allegiance and the long-term reputation of the firm.[15]

Some call the next step "the caring organization." This model, coming from the feminist perspective, embraces all the above. In addition, it builds into the fabric of a firm the caring attitude for all employees and those people touched by the organization.[16]

These internal efforts are not always noticed by the public and thus are not so useful as public-relations aids. Yet they affect many more of the firm's stakeholders, since potentially they will have an impact on all employees, as well as customers and suppliers. This step will achieve a more profound and long-lasting impact than did the few socially responsible programs that some firms started twenty-five years ago.

Ford Motor Company's CEO, Alex Trotman, offers a recent example. The new model Mustang automobile was designed from the beginning by a team, in a "skunk works"; designers, engineers, purchasing, and service employees were all brought together and given a separate space, isolated from the rest of the Ford bureaucracy. They were able to design the car in thirty-five months, in about 30 percent less time and at 30 percent less cost than comparable new designs at Ford.[17] Global competitiveness has driven Ford toward teamwork, better communication, and more effective work-groups.

Mr. Trotman also noted that, since 20 percent of the people of the world purchase 80 percent of the automobiles, there is a tremendous potential market among the remaining 80 percent of the people. Ford plans to greatly increase its presence in developing countries. They have twenty dealers on mainland China, two hundred in Eastern Europe, and are expanding their presence in other developing countries. Ford already manufactures millions of vehicles overseas. It exports 100,000 vehicles per year from the United States alone, and aims to raise that to 250,000 vehicles per year.

Mr. Trotman recently announced a reorganization that will integrate worldwide operations. Ford's plants in North America and Europe will produce the same models and use the same production systems, in an effort to get people to forget about geographical boundaries.[18] Such actions also demonstrate financial results. Ford has gone from losing billions of dollars just a few years ago to generating more than $2.5 billion in net earnings in 1993.

The Values of the Firm and Society

Let us shift our view to the values of the firm and of society. Intellectual life in the United States over the last few generations has put the individual, and the rights of the individual, at its center. Deconstructionists and postmodernist ideologies have been the vanguard of these recent intellectual movements. Deconstructionism makes an important contribution in praising the autonomous individual. Some deconstructionists are libertarian in their political and economic views, while others maintain that, since Western culture and Christianity are so culture-bound, our society has no real moral foundation from which to judge or speak. Under these circumstances there is only one objective moral truth which is: "Everybody has the right to determine his or her own morality. At the end of this anti-objective road lies this one objective claim."[19] The deconstructionists and postmodernists have been described by Clarence Walton as "anti-capitalist, anti-Christian and in many respects anti-democratic."[20]

The basic values of the business enterprise, good and bad, are also the values of most Americans; thus, there is a congruence between business values and U.S. culture. Some observers go so far as to say that business values *are* American values. As responsible citizens of this or any society, we must be explicitly aware of our own values.

Let us examine the content of business values. For long-term success, entrepreneurship requires imagination and creativity, flexibility, willingness to work hard and long hours for a reward, effective leadership of the team, the ability to articulate a vision that will inspire coworkers, and an honesty with all stakeholders. Competition is also an important value for entrepreneurs and most Americans. Competition in the marketplace brings efficiencies, lower costs to consumers, and encourages new ideas, new products and, ultimately, new jobs. However, competition has its costs.[21]

While acknowledging the importance of trust in the current marketplace, competitiveness brings some dangers to the business system—it can bring an unrelenting pressure to perform, which can encourage unethical shortcuts. We have witnessed "the breakdown of traditional bonds of loyalty and commitment between employers and employees." The huge layoffs in many established firms are clearly "taking an enormous financial, psychological, and ethical toll."[22]

Some institutional shareholders have become demanding of management, and these demands are often shortsighted. Institutional shareholders and their portfolio managers want quarterly, even daily, financial performance results from a firm, and they do not acknowledge the importance of longer-term efforts in research and product development.

An overemphasis on competition encourages individualism, self-centeredness, and even selfishness. The media provide an example. Attempts to lure readers, viewers, and advertising revenue have brought us violence in television and film, which undermine the family and its values. The average child views eight thousand murders on television before that child leaves elementary school.[23] The never-ending local television news accounts of murder in cities also encourages racism; they promote the stereotype among white suburban Americans that Blacks are innately prone to crime and violence.[24]

Violence and antifamily sex in the media are similar to pollution. Violence and antifamily sex on television attract viewers and hence advertisers and revenue. Similarly, corporations save money by dumping their refuse on others and letting them bear the costs of cleaning it up. A responsible firm that pays, on its own initiative, for safe disposal of its toxic wastes can raise its own costs compared to competitors and put itself at a competitive disadvantage. In a similar fashion, media firms that are socially responsible and try to avoid violence and antifamily sex place themselves at a competitive disadvantage. They can lose advertising revenue to those producers and advertisers who pander to the lowest common denominator of the general public's individualistic and sometimes selfish curiosity and desires.[25]

In the case of pollution, we have recognized that common standards, albeit achieved through government regulation, are necessary to ensure that cleanup costs are born by all. In the case of violence and antifamily sex, we have been afraid to suggest standards, frightened by an exaggerated sense of individual rights, fear of censorship, and threats led by the American Civil Liberties Union. The media also need ground rules under which all will operate. Is this censorship? Perhaps. But after considering what is at stake, censorship might be considered a necessary societal trade-off. Achieving basic, long-term freedoms for many often demands that other freedoms be limited. Children who are safe in the streets, intact households with both a father and a mother, and quality education are more important to a society than a media that is free to exploit violence and antifamily sex.

Salaries of Entertainers

Salaries are another example of how business values are acted out in the marketplace. Some of these salaries do not represent the contribution made by the individual to the firm or to society. Great disparities exist between the salaries of some entertainers and a few executives and professionals, compared to those of most working people who may provide more proportional good for society and the country. Derek Bok, the former president of Harvard University, points out that the salary of television entertainer David Letterman is more than fifty times that of President Bill Clinton. The partners in a

New York law firm make more than seven times the salary of a Supreme Court justice.[26]

Let us critically examine an American idol: a professional athlete and his/her pay. Fox television network recently outbid CBS television for the National Football League contract to broadcast the season's games. Fox will pay $1.5 billion for this contract.[27] CBS lost hundreds of millions on their last NFL contract, and believed they could not meet Fox's bid. The average salary of professional baseball players in 1993 was $1.1 million.[28] What do these huge dollar amounts say about how our national priorities are spelled out in the marketplace? What image of American success does this present to young people here and around the world? The corrosive influence of huge sums of money also has affected college athletics. Football and basketball, the sports that can bring in millions of dollars, determine schedules, leagues, and often even academic programs and policies for athletes and others.

Let us ask a further question with regard to professional athletics, Why do we pay people to play games? The very notion of play and games implies that one enjoys playing the game. Thus, one plays a game because one enjoys it, not because it is a business. It is a misdirection of priorities and resources to pay players such huge salaries. Entertainment it is, and we pay some entertainers also disproportionate salaries.

Chief Executives' Salaries

The salaries of some chief executives officers (CEOs) of corporations present the same problem. In 1993 "the average CEO of a major company made one hundred and forty-nine times the average factory worker's pay of $25,317." In 1974 CEOs made thirty-five times the average.[29] Relevant to increasing costs of health care, several of the highest-paid chief executives have been in the health-care industry (National Medical Enterprises, U.S. Surgical, and Humana Hospitals); one is in the environmental clean-up business (Waste Management Corp).[30]

In 1990 the chief executive of United Airlines earned $18.3 million, about twelve hundred times the starting salary of a flight attendant. In that same year United lost $331 million. We are hardly witnessing pay for achievement.[31]

Global competition has increased the demands on CEOs. However, it requires all employees to work as teams, develop their skills, and work longer and harder. But the compensation for the average worker, in the United States or in poor countries, compared to the American CEO, does not reflect this.

We Americans often judge our own self-worth by the amount of money we make. One of the results of the computer is the ease with which we can generate ordered lists of everything, including salaries; thus, everyone can make comparisons such as that cited above. Each CEO can see where he stands. I use "he" advisedly here; there are no women among the highest-paid CEOs. In our competitive culture, every CEO wants to be number one. This is dysfunctional and ultimately wasteful of limited resources. The CEO and others with large salaries need only a fraction of what they receive to purchase a very fine standard of living. Moreover, it is doubtful they would refuse to work if they were offered a fraction of their bloated salaries.

A culturally supported and voluntary stabilization or even a rollback of the immense salaries provided to athletes, entertainers, and CEOs would build a greater sense of teamwork and consensus among all people. These are exactly the values we are trying to support to enable us to operate effectively in a global economy. Furthermore, negotiating rollbacks and flexible limits on such salaries would not undermine the free market, nor would it violate substantially the freedom of the individual. Failing voluntary restraint, I submit that a steeply graduated income tax would be appropriate.

There is an irony here. With increasing salary as our goal, we are caught up in chasing a goal that can never be achieved. We want to be on the top of the list, or at least we want to earn more than our neighbor. That inevitably leads to satisfaction for one and dissatisfaction for everyone else. John Paul II is eloquent on this issue:

> It is not wrong to want to live better; what is wrong is a style of life which is presumed to be better when it is directed toward "having" rather than "being", and which wants to have more, not in order to be more but in order to spend life in enjoyment as an end in itself. It is therefore necessary to create life-styles in which the quest for truth, beauty, goodness and communion with others for the sake of common growth are the factors which determine consumer choices, savings and investments. . . . I am referring to the fact that even the decision to invest in one place rather than another, in one productive sector rather than another, is always *a moral and cultural choice*. . . . The decision to invest, that is, to offer people an opportunity to make good use of their own labor, is also determined by an attitude of human sympathy and trust in Providence, which reveal the human quality of the person making such a decision.[32]

We learn as we mature that we cannot have all good things simultaneously. We must choose our personal goals in life and not drift into merely accepting the values and goals that a secular, materialistic society presents to us. In addition, as a people, we must choose the type of a society we want for ourselves and for our children.

In the contemporary United States, we have witnessed the undermining of some of the most cherished values of our society: centrality of the two-parent family, care for children, strong neighborhoods, and the importance and effectiveness of schools. If twenty-five years ago we had set out as a society deliberately to undermine these basic values, we could hardly have done a more effective job of it.

Influencing Our Common Values: Considering Others

On the other hand, if values can be undermined, why can they not be supported? Can we not decide which values are important for us and then set out to communicate and support these values through schools, churches, families, and the media? Mission statements do this for colleagues in a corporation; public relations advertisors do it for the external public. In political affairs, public-relations experts put a particular emphasis on the news and thus affect both the information we receive and our values. In his classic work on personal motivation, *The Achieving Society*, David McClelland points out how the values and motivation of a culture are influenced profoundly by children's books and the stories told to children.[33] Children's books, television, and stories have a large impact on contemporary young people. Television, film, stories, and books form character, yet we leave the stories our children encounter to chance, taste, and market appeal. It is the occasional religious or political leader who will challenge destructive values and propose and support constructive human values.

The values needed for a successful society operating in a global economy are no mystery. Such a culture must support the values of initiative, self-reliance, and self-development. In addition, we need the values of listening, cooperation, teamwork, and sharing. The skills of consensus-building, conflict-resolution, and peace-making also are needed in our own country and worldwide. Meredith's CEO, James A. Autry, points out in his popular book, *Love and Profit*, that the last decade has seen business books consistently on the best-seller list: "And most of those books are dealing with values and relationships, not high finance."[34]

Self-determination: Detroit and Religion

Here is one example of a person who is proactive in affecting values. Detroit's mayor, Dennis W. Archer, asks people to be aware of the needs of children and to share responsibility for the city. Archer is a man of prayer. He began his inauguration address with a quote from Psalm 127, "Except the Lord build the house, they labor in vain that build it; except the Lord keep the city, the watchman waketh but in vain."

In that speech, Archer gave these examples:

> For this great crusade to redeem our city to succeed, everybody must pitch in. . . . Sweep the sidewalk in front of your house. Clean the rubbish from the storm sewer on your street. Pick up the broken glass in your alley. Go with your neighbors to cut the weeds in the lot on the way to your street. Demand that I get the trash picked up on time. . . . Get a grip on your life, and the lives of your children. With our children rests the destiny or the destruction of our community. In their hands is the future of our society.[35]

Our major religious traditions in the United States can help us. The Protestant, Catholic, and Jewish traditions have been very influential in the United States. Although their records have some notable blotches, our churches generally have had an important, positive role in shaping the generous, cooperative, and community-building values of the American people. The Black churches have been a very important element in the lives of most African-Americans. The church has been a source of leaders, models, community spirit, and many programs for neighborhoods. In recent years other religious traditions also have had an influence on public values.

In most religions, and certainly in the Catholic tradition, the poor have a "special claim to consideration."[36] Wealthy people have the means to protect themselves through the economic and political system. The poor generally do not have those same opportunities, even in a democracy. This concern stems from the "principle of solidarity," in which we recognize that all people are bound together. If anyone is suffering, we all suffer.

These important questions that touch on personal values cannot, some argue, effectively be examined at state-run universities in the United States. Many universities avoid such ethical and moral issues. It is even more difficult to discuss our religious values at these institutions, yet religion is a strong integrator of personality and a strong motivator of most Americans. Recognizing the importance of all religions and yet refusing to discuss religion in most public settings has left us schizophrenic.[37]

We Americans have isolated and privatized our religious experience and this has hindered our development of adequate public policy. We have gone beyond the intention of most of the Founding Fathers of the country when we keep religion separate from any significant influence on our common attitudes and public policy. Our individualism, stemming from the Enlightenment-inspired lack of respect for religion and religious experience, has caused us to challenge the constitutionality of acts and legislation that embody religiously influenced moral principles. However, we may be witnessing a reversal of this. The new majority on the U.S. Supreme Court "accepts the constitutionality of both the inclusion of religious institutions in publicly funded programs and legislation that embodies religiously influenced moral principles."[38]

President Bill Clinton visited a Catholic University—Georgetown— recently and commented on the religious influences on him. He said that his Baptist roots gave him a deep belief in the importance of the religious freedom of each person and the Catholic influence on him is manifested in two ways:

1. Belief in respect for the obligation to develop one's mind, that religious convictions involve more than emotions, that there is an intellectual vigor, that if you have a mind you have an obligation to develop it;
2. A sense that we are morally obliged to try to live out our religious convictions in the world, that our obligation to social mission is connected to religious life.[39]

Mr. Clinton acted on his conviction that he had an obligation to society when he ran for the office of President of the United States. Partners in most large law firms make far more money than does the President of the United States. We need more people who are willing to contribute something to society, even though it may require some personal financial sacrifice.

Good Habits in Business

A leader of a firm who wants the employees to act ethically will undoubtedly follow the procedures listed earlier—a clear statement of policy, models of behavior, etc. That business leader will try to hire people who are disposed to behave ethically and to encourage current colleagues to have good or virtuous habits.

Interest in good habits or virtue is not new, indeed, it goes back to Aristotle.[40] Nevertheless, this interest has resurfaced as we have come to understand how people act and the limitations of much of current ethics. Business ethics provide structures to aid us in making ethical judgments, which is very helpful but does not address the question of what leads a person to select either the ethical or the unethical option.[41]

Virtues are good habits, so the questions leaders of the firm must ask are: (1) How can we encourage the development of good habits or virtue among our colleagues? (2) What kind of an organizational environment supports such behavior?

Once a person develops a virtue, he or she will act in that fashion almost instinctively, without considerable new reflection at each instance. From the person's own long-term viewpoint, being virtuous is a very efficient way of acting correctly. Once the good habit is developed by early effort, it becomes part of an individual's ordinary way of acting. Tying our shoelace is a habit but, since it is not a moral act, it is not a virtue. Someone who regularly treats colleagues in business honestly and respectfully, however, has developed a good moral habit, a virtue. Moreover, each successive act of honesty and respect becomes easier for the person, as the virtue becomes more and more an integral part of his or her personality.

James Burke, CEO of Johnson & Johnson, implicitly cited good habits as the reason why his firm responded to crisis in an ethical way. When Tylenol capsules were implicated in consumer deaths, it presented a serious problem for executives: Should they recall all the product, even though evidence showed that it was not their fault? The Johnson & Johnson *Credo* provided the foundation that influenced the basic moral habits and virtues for Mr. Burke and the other officers of the firm. That *Credo* indicates that "our first responsibility is to . . . mothers and fathers and all others who use our product." As Williams and Murphy put it:

> The Johnson & Johnson decision was determined largely, then, by its way of seeing the problem, and its ingrained habits (not by reasoning about core values). Virtues such as courage, compassion and lucidity, long operative in the organization, came to the foreground in the quandary over the Tylenol crisis.[42]

Positive moral values and virtues are formed in people within the corporation in a variety of ways, but oral tradition—stories about its heros or the founder—is an important way of communicating both the importance of and the content of virtue. Such structures and stories also encourage the development of virtue.

Educating Virtuous Entrepreneurs

When universities educate for the global economy, they are doing far more than that. They are responding to the calls of many who have examined the larger needs of U.S. society and higher education.

Two recent national reports urged universities to provide instruction on values. The first report charged that universities have not provided basic knowledge and skills for students and have contributed to the crisis in values. A principal need that has been recognized throughout the history of American education is "the development of student character and the transmission of the values supporting that character as an essential responsibility of faculty and administration."[43] Although, in the last generation, universities have been slow to embrace this responsibility, it has become even more important in recent years because of "the weakening of the role of the family and religious institutions in the lives of young people." This same report goes on to challenge us to put students first, to design experiential learning systems, and to create a thirst for continual learning through the positive experience students have of learning.

In his annual report, Harvard President Neil Rudenstine called for students "to serve society by addressing the most important problems that confront the nation and the larger world."[44] He asked the university also to become more involved in life and learning, and to challenge students to contribute to the society in which they live.

Indeed, a new model of leadership education is emerging on campuses, especially at Catholic universities. At the University of Detroit-Mercy, undergraduate students learn the meaning of servant leadership; they work together with a community agency to study the needs and plans of machine shops in the metropolitan Detroit area. In a graduate class, students are required to perform ten hours of community service.

Students at Loyola Marymount University replanted trees in a section of a national forest. They also raised the money for and painted several rooms in an inner-city Los Angeles public school.

Most graduate business students at Georgetown University volunteer their time for various community agencies. Bentley College students also volunteer their time for various social service agencies.[45]

Beyond these educational initiatives, some business executives have formed groups to encourage each other in their sense of social responsibility. Business for Social Responsibility[46] and The Social Venture Network both met in October 1993 in Washington, D.C. Some of the firms active in these groups are Levi Strauss, Ben and Jerry's, Reebok, The Body Shop, Stonyfield Farm, and Lotus Development.

The Social Venture Network has helped found Students for Responsible Business (SRB), composed of business students. SRB sponsors a newsletter, national and regional meetings, a list of speakers for local meetings and events and, most important for many students, a summer internship program.[47] The summer internships are offered by the member firms of Business for Social Responsibility and the Social Venture Network.

Businesspeople who seek to explore the Judeo-Christian roots of their own values and business values in general have formed the Business Vocation Conference.[48] This organization goes beyond the other by "affirming the relevance of religious faith to business practice." There are several chapters in cities across the United States.

We at universities must examine what we are teaching and our own organizational climate. Are we educating students to recognize and appreciate teamwork, cooperation, and community? Are we ourselves a community? Are we in universities educating students to be alert to the needs of other people? Are we training servant leaders? How are our graduates affecting the world?

Conclusions

The need to weave corporate social responsibility into the fabric of the firm is a challenge to businesspeople. It is also a challenge to those who educate future business leaders—universities and business schools. It is a special challenge to a Catholic university, which especially espouses ethics, virtue, and concern for the needs of others.

Notes

I want to thank Bing Li, graduate student in Business Administration, for her help in researching this paper.

1. See, for example, "Xerox Programs in Business Ethics and Corporate Responsibility," in *Corporate Ethics: A Prime Business Asset* (New York: The Business Roundtable, 1988): 131–138.

2. See Paul Carroll, *The Unmaking of IBM* (New York: Crown, 1993).

3. See William C. Norris, "Responding to Society's Needs," in *Corporations and Their Critics*, Thornton Bradshaw and David Vogel, eds. (New York: McGraw-Hill, 1981): 103–113.

4. For examples of public-service advertisements, see Donna Wood, *Business and Society* (Glenview, Ill.: Scott, Foresman, 1990): 268–272.

5. Thanks to Marina v.N. Whitman for this information on General Motors' socially responsible activities and their *Public Interest Report*.

6. Committee for Social Measurement of the American Institute of Certified Public Accountants, *The Measurement of Corporate Social Performance* (New York: AICPA, 1977); David H. Blake, William C. Frederick and Mildred S. Myers, *Social Auditing: Evaluating the Impact of Corporate Programs* (New York: Praeger, 1976); Report of Task Force on Corporate Social Reporting, *Corporate Social Reporting in the United States and Western Europe* (Washington, D.C.: U.S. Department of Commerce, 1979).

7. See Anthony Sampson, *Sovereign State of ITT* (Greenwich, Conn: Fawcett, 1973); see also "Harold Geneen's Tribulations," *Business Week*, 11 August 1973, 102–107, and "ITT, Exxon on the Spot," *Newsweek*, 13 November 1978, 101.

8. See "G&W and Bluhdorn Are Sued by the S.E.C.," *New York Times*, 27 November 1979, A1; Gerald F. Cavanagh, *American Business Values*, 2nd ed. (Englewood Cliffs: Prentice-Hall, 1984): 172.

9. See Paula Dwyer and Seth Payne, "The General Dynamics Case Sets a Bad Precedent," *Business Week*, 8 June 1987, 41; Eileen White and Debbie Goldberg, "Litton Pleads Guilty to Defrauding U.S. on Pentagon Work, Will Pay $15 Million," *Wall Street Journal*, 14 July 1986; "Kickbacks Reported Widespread in Subcontracts for Military Work," *New York Times*, 26 April 1986, 1, 36; John Koten and Tim Carrington, "For General Dynamics, Scandal Over Billing Hasn't Hurt Business," *Wall Street Journal*, 29 April 1986, 1, 20; and Eileen White, "Suspended Contractors Often Continue to Get More Defense Business," *Wall Street Journal*, 6 May 1986, 1, 23.

10. See the cover stories, "Whatever Happened to Ethics," *Time Magazine*, 25 May 1987, 14–17. The article describes and pictures thirty-nine federally appointed officials during the Reagan era who were indicted or resigned because of illegalities or irregularities, 18–20. See also the account of fourteen very successful businessmen (all male—CEOs and financiers) who were indicted and served prison terms for acting out their greed, "Having it All, Then Throwing it Away," 22–23.

11. See *Corporate Ethics: A Prime Business Asset* (New York: The Business Roundtable, 1988). One hundred companies provided information and ten firms were studied in detail. Conclusions were drawn about the firms' ethical histories, climates, policies, and procedures.

12. Ibid. 4–10.

13. See Richard Blackburn and Benson Rosen, "Total Quality and Human Resources Management: Lessons Learned from Baldridge Award-winning Companies," *Academy of Management Executive* 7(3)(1993): 49–66.

14. See Dominic A. Tarantino, "Trust + Ethics = Competitiveness" in *Business Ethics: Generating Trust in the 1990s and Beyond* (New York: The Conference Board, 1994): 15–16. In addition, among the seven principles in a recent report are: (1) Use teams to manage everything; (2) Reward team performance; (3) Inform and train all employees; (4) Let customers drive performance; (5) Maximize supplier and customer contact. Even the remaining two contribute to the point: (1) Organize around process, not task; and (2) Flatten hierarchy. See "The Horizontal Corporation," *Business Week*, 20 December 1993, 76–81.

15. See Rabindra N. Kanungo and Jay A. Conger, "Promoting Altruism as a Corporate Goal," *Academy of Management Executive*, 7(3)(1993): 37–48.

16. For a summary of these views see Rosemarie Tong, *Feminine and Feminist Ethics* (Belmont, CA: Wadsworth, 1993). See the chapters on the ethics of care of Carol Gilligan, 80–107, and Nel Noddings, 108–134, also that on maternal ethics, 135–157.

17. See Alex Trotman, Emmet E. Tracy Lecture, University of Detroit-Mercy, 14 February 1994.

18. See "Ford Remakes Itself," *The Detroit News*, 22 April 1994, 3D–4D.

19. Alasdair MacIntyre, "Contemporary Moral Culture," *The Catholic Commission on Intellectual and Cultural Affairs*, Annual Meeting, 1982: 40.

20. Clarence C. Walton, "The Moral Education of Business Students in an Immoral World," paper delivered to deans of business schools of Jesuit colleges and universities in Spain, 5 May 1993: 26.

21. For a much fuller treatment of these issues, see Gerald F. Cavanagh, *American Business Values*, 3rd ed. (Englewood Cliffs, N.J.: Prentice-Hall, 1990). See chap. 1 for a description of contemporary values; chaps. 2 and 3 for the historical roots of American business values; and chap. 5 for the influence of business values on personal values.

22. Dominic A. Tarantino, "Trust + Ethics = Competitiveness," in *Business Ethics: Generating Trust in the 1990s and Beyond*. (New York: The Conference Board, 1994): 15.

23. An American Psychological Association study reported in "The War Over 'Family Values'," *U.S. News and World Report*, 8 June 1992, 36.

24. "Holiday Spirit and Body-Bag Coverage," *U.S. News and World Report*, 7 December 1992, 11.

25. For a discussion of the difficulty that responsible media face when a story surfaces that is scandalous, probably untrue, destructive to individuals, family, and the country in the national media, see Anthony Lewis, "Freedom of the Press," *New York Times*, 24 December 1993, A27.

26. Derek Bok, "It's Time to Trim Hefty Paychecks," *New York Times*,

Sunday, 5 December 1993, F13. See also Bok's fuller treatment of the same issues in his book, *The Cost of Talent* (New York: Crown, 1993).

27. "The Thrill of Victory, The Agony of Paying for It," *Business Week*, 31 January 1994, 36.

28. "A New Game for Baseball," *Fortune*, 4 April 1994, 12.

29. "That Eye-Popping Executive Pay," *Business Week*, 25 April 1994, 55, 146.

30. See the list in *Business Week*, "Stock Options: The Gravy Train Could Derail," 15 March 1993, 31; "National Medical Enterprise: CEO Makes One of 1991's Top Salaries," *Forbes*, 25 May 1992, 40; and "The Flap Over Executive Pay," *Business Week*, 6 May 1991, 90–110.

31. Walter Olesky, "How Come the Boss is Getting \$10 Million?" *Career World*, 3 February 1992, 27.

32. John Paul II, *Centesimus Annus* as in United States Catholic Conference Publication No. 436–8, No. 36, 72–73.

33. David C. McClelland, *The Achieving Society* (Princeton, N.J.: Van Nostrand, 1962), points out every culture that brought about breakthrough accomplishments (e.g., Ancient Greece, Rome, the British Empire, the American Frontier, etc.) all set out to influence the values of the people of that society—especially the children. Grade-school readers were rewritten to capture the values that would bring initiative, self-reliance, and respect for other people.

34. James A. Autry, *Love and Profit: The Art of Caring Leadership* (New York: Avon, 1991): 158.

35. Dennis W. Archer, " 'We Must Believe Again': Mayor Asks Detroiters to Share Responsibility," *Detroit Free Press*, 4 January 1994, 1, 7A.

36. *Centesimus Annus*, No. 10 and 15, 20–21, 31–33.

37. The dictionary definition of schizophrenia might be applied to our society, at least with regard to this issue: "psychosis marked by withdrawal, bizarre, and sometimes delusional behavior and by intellectual and emotional deterioration." *Random House Dictionary* (New York: Random House, 1980): 798.

38. See Richard S. Myers, "The Supreme Court and the Privatization of Religion," *Catholic University Law Review* 41(1)(Fall 1991): 19–80. See also the excellent book by Stephen L. Carter, *The Culture of Disbelief* (New York: Basic Books, 1993).

39. "President-elect Bill Clinton: 'My Catholic Training' " in *National Jesuit News*, January 1993, 7.

40. Aristotle, *The Nicomachean Ethics*. Trans. by Hippocrates G. Apostle (Dordrecht, Holland: D. Reidel, 1975). For his superb treatment of how one acquires virtue, see 1103–1109, 21–34. He then goes on to discuss specific virtues in some detail. See also the excellent book, Robert C. Solomon, *Ethics and Excellence: Cooperation and Integrity in Business* (New York: Oxford University Press, 1993). Solomon builds upon Aristotle's analysis.

41. See Oliver F. Williams and John W. Houck *A Virtuous Life in Business: Stories of Courage and Integrity in the Corporate World.* (Lanham, Md: Rowman & Littlefield, 1992).

42. For more information on the incident and the full *Credo*, see *ibid.,* Oliver F. Williams and Patrick E. Murphy, "The Ethics of Virtue: A Moral Theory for Business," 12–16.

43. *An American Imperative: Higher Expectations for Higher Education.* (Johnson Foundation, 1993):4.

44. "President of Harvard Cites Need for Commitment to Social Service," *New York Times*, 1 November 1993,16.

45. "Developing Student Leaders: Reducing Barriers Between the University and the Community," Mary Ann Hazen, David Boje, Karen Newman, Amy Kenworthy and Gerald Cavanagh. A Symposium submitted to The Academy of Management, annual meeting, August 1994, Dallas, Texas.

46. Business for Social Responsibility is open to any business organization; its dues are proportionate to the size of the business firm. It is located at 1030 15th Street N.W., Suite 1010; Washington, D.C. 20005.

47. Students for Responsible Business, c/o Social Venture Network, 1388 Sutter St., San Francisco, CA 94109.

48. Business Vocation Conference, James L. Nolan, Executive Director, c/o Woodstock Theological Center, Georgetown University, Washington, D.C. 20057–1097.

11

Seven Corporate Responsibilities

Michael Novak

What Is a Corporation?

In the long view of history, the business corporation is a fascinating institution. It is a social institution, independent of the state. Its legal existence is transgenerational; it goes on when its progenitors die and may endure across many generations. Its members come to it voluntarily. They do not give it all the commitment and all the energies of life; it is not a total institution.[1] But they may well commit more of their time and energy to it, on a sustained basis, than to any other institution of their lives, except possibly their families.

The business corporation is also a mediating structure, a social institution larger than the individuals who make it up but smaller than the state. An institution both voluntary and private, it stands between the individual and the state and is, perhaps, (after the family) the crucial institution of civil society.

Civil society is composed of all those associations, freely chosen or natural (such as the family), through which citizens practice self-government independently of the state. Through the institutions of civil society and its mediating structures, citizens pursue their own affairs, accomplish their social purposes, and enrich the texture of their common life. Civil society is a larger, more basic, and more vital component of social life and the common good than is the state. The state is a servant of civil society. This is caught in Lincoln's classic phrase, "government of the people, by the people, and for the people."

189

Michael Novak

The private business corporation is a necessary (but not sufficient) condition for the success of democracy. This insight is one of the crowning achievements of this nation's founders who inherited parts of it from Montesquieu. They saw quite clearly that democracy would be safer if built upon the commercial and industrial classes than if built upon the military, aristocratic, clerical, or landed classes, the basis of most regimes.

At the same time, the founders of this nation looked to commerce and manufacture as essential keys to economic prosperity. In Article 1, section 8 of the Constitution, they looked to the private business corporation for the advancement of the arts and practical sciences, they looked to invention and discovery and saw in ideas a new form of property far more significant than land. Only in this one place in the body of the Constitution did the founders use the word "right" to protect the "right" of authors and inventors to the fruit of their original ideas.[2] The founders saw that the primary cause of the wealth of nations lies in the mind.

To genius of mind they added, as Lincoln admiringly noted, the "fuel of interest."[3] To mind they gave incentives. In subsequent years, through a land grant college act, they gave intellectual activity a basis of institutional support through the research of an entire array of state-funded universities.[4]

One of the most striking features of early American life, according to Tocqueville, was the delight Americans took in forming associations, in cooperation, and in teamwork.[5] (Given this tendency, is it little wonder that the only sports to attract universal acclaim in the early United States were team sports—baseball, football, and basketball?) A major preoccupation of the early decades was building communities—entire cities sprang up where none had existed. To create these cities, Americans had to learn to work together under private auspices, while keeping the state both as weak and as strong as was consistent with self-government. In this climate, the private business corporation became a prime model of public association, common motivation, mutual dedication, widespread optimism and the can-do spirit. "The impossible takes a little longer," is the sort of motto that members of enterprising institutions still like to exchange.

Despite the obvious importance, theological or religious writing on the business corporation that meets two conditions has until recently been rare. These conditions are that it not be positively hostile to business and not be patronizing but fair and sympathetic. Sections 32, 33, and 42 of Pope John Paul II's magnificent encyclical of 1991, "The

Hundredth Year," *Centesimus Annus* meet these tests.[6] They are, by far, the most religiously helpful passages that people involved in business are likely ever to encounter.

> Many goods cannot be adequately produced through the work of an isolated individual; they require the cooperation of many people in working towards a common goal. Organizing such a productive effort, planning its duration in time, making sure that it corresponds in a positive way to the demands which it must satisfy, and taking the necessary risks—all this too is a source of wealth in today's society. In this way the *role* of disciplined and creative *human work* and, as an essential part of that work, *initiative and entrepreneurial ability* become increasingly evident and decisive.[7]

At this point, the pope makes a startling claim. Speaking of the process of organizing the productive effort, he writes: "This process . . . throws practical light on a truth about the person which Christianity has consistently affirmed" and this process "should be viewed carefully and favorably."[8] He highlights some of the lessons that become evident in the life of the business corporation:

> Indeed, besides the earth, man's principal resource is *man himself*. His intelligence enables him to discover the earth's productive potential and the many different ways in which human needs can be satisfied. It is his disciplined work in close collaboration with others that makes possible the creation of ever more extensive *working communities* which can be relied upon to transform man's natural and human environments. Important virtues are involved in this process such as diligence, industriousness, prudence in undertaking reasonable risks, reliability and fidelity in interpersonal relationships as well as courage in carrying out decisions which are difficult and painful but necessary, both for the overall working of a business and in meeting possible set-backs.[9]

Pope John Paul II also has a sound word on profit:

> The church acknowledges the legitimate *role of profit* as an indication that a business is functioning well. When a firm makes a profit, this means that productive factors have been properly employed and corresponding human needs have been duly satisfied. . . . In fact, the purpose of a business firm is not simply to make a profit, but is to be found in its very existence as a *community of persons* who in various ways are endeavoring to satisfy their basic needs, and who form a particular group at the service of the whole of society. Profit is a regulator of the life of a

business, but it is not the only one; *other human and moral factors* must also be considered which, in the long term, are at least equally important for the life of a business.[10]

The private business corporation is, then, an extraordinary institution. It is a practical model for the Christian church to reflect on "carefully and favorably." Carefully—since, after all, "The first moral responsibility is to think clearly."[11] The corporation is not a church, not a state, not a welfare agency, not a family. A corporation is an economic association with specific and limited responsibilities. In this light, seven corporate responsibilities may be said to constitute its primary moral duty.

Seven Corporate Responsibilities

Some who work in the field of business ethics were trained first in ethics and tend to think of business corporations as morally naked, unless hung with baubles and jewels from ethics to disguise that nakedness. They do not see the ethical dimensions inherent in business activities. As a consequence, one detects a certain dualism in many discussions of business ethics: on the one side is business and on the other are all those other responsibilities that business needs to add on to be, or appear to be, ethical. In an analogous way, parents sometimes try to impose on one of their children an ideal of behavior that seemed appropriate to their other children but is not for this child; they have not taken the time to listen to that child as a distinct individual.

Thus, we must first discern the moral ideas inherent in business qua business. A business corporation is not a church; it is not a state; it is not a welfare agency; it is not (except rarely) a religious association; it is not a political association; it is not a total institution. It is an economic association, which in several ways serves the common good of the community simply by being what it is. Accordingly, among the corporate responsibilities of business that spring from its own nature are at least these seven:

1. *To satisfy customers with goods and services of real value.* This is not as easy as it seems. Three out of five new businesses fail—perhaps because the founders lack a realistic conception of how to serve the customer, perhaps because the conception itself is flawed, or its execution. Like other acts of freedom, launching a new business is an act of faith; one has to trust one's instincts and one's vision and

hope that these are well enough grounded to build success. It is the customers, in the end, who decide.

2. *To make a reasonable return on the funds entrusted to the business corporation by its investors.*[12] It is more practical to think of this responsibility in the second place, rather than in the first, where some writers place it, because only if the first is satisfied will the second be met.

3. *To create new wealth.*[13] This is no small responsibility; if the business corporation does not meet it, who in society will? Probably more than one-third of American citizens who are employed receive their salaries from nonprofit institutions. But nonprofit institutions receive their funding from the benefactions of others, which in the end come from the new wealth created by the business corporations. It is also from this new wealth that the firm finds it possible to pay a return to investors, in addition to returning their principal. From this new wealth, provision must also be made for the future, including a fund to underwrite all those failed projects that are certain to accompany successes. If a company is not creating new wealth, it is spinning its wheels, going into debt, or consuming its capital; all of these processes are self-destructive. On the other hand, the steady, incremental creation of new wealth is the road to what Adam Smith called "universal opulence," the condition in which the real wages of workers keep growing over time until even the poor live at a level, with new technologies and other benefits, that even kings and dukes did not enjoy in 1776.[14]

4. *To create new jobs.* It is better to teach a man how to fish than to give him a fish. In the same way, it is far better to provide all willing citizens with jobs rather than with government grants that keep them permanently dependent and in the condition of serfs. This is one of the great social responsibilities for whose accomplishment democracies look to business corporations, and in particular to new entrants into the field. The rate of small business formation is usually a very good index of the general health of society, and not only its economic health, but also its morale, hopefulness, and spirit of generosity toward others. When economic horizons contract and large masses of people are unemployed, divisive, and self-destructive, passions such as envy, leveling, and resentment multiply.

In South America, for example, with nearly 110 million persons fifteen years old and under, youngsters enter the labor force cohort by cohort with every year that passes, looking for employment, with little employment to be found.[15] In the future, surely there will be fewer agricultural workers in Latin America, and perhaps even fewer working in large industrial factories. Without a rapid expansion of the small-business sector, in firms employing from two or three to one hundred workers, it is not easy to see how economic health will come to Latin America. The creation of jobs is a very high priority, but you cannot create employees without creating employers. Like other societies, Latin America will have to look to its small-business sector for a realistic hope of liberating the poor.

5. *To defeat envy through generating upward mobility and putting empirical ground under the conviction that hard work and talent are fairly rewarded.* The founders of the American Republic recognized that most other republics in history had failed, and that one reason they failed was envy: the envy of one faction for another, one family for another, one clan for another, or of the poor toward the rich.[16] If a republic is to have a long life, it must defeat envy. The best way to do this is to generate economic growth through as many diverse industries and economic initiatives as possible, so that every family has the realistic possibility of seeing its economic condition improve within the next three or four years. Poor families do not ask for paradise, but they do want to see tangible signs of improvement over time. When such horizons are open, people do not compare their condition with that of their neighbors; rather, they compare their own position today with where they hope to be in three or four years. In this way, they give no ground to envy. The realistic hope of a better future is essential to the poor, and this hope is made realistic only through the provision of universal chances for upward mobility such that, in general, people see that hard work, good will, ingenuity, and talent pay off. When people lose their faith in this probability, they become cynical and destructive. For this reason, a dynamic economy is a necessary (although not sufficient) condition for the survival and success of democracy. If they do not see real improvement in their economic conditions, people in the formerly communist countries of Central Europe, for example, are not likely to be satisfied merely with the opportunity to vote every two years.

6. *To promote invention, ingenuity and in general, "progress in the arts and useful sciences"* (Article 1, Section 8, U.S. Constitution). The heart of capitalism is *caput*; the human mind, human invention, human enterprise. Pope John Paul II puts it well: "Today the decisive factor is increasingly *man himself*, that is, his knowledge, especially his scientific knowledge, his capacity for interrelated and compact organization, as well as his ability to perceive the needs of others, and

to satisfy them.''[17] The great dynamo of invention, discovery, and ingenuity is the business corporation. To repeat Abraham Lincoln's formulation, the property in ideas made possible by the patent and copyright clause of the Constitution "adds the fuel of interest to the fire of genius.''[18] The Constitution gives an incentive to discover new practical ideas and to bring them to the realistic service of one's neighbors. Perhaps no other practical device in history has so revolutionized the daily conditions of life and actually brought about a higher level of the common good than any people ever experienced before.

7. *To diversify the interests of the Republic.* One of the least observed functions of the business corporation is to solidify the economic loyalties of citizens and to sort out their practical knowledge into diverse sectors of life. The interests of the road-builders is not that of the canal-builders, nor of the builders of the railroads, nor of the airline companies. The sheer dynamism of economic invention makes far less probable the coalescing of a simple majority that could tyrannize minorities. The economic interests of some citizens are, in an important sense, at cross-purposes with the economic interests of others, and this is crucial to preventing the tyranny of a majority.

All seven of these economic responsibilities need to be met by a nation's business corporations. All seven are crucial to the health of the state and, more importantly, to the health of civil society, which is the master social reality. But there are also other responsibilities, inherent not so much in business qua business as in the convictions of its practitioners.

Should the Christian Businessperson be Different?

The cult of the Catholic Church is culture-forming.[19] The liturgy is intended to inspire a distinctive style of life. Thus, while the business corporation has a set of inherent responsibilities, proper to itself, these do not exhaust the responsibilities of the Christian whose vocation calls him or her to the business world. Without intending to be exhaustive, one might discern seven further sets of moral responsibilities proper to the business worker qua Christian. I have taken pains to state them in a way that shows their relevance to business, and makes them analogously compelling to those who are not Christian. Among these responsibilities:

1. *To establish within the culture of the firm a sense of community and respect for the dignity of persons.* This should include a respect

for the standards, the discipline, the motivation, and the teamwork that brings out the best in people and helps them gain a sense of high achievement and human fulfillment.[20]

2. *To protect the political soil of liberty.*[21] Since free business corporations are permitted to operate freely only in a minority of countries, those involved in business must come to see how fragile their activities are—how they can be crushed by war, revolution, tyranny, and anarchy. Most people today, like most in history, have suffered from such devastations. Many individuals have hardly ever (or never) experienced that peace, stability, and institutional environment that supports the daily activities and long-term hopes of business. Businesses will not grow in just any soil; they depend on specific sorts of political environments. People in business, therefore, have a responsibility to be watchful over the fate of their political society, even as a matter of self-survival. It is no accident that they have had reason to learn to love liberty as ardently as any others in history and, indeed, have often been instigators of free societies.

3. *To exemplify respect for law.* Business cannot survive without the rule of law. Long-term contracts depend upon respect for law for their fulfillment. Often in the United States we take the rule of law for granted and hardly appreciate its fragility. Hardly any institution is as much at risk as the business corporation and hardly any is so dependent on the reliability, speed, and efficiency of the daily operation of the rule of law. Thus, it is doubly scandalous for people in business to break the law. It is wrong in itself, and it is also suicidal, since to the extent that the law falls into disrespect, the life of corporations is rendered insecure if not impossible.

4. *To win the allegiance of the majority.* Since the survival of business depends on the survival of free institutions, the responsibilities of people in business go well beyond their strictly economic responsibilities. A look at the top 20 percent of American society—i.e., its elite, defined in terms of income, education, and status (professionals, managers, the self-employed versus employees)—shows that our elite is roughly divided into two parts. One part we will call the "Old Elite," whose income and status depend upon the expansion of the private sector, particularly the business sector. The "New Class" are those who see their own income, power, and status as dependent upon the expansion of the state.[22] These two rivals vie for the allegiance of a democratic majority. A society simultaneously democratic and capitalist benefits when these two perennial rivals are of roughly equal strength, so that the free political system and the free economic system

are in healthy equilibrium. (Given the tendency of the state to amass power and even coercive force, however, a society is probably closer to healthy equilibrium when at least a slight majority favors economic liberty.)

5. *To overcome the principle of envy.* Benjamin Franklin and Thomas Jefferson ransacked the libraries of London and Paris, respectively, in an attempt to understand what brought about the downfall of earlier republican experiments. Virtually all republics failed, often after only a few generations. Typically, the cause of failure was envy and the division it caused between rich and poor, family and family, dynasty and dynasty, or one section of the republic and another. No vice is deeper or more destructive than envy, not even hatred. Hatred is visible, and everyone knows it is wrong. Envy is typically invisible, like a colorless gas, and normally it presents itself under a beautiful (but deceptive) name, such as "justice," "fairness," "equality," or even "social justice." All these are good names, and for this reason envy often hides behind their skirts. Envy is so pervasive among the human race that in the Ten Commandments, under the name "covetousness," God forbade it seven times.[23]

What people in business need to learn from this is that envy, once mobilized in society, can strangle the open society. They need to be on the alert to defeat envy. For this reason, they should avoid some things which are otherwise innocent in themselves. Conspicuous privilege, ostentation, and other forms of behavior, even when not necessarily wrong, typically provoke envy among others. Unusually large salaries or bonuses, even if justified by competition in a free and open market (since high talent of certain kinds is extremely rare), may offer demagogues fertile ground on which to scatter the seeds of envy. It is wise to take precautions against these eventualities.

6. *To communicate often and fully with their investors, shareholders, pensioners, customers, and employees.* A business firm represents everwidening circles of people, and it is much to its advantage to keep all of them informed about its purposes, needs, risks, dangers, and opportunities. In a democratic society, the corporation needs the support of a great many, and it is of itself—especially over against the omnivorous administrative state of the late twentieth century—exceedingly fragile.

7. *To contribute to making the surrounding society, its own habitat, a better place.* It is much to the advantage of the business firm that the republican experiment in self-government should succeed and that also, therefore, there should be an active private sector as an alternative

to the state. The business firm does well to become a leader in civil society and to contribute to the good fortune of other mediating structures in the private sector, whether in areas such as education and the arts, healthful activities for youth, the environment, care for the elderly, new initiatives to meet the needs of the homeless and the poor, or other such activities. The business corporation cannot take primary responsibility for these things; it is not, in itself, a welfare organization. Nevertheless, it does well to strengthen the networks of civil society and those of its allies who provide an alternative to government. Government is not the enemy of business nor of the citizens, although it has been, historically, a fertile source of tyranny, corruption, the abuse of rights, and plain arrogance of power.

In sum, the business corporation is, in its essence, a moral institution of a distinctive type. It imposes some moral obligations that are inherent in its own ends, structure, and modes of operation. Other moral obligations fall upon it through the moral and religious commitments of its members. Thus, those who labor within the business corporation have many moral responsibilities and a richly various moral agenda, of which the fourteen responsibilities mentioned here are basic but not exhaustive.

Those academics (and journalists) who do not take the high moral responsibilities of business with due seriousness are making a grave mistake on two levels. First, they are guilty of intellectual blindness or, perhaps, professional prejudice. Second, since a capitalist economy (indeed, a healthy, thriving capitalist economy) is a necessary condition for the success of democracy—including the rule of law, the protection of the rights of minorities, resistance against the voracious power of the state, and a flourishing of civil society—this error is in the long run self-destructive.

Notes

1. See Erving Goffman, *Asylums: Essays on the Social Situation of Mental Patients and Other Inmates* (New York: Doubleday, 1961).

2. *The Constitution of the United States of America*, Article 1, Section 8: "The Congress shall have Power to . . . promote the Progress of Science and useful Arts, by securing for limited Times to Authors and Inventors the exclusive Right to their respective Writings and Discoveries."

3. *Abraham Lincoln: Speeches and Writings, 1859–1865* (New York: Library of America, 1989), 10–11: "Next came the Patent laws. These began in England in 1624; and, in this country, with the adoption of our constitution.

Before then, any man might instantly use what another had invented; so that the inventor had no special advantage from his own invention. The patent system changed this; secured to the inventor, for a limited time, the exclusive use of his invention; and thereby added the fuel of *interest* to the *fire* of genius, in the discovery and production of new and useful things.''

4. *Morrill Act.* Signed 2 July 1862 by President Lincoln. Mandated the states to set aside land for the establishment of specialized colleges of research and teaching to promote the scientific advancement of agriculture.

5. Alexis de Tocqueville, *Democracy in America*, trans. George Lawrence (Garden City: Doubleday, 1969): 513: "Americans of all ages, all stations in life, and all types of disposition are forever forming associations. There are not only commercial and industrial associations in which all take part, but others of a thousand different types—religious, moral, serious, futile, very general and very limited, immensely large and very minute. Americans combine to give fetes, found seminaries, build churches, distribute books, and send missionaries to the antipodes. Hospitals, prisons, and schools take shape in that way. Finally, if they want to proclaim a truth or propagate some feeling by the encouragement of a great example, they form an association. In every case, at the head of any new undertaking, where in France you would find the government or in England some territorial magnate, in the United States you are sure to find an association.''

6. *Centesimus Annus* commemorates the 100th anniversary of Pope Leo XIII's 1891 encyclical *Rerum Novarum*, which is usually understood to be the first document in modern papal social teaching.

7. *Centesimus Annus*, no. 32.

8. *Centesimus Annus*, no. 32.

9. *Centesimus Annus*, no. 32.

10. *Centesimus Annus*, no. 35.

11. See Blaise Pascal, *Pensees*, trans. A. J. Krailsheimer (London: Penguin Books, 1966): 95:

> 200 H3. Man is only a reed, the weakest in nature, but he is a thinking reed. There is no need for the whole universe to take up arms to crush him: a vapour, a drop of water is enough to kill him. But even if the universe were to crush him, man would still be nobler than his slayer, because he knows that he is dying and the advantage the universe has over him. The universe knows none of this.
>
> Thus all our dignity consists in thought. It is on thought that we must depend for our recovery, not on space and time, which we could never fill. Let us then strive to think well; that is the basic principle of morality.
>
> (347)

12. Milton Friedman has made the classic case for this fundamental social responsibility. I agree with him in stressing how basic it is, but would place it also in the context of other responsibilities. Friedman's classic statement is:

The view has been gaining widespread acceptance that corporate officials and labor leaders have a "social responsibility" that goes beyond serving the interest of their stockholders or their members. This view shows a fundamental misconception of the character and nature of a free economy. In such an economy, there is one and only one social responsibility of business—to use its resources and engage in activities designed to increase its profits so long as it stays within the rules of the game, which is to say, engages in open and free competition, without deception or fraud. Similarly, the "social responsibility" of labor leaders is to serve the interests of the members of their unions. It is the responsibility of the rest of us to establish a framework of law such that an individual in pursuing his own interest is, to quote Adam Smith again, "led by an invisible hand to promote an end which was no part of his intention. Nor is it always the worse for the society that it was no part of it. By pursuing his own interest, he frequently promotes that of the society more effectually than when he really intends to promote it. I have never known much good done by those who affected to trade for the public good." Few trends could so thoroughly undermine the very foundations of our free society as the acceptance by corporate officials of a social responsibility other than to make as much money for their stockholders as possible. This is a fundamentally subversive doctrine. *Capitalism and Freedom* (Chicago: University of Chicago Press, 1962): 133.

Note that Friedman's own definition includes further moral responsibilities such as maintaining open and free competition, establishing a framework of the rule of law, avoiding deception and fraud, and exemplifying fair play within the rules of the game—altogether no small moral agenda.

13. See Peter F. Drucker, *Concept of the Corporation* (New York: Harper and Row, 1983): 193:

Just as it is nonsense to say that economic life is possible without profit, it is nonsense to believe that there could be any other yardstick for the success or failure of an economic action but profitability. Of course, it is always necessary for society to go in for a good many unprofitable activities in the social interest. But all such activities that are undertaken in spite of their economic unprofitability must be paid for out of the profits of some other branch of economic activity; otherwise, the total economy shrinks. Profitability is simply another word for economic rationality. And what other rationality could there be to measure economic activity but economic rationality?

Note that Drucker, like Pope John Paul II, refers to profit as a "yardstick" or "indication."

14. Adam Smith, *An Inquiry into the Nature and Causes of the Wealth of Nations*, R. H. Campbell and A. S. Skinner, eds., vol. I (Indianapolis: Liberty Press, 1981): 22:

It is the great multiplication of the productions of all the different arts, in consequence of the division of labour, which occasions, in a well-governed society, that universal opulence which extends itself to the lowest ranks of the people. Every workman has a great quantity of his own work to dispose of beyond what he himself has occasion for; and every other workman being exactly in the same situation, he is enabled to exchange a great quantity of his own goods for a great quantity, or, what comes to the same thing, for the price of a great quantity of theirs. He supplies them abundantly with what they have occasion for, and they accommodate him as amply with what he has occasion for, and a general plenty diffuses itself through all the different ranks of the society.

For a good recent discussion of Adam Smith, see Jerry Z. Muller, *Adam Smith in His Time and Ours: Designing the Decent Society* (New York: The Free Press, 1993).

15. United Nations Population Division, *World Population Prospects 1990* (New York: United Nations, 1991). Quoted in *World Resources: 1992–93*, A Report by The World Resources Institute in collaboration with the U.N. Environmental Programme and the U.N. Development Programme (New York: Oxford University Press, 1992): 76, 246, 248, 257.

16. Alexander Hamilton, James Madison, and John Jay, *The Federalist Papers*, No. 10:

Among the numerous advantages promised by a well constructed Union, none deserves to be more accurately developed than its tendency to break and control the violence of faction. The friend of popular governments, never finds himself so much alarmed for their character and fate, as when he contemplates their propensity to this dangerous vice. He will not fail therefore to set a due value on any plan which, without violating the principles to which he is attached, provides a proper cure for it. The instability, injustice and confusion introduced into the public councils, have in truth been the mortal diseases under which popular governments have everywhere perished; as they continue to be the favorite and fruitful topics from which the adversaries to liberty derive their most specious declamations.

17. *Centesimus Annus*, no. 32.

18. See no. 3 above.

19. See Romano Guardini, *The Church and the Catholic & The Spirit of Liturgy* (New York: Sheed & Ward, Inc., 1935).

20. *Centesimus Annus*, no. 31. See also nos. 7–9 above.

21. For elaboration, see my essay on "The Moral, Cultural, and Political Responsibilities of Business," in *This Hemisphere of Liberty: A Philosophy of the Americas* (Washington, D.C.: American Enterprise Institute Press, 1992): 89–99.

22. See my discussion of "The New Class" in *The American Vision: An*

Essay on the Future of Democratic Capitalism (Washington, D.C.: American Enterprise Institute Press, 1978): 29–34. Cf. *The New Class?* B. Bruce-Briggs, ed. (New Brunswick, New Jersey: Transaction, 1979). For more recent tendencies in the new class, see Peter Berger, "Furtive Smokers: And What They Tell Us About America," *Commentary* 97 (June 1994): 21–26.

23. Exodus 20:17: "You shall not covet your neighbor's house; you shall not covet your neighbor's wife, or his manservant, or his maidservant, or his ox, or his ass, or anything that is your neighbor's."

12

The Apartheid Struggle: Learnings from the Interaction between Church Groups and Business

Oliver F. Williams

Under what circumstances are multinational corporations ever morally required to terminate all business transactions in a host country? That question was the subject of intense debate in the United States and, to a lesser extent, in other developed nations throughout the 1980s, sparked by the issue of the ethics of investing in an apartheid South Africa. Much may be learned from that situation about how to deal with other human-rights violations in various countries. Apartheid literally means "separate development" and, although there may have been more oppressive systems, apartheid was the only one based on skin color and codified in elaborate laws.

Finally, in April 1994, statutory apartheid was completely ended when, in a move almost as dramatic as the fall of the Berlin Wall, South Africa had its first national election in which all—whites and blacks—could vote. This vote was the culmination of several years of intense negotiation among all the major groups in the country and was, very likely, in large measure the result of strong internal pressure from the disenfranchised blacks as well as external pressure from the community of nations. One issue in contention was what sort of response was morally required by a multinational business with operations in South Africa during the apartheid regime. Must a company terminate all business transactions or could a moral argument be made that the companies should remain in the country, assist the blacks in their struggle and prepare the way for a strong economy in the post-apartheid South Africa?

In discussing the issue of South Africa with managers of major businesses in the United States, one common theme that emerges is almost a disbelief that, in fact, the pressures became so great that almost one hundred fifty U.S. companies decided to leave the country between 1985 and early 1990. These pressures were largely orchestrated by the church groups and associated antiapartheid organizations that had begun that struggle in the 1970s. In one way or another the "hassle factor" reached a threshold where, for many companies, it made little sense to stay. Quoting Xerox chairman David T. Kearns, discussing the 1987 Xerox disinvestment, the *Wall Street Journal* captured the sentiment of many top managers:

> "It was clear things were continuing to deteriorate on all fronts," he said. The nation's economy and social climate were worsening; pro-disinvestment groups' criticism was rising; and Xerox was beginning to lose sales in the U.S. to local governments that were banning contracts with companies doing business there.[1]

How is it that prodisinvestment groups captured the minds and hearts of many Americans? By the late 1980s, over one hundred college and university endowments divested of stocks of companies with holdings in South Africa, and sixty-eight cities and counties and nineteen states passed selective purchase ordinances banning contracts with companies with operations there. Can interest groups mount that kind of pressure on other contemporary issues? How did such a broad constituency for disinvestment coalesce?

While asking businesses to use their power to help solve a host country's social issue was not a new idea, demanding that all companies completely leave such a country was without precedent. This article argues that because business leaders never explicitly championed the civil and political rights of the oppressed blacks when they formed the Sullivan Principles in 1977, they were never really trusted by church groups concerned about South Africa. In 1985, when, under tremendous public pressure, the principles were finally amplified to include political rights, it was considered too little, too late. Business leaders were perceived as doing whatever they had to do to continue making profits in South Africa—no more, no less. If they were operating from an ethical principle, most church leaders could not find it.

After several decades of strategizing and lobbying by the various parties, there emerged in the 1980s two major policy proposals designed to overcome apartheid. One proposal, championed by affiliated church and various other groups, argued for complete withdrawal of all U.S. companies in South Africa. The other policy, spearheaded by the coalition of U.S. companies known as the Principles Program, founded by the civil-rights leader, the Reverend Leon Sullivan, argued for American companies to remain in South Africa and use their power to advance the struggle for black political and economic rights.

In the 1970s, however, there was plurality of policy proposals among antiapartheid church groups; some, for example, wanted U.S. companies to use their leverage to nudge the white South African government to the negotiating table. At this time, it may have been quite possible to forge a coalition of business and some church groups that would have enabled a concerted U.S. effort to dismantle apartheid. Why did such a coalition never emerge? As will be demonstrated below, the business leaders could not begin to think about challenging the laws of a sovereign nation in the 1970s, and thus church groups arguing such a case were dismissed, politely but firmly. It was clear to many church leaders that business managers would not be a willing partner in the struggle to overcome apartheid. A brief history of the interaction between business and the church advocates, as well as a discussion of other major factors in this struggle, may shed light on these issues.

A Brief History

Although disagreeing over the means of dismantling apartheid, almost all Americans believed apartheid was wrong. Apartheid in South Africa was controlled by over three hundred racial laws denying blacks the rights many people of the world take for granted—the right to vote, to move freely within the country, to attend decent schools, and to have the opportunity to live in suitable housing. Focusing on human rights, concern about these racist policies on the part of U.S. groups dates back to 1912 when the National Association for the Advancement of Colored People (NAACP) provided assistance to what later became the Africa National Congress of South Africa. The momentum only began, however, in 1953 with the founding of the American Committee on Africa (ACOA) by the white U.S. Methodist minister, George Houser. Under Houser, the ACOA campaigned for total U.S. disinvestment from South Africa. In 1957 the ACOA sponsored a Declaration

of Conscience campaign with the "World-Wide Day of Protest" that
featured Eleanor Roosevelt and Martin Luther King, Jr. For the most
part, the ACOA campaign of the 1950s did not attract much interest in
the United States.

In Houser's view, it was the media attention given to official violence
against blacks in South Africa that especially caught the attention of
Americans.[2] On March 21, 1960, a demonstration against the pass laws
in Sharpeville resulted in the police killing sixty-seven and wounding
one hundred eighty people. Later in 1976, fifteen thousand school
children, demonstrating in Soweto, were fired upon by security forces.
Finally, the 1984–87 unrest and violence throughout the country
between 1984 and 1987 added to the ever-growing American interest
group supporting total disinvestment.

Defining the Situation: Business as Part of the Problem from the Church Perspective

To be sure, the television and other media coverage of these tragic
events brought the apartheid problem into the living rooms of middle
America, but does it explain the ever expanding pressure for total
disinvestment? Houser and others think not and focus instead on the
fact that business, at least until 1984, was perceived as being too cozy
with the white government in South Africa and relatively unconcerned
with the plight of the majority of the people who suffered under
apartheid.

What was the proper role of business in advancing the civil and
political rights of blacks in South Africa? While from the 1950s to early
1970s business leaders made no concerted efforts to determine a
consensus response, church groups were busy formulating their answer. In the 1950s Methodist minister George Houser was fashioning
an action-oriented organization (ACOA) that was destined to be most
influential. It was not until the middle to late 1960s, however, that
college students, civil-rights leaders, and church groups began to
devise strategies in response to the evil of apartheid. In 1975, building
on work begun in the 1960s by ACOA, a major offensive was launched
by church groups coordinated by the ICCR (the Interfaith Center on
Corporate Responsibility, a large coalition of Protestant denominations
and an ad hoc group of Catholic dioceses and religious orders, housed
in the New York City headquarters of the National Council of
Churches), against bank loans to the Republic of South Africa
(R.S.A.). Forty-seven banks, including some of the major banking

institutions in the United States, were threatened with a mass with-drawal of deposits and continued shareholder pressure unless loans to the R.S.A. ceased. Although initially the campaign did not have a significant effect on the loan policy of the banks, it did give much visibility to the apartheid problem. Tim Smith, executive director of the ICCR, the church coalition that led the bank campaign, reflecting on the discussions with bank officials, noted that he observed a major shift in the thinking of managers.

Initially, as the ICCR and its religious investors challenged managers to take responsibility for supporting the evils of apartheid with their bank loans, the managers responded that their sole responsibility was to find reliable businesses that would return on investment (the market capitalism model). As the campaign progressed, however, Smith ob-served a gradual opening on the managers' part to hear and act upon the social and moral concerns of the church groups. Business came to realize that what was at stake was the very legitimacy of business in the minds of some important constituencies and that it was in the interest of business to interact with those forces impinging on the business system.

What was happening here was a gradual paradigm shift from the market-capitalism model to what has been called the business-ecology model.[3] While it was never clear to the interest groups whether the banks were acting on principle or protecting self-interests, after mounting enormous public pressure, the religious coalition was finally successful in terminating all loans. To be sure, this process took over ten years. Were the bank managers actually convinced that they, as bank officers, had an ethical obligation to advance the human rights of the South African blacks or did they simply capitulate in the face of overwhelming public opinion in the United States? At least two banks (Chemical and Chase Manhattan) did state their opposition to apart-heid as the reason for ending loans. Did they have an adequate model to conceptualize the ethical issues in the context of a business environment? Might the integrative social-contracts theory provide the underlying justification to make normative judgments and to discuss these judgments with shareholders and other stakeholders?[4]

The shareholder resolution campaign developed into a major avenue of mobilizing public pressure on business. In 1971 the first shareholder resolution ever to come to a vote called for the termination of General Motors (GM) operations in the R.S.A. and was presented by the Episcopal Church. (By 1990 over five-hundred shareholder resolutions had been presented to over ninety companies with operations in South

Africa.) Although the resolution in 1971 garnered only 1.29 percent of
the votes, it was a watershed event in that it was the occasion for the
Reverend Leon Sullivan, a new member of the board of GM, to call
for the withdrawal of GM and all U.S. business from South Africa until
apartheid was dismantled. While Sullivan clearly did not carry the day
at the GM board meeting, he did make a very significant point: that
human-rights concerns were the province of the board and that he
would not rest until that notion was accepted. According to Sullivan,
in 1971 most of the board of GM or any other company were not
prepared to consider factoring human-rights considerations into business decisions. As will be discussed later, by 1991 this broader agenda
for business had become almost standard practice for a growing
number of companies. This study hopes to shed light on that transition
in thinking.

While Sullivan was unable to persuade the GM board to take a stand
in 1971, he continued to mull over the various options to overcome
apartheid in South Africa. There was a growing expectation in the
United States that business should be involved in social issues, and
advocacy groups, encouraged by the success of Ralph Nader's initiatives, began to grow in importance. What gave rise to this rather
sudden increase in nonmarket forces or interest-group activism? One
of the most formative experiences that may have set the tone for
activism in the United States was the civil-rights movement of the
1960s. The many who participated in this event, actively or passively,
came to feel a new power to transform society. Evil did not have to be
tolerated; unjust social structures could be changed with strategy and
persistence. In my view, the antiwar movement, the rise of local
community organization, and the experience of the civil rights movement and its use of the media and creation of heroes provided the
model and the power that brought the current activist movements
to birth.

At the same time, several other important developments have provided fertile soil for the growth of the activist movements. During the
last thirty years the media has achieved significant power to shape
public opinion on social issues, and informed public opinion has led
to financial and other support for a wide variety of organizations
championing social issues. In addition, the two major political parties
were the vehicles that carried the concerns of the people through the
public-policy process, but they no longer function effectively in the
eyes of many people; today's interest groups perform many of the
roles that were abdicated by the political parties. That U.S. business

should avoid racist policies in South Africa has had an especially compelling claim on Americans because of their own, often unsuccessful, experience in trying to overcome a racist past.

It was in this climate that the Reverend Sullivan, acting independently of the ICCR affiliates, invited the top executives of fifteen of the largest U.S. corporations with operations in South Africa to attend a meeting to discuss the means of overcoming apartheid. Held on January 29, 1976, at Sands Point, Long Island, an IBM facility, the meeting focused on Sullivan's agenda: either the companies use their power to overcome apartheid or they leave South Africa. There was a preliminary agreement at the meeting to seek a consensus on a set of principles that would guide all U.S. businesses in South Africa in a common task of dismantling apartheid.

It was not until over a year later and after much compromise that, on March 1, 1977, Sullivan was able to announce that twelve of the companies had found consensus on six principles. The companies were American Cyanamid, Caltex Petroleum, Citicorp, Ford Motor, IBM, International Harvester, Minnesota Mining and Manufacturing, Mobil Oil, Otis Elevator, Union Carbide, Burroughs, and General Motors. The original principles, listed below, did not touch on seeking civil and political rights but focused only on employment practices in the workplace. The original principles called for:

- nonsegregation of the races in all eating, comfort, and work facilities;
- equal and fair employment practices for all employees;
- equal pay for all employees doing equal or comparable work for the same period of time and minimum wages well above the minimum living level;
- initiation of and development of training programs that will prepare, in substantial numbers, Africans and other blacks for supervisory, administrative, clerical and technical jobs;
- increasing the number of Africans and other blacks in management and supervisory positions;
- improving the quality of employees' lives outside the work environment in such areas as housing, transportation, schooling, recreation and health facilities.

Sullivan struggled during 1976 to persuade the companies to use their power to pressure the South African government to dismantle the apartheid laws and grant all full civil and political rights, but he was not successful. He finally settled for the original six principles. While Sullivan was hoping to bring the companies in compliance with the emerging social contract for business, stressing civil and political rights, what is sometimes called "bridging," the business leaders prevailed so that the final version of the 1977 principles were more of a buffering strategy;[5] that is, they were an attempt to influence the social contract so that it would be less intrusive on business. The principles, while meeting some of the concerns for human rights, were largely seen by church groups as an ineffective attempt to influence the emerging social contract and avoid overwhelming pressures for complete disinvestment. In terms of strategic response patterns,[6] from the church point of view, the companies were involved in "domain defense" while seeming to accede to domain expansion; that is, they were preserving their position in South Africa by responding to some of the concerns of those who threatened to undermine their legitimacy. The principles may have been perceived partly as an attempt to co-opt those church groups that were championing complete disinvestment and replace them by the Reverend Sullivan and the principles program (Domain Offense—Encroachment). To be sure, Sullivan is and was thought by church leaders to be an honorable man with great charisma and deep convictions about the dignity of all people. His 1977 Principles for U.S. business in South Africa, however, appeared to the active church interest groups to divert attention from the real issues rather than help in the struggle for political rights. The ICCR led the opposition. While in retrospect, it is clear that in 1977 the companies had a golden opportunity to forge a new alliance with the coalition of religious groups under the umbrella of the ICCR, because they chose not to include political rights in the principles, any new initiative did not have a prayer. Timothy Smith, executive director of the ICCR, promptly issued the coalition response in a public statement:

> Is the "Statement of Principles" a case of offering a stone when a child asks for a fish? The issue in South Africa at this time is black political power; it is not slightly higher wages or better benefits or training programs, unless these lead to basic social change. As one South African church leader put it, "These principles attempt to polish my chains and make them more comfortable. I want to cut my chains and cast them away."[7]

George Houser, the executive director of the ACOA, wrote a letter to the Reverend Leon Sullivan shortly after the principles were issued, severely criticizing them. Sullivan responded, indicating that he too was less than satisfied with the principles but hinting that he had plans to amplify them:

> The Statement of Principles you received represents only a "first step" in an attempt to see if American-based companies operating in the Republic of South African can be a significant influence for change in getting rid of apartheid as a system and totally unacceptable way of life. The ultimate objective of my effort is to assist in the ending of apartheid and the ending of the oppression and destruction of human life that has already reached unendurable, inhumane, and savage proportions.[8]

Sullivan, in a 1977 letter to the director of the National Council of Church of Christ in the U.S.A., Robert C. S. Powell, explicitly states his ultimate goal to have the companies aggressively oppose the government:

> Further, it is our aim to have all companies participate in intensive lobbying efforts to let the South African Government know that participating American businesses want to see all industrial discriminatory laws changed, and want to see an end to oppression and terrorism, and want to see an end to the apartheid system.[9]

Lest anyone have any doubts that the Sullivan Principles were not sufficient to meet the concerns of many religious leaders, twenty-six U.S. officials representing a number of Catholic organizations and most major mainline Protestant denominations, coordinated by the ICCR, issued a letter to corporations in South Africa indicating their position:

> We call on all U.S. corporations investing in South Africa to adopt a policy to cease any expansion and begin to terminate present operations in the Republic of South Africa unless and until the South African government has committed itself to ending apartheid and has taken meaningful steps toward the achievement of full political, legal and social rights for the black majority.[10]

From the perspective of 1995, there would be good cause to wonder why the twelve CEOs who agreed upon the original principles in 1977 did not include a strong statement on the need to aggressively seek political rights for blacks, even if such a campaign would violate South African law. Even a statement indicating that the companies would reassess remaining in South Africa if some movement on political rights did not transpire would have been acceptable to many. Most in the United States thought this was the moral thing to do. Furthermore, such a move would have pleased some in the large coalition of church groups and may have drawn business and at least some of the church groups together in common cause. This, of course, was the original intention of Reverend Sullivan, and it was the strategy that ethicists and most commentators counseled. Seven years later, in 1985, under enormous pressure from religious groups, Sullivan finally insisted on adding opposition to government apartheid policies to the principles; even then there was still strong opposition from the business community. An editorial in the *New Republic* captures the dilemma that seems to have eluded many in the business community:

> The Reverend Leon Sullivan wants to add to his principles a requirement that companies lobby politically for free movement of labor—that is, for the end of pass laws, and so on. But even some of Sullivan's staunchest corporate backers are resisting the notion of political involvement. Yet this goes to the essence of the claim that capitalism and apartheid are incompatible. Companies that profit from investments in South Africa are morally implicated in that nation's political system. If they wish to discharge that moral burden with the assertion that they're helping to change the system, they have to be ready to prove it. Otherwise, they should get out.[11]

To understand the resistance of the business community, one has to realize that such business involvement in political affairs was considered out of the question in the market capitalism model. Several comments from business leaders in 1977 may illustrate the adamantine resistance. For example, Henry Ford II, chairman of the board of Ford Motor Company, wrote to Leon Sullivan on November 11, 1977: "We are making good progress in implementing the Statement of Principles agreed to earlier this year. . . . *As a businessman, I don't know what more the U.S. companies can or should do in South Africa* (italics added) to try to solve a problem which is political, social and moral, as well as economic, in nature."[12]

Again, in a letter to Sullivan, dated November 1, 1976, R. H. Herzog, chairman of the board and chief executive officer of 3M, said: "To the degree that South African law and South African Government policy allows, our subsidiary there has taken aggressive action to conform to these principles."[13]

Finally, the Conference Board had a meeting on South Africa on

March 15, 1987, in New York City, where top officers of some twenty-six U.S. companies attended, most of whom were signers of the principles. Although no formal minutes "were allowed to be taken," the informal notes of Sal G. Marzullo of the Mobil Corporation, retained in the archives of Temple University, report as follows:

> It was agreed business cannot do more than improve the conditions of its workers. We cannot transform the nature of South African society and we will have serious problems with South Africa if we try, but we must do all that we can as quickly as we can to improve the social and economic well-being of all of our black and other non-white employees.[14]

Because of the omission of political-rights concerns, the coalition of religious groups opposing apartheid not only did not perceive the Sullivan Principles as helping to enable democratic change, but they found them subversive to the cause of liberation, and thus they continued to press for the complete disinvestment of all U.S. firms. Elizabeth Schmidt, a prominent activist, was most critical and adopted a cynical response in her work on the principles, *Decoding Corporate Camouflage: U.S. Business Support for Apartheid.*[15] In a 1982 address to the State of Connecticut's Task Force on South African Investment Policy, Schmidt quotes Bishop Tutu who gives a capsule summary of the key issue:

> Our rejection of the code is on the basis that it does not aim at changing structures. The Sullivan Principles are designed to be ameliorative. We do not want apartheid to be made more comfortable. We want it to be dismantled.[16]

Between 1977 and 1982 enormous pressures were brought to bear on U.S. corporations to leave South Africa. Shareholder resolutions continued as did university and college divestment initiatives. In 1982 the pressure tactics took a new turn when three state legislatures (Connecticut, Michigan, and Massachusetts) passed bills restricting investment of state funds (pension funds, endowments, etc.) in companies and banks with business connections in South Africa. This was only the beginning of a powerful trend, much of which was a response to the "constructive engagement" of the Reagan administration that eased many of the existing federal government restraints.

It was in this climate that Sullivan was able to persuade the companies, now over ninety signatories, to be more even more aggressive in seeking black equality. Three amplifications were added to the principles prior to 1982. In addition to the six principles, companies must:

- acknowledge the rights of Africans to form and belong to trade unions, whether registered with the government or not;
- support changes in South Africa's influx-control laws to provide for the right of African migrant workers to normal family life;
- assist in the development of African and black business enterprises, including distributors, suppliers of goods and services, and manufacturers.

As with the other points in the code, companies were graded by the consulting firm of Arthur D. Little on the basis of a written report required from each.

In 1983, a few of the U.S. companies made some tentative efforts to lobby the government on noneconomic issues, a major breakthrough in practice. Specifically, the companies, through the American Chamber of Commerce in Johannesburg, protested a bill that would have, in effect, required employers to enforce influx-control laws in the workplace.

Pressures on the companies continued to mount. In 1983 the South African Council of Churches (SACC), a coalition of Protestant churches, passed a resolution asking the world community to refrain from investing in institutions that supported apartheid. In June 1983 Bishop Desmond Tutu, a former head of the South African Council of Churches, proclaimed the Tutu "Principles." In November 1983 Sullivan announced the fourth amplification which largely followed the Tutu principles and required companies to lobby against apartheid laws. Notably, Sullivan's amplification differed from Tutu's principles in that he did not use the threat of withdrawal of all investment as leverage to move the government to dismantle apartheid. In November 1983, a large, black trade union coalition in the R.S.A. (COSATU), endorsed disinvestment. In 1985, meeting at a World Council of Churches (WCC) consultation in Harare, the SACC issued a definitive call for comprehensive economic sanctions until apartheid was dismantled. In November 1986 the fourth amplification was expanded and designated as principle seven of the Sullivan Principles. Principle seven is as follows:

- press for a single education system common to all races;
- use influence [to] support the unrestricted rights of black businesses to locate in the urban areas of the nation;

- influence other companies in South Africa to follow the standards of equal rights principles;
- support the freedom of mobility of black workers, including those from "so-called" independent homelands, to seek employment opportunities wherever they exist and make possible provision for adequate housing for families of employees within the proximity of workers' employment;
- use financial and legal resources to assist blacks, Coloreds, and Asians in their efforts to achieve equal access to all health facilities, educational institutions, transportation, housing, beaches, parks and all other accommodations normally reserved for whites;
- oppose adherence to all apartheid laws and regulations;
- support the ending of all apartheid laws, practices and customs;
- support full and equal participation of blacks, Coloreds, and Asians in the political process.

Meanwhile, in 1984, Bishop Tutu was awarded the Nobel Peace Prize, and his campaign for economic sanctions against South Africa was given prominent global media coverage. All this additional pressure on the companies to leave South Africa no doubt influenced them in their willingness to support political rights for blacks. It is noteworthy that the 1984 Arthur D. Little report on the companies' progress on the principles includes the following observation on the new requirements of the program:

It is significant that there are today several areas in which companies are being requested to be active which would not have been tolerated by the companies when the program was initiated.[17]

In May 1985, in the face of enormous pressure at home and a rapidly deteriorating situation in South Africa, Sullivan announced an ultimatum: If statutory apartheid was not dismantled in two years, he would not continue to support the principles and would call for all companies to disinvest. While most U.S. business leaders hoped that Sullivan would not issue such a call in 1987 (he did issue it in June 1987), the ultimatum pushed companies to be radical beyond their wildest dreams.

In June and August 1986 the U.S. companies, in a watershed event, explicitly and publicly championed political rights in advertisements in major South African newspapers.

Organized by the American Chamber of Commerce (AMCHAM), the advertisement proclaimed that "apartheid is totally contrary to the idea of free enterprise" and encouraged the government "to create a climate for negotiation." It listed the "urgent issues" that Pretoria must address:

> Release political detainees; unban political organizations; negotiate with acknowledged leaders about power sharing; grant political rights to all; repeal the Population Registration Act; grant South African citizenship to all; repeal the Group Areas Act; provide common, equal education; and equalize health services.

The U.S. companies that remained in South Africa took up the challenge and began to oppose the government on various fronts. Between 1986 and 1990 over 140 U.S. companies departed South Africa under intense pressure at home. In 1990 the annual report on the activities of the U.S. companies in South Africa, compiled by Arthur D. Little, Inc., as a part of the requirements of the Statement of Principles Program, notes that some fifty-four U.S. companies continued to have operations there and that they provided more than $30 million a year to programs designed to eliminate apartheid. Some of these dollars were to assist in black educational endeavors, but many went to activities that most South Africans considered too risky because they directly challenged the status quo and advanced social change. For example, the Colgate Palmolive Company provided the funds and personnel to organize a black consumer boycott of the stores in Boksburg after the local city council tried to restore segregation in the downtown city park. Other companies directly challenged white merchants in Johannesburg by assisting blacks in exercising their newly legislated freedom to do business in the downtown areas; this assistance was not only start-up funding, but also training in business skills and entrepreneurship.

Several companies such as the Kellogg Company used their influence and resources to secure the freedom of union leaders who were being detained by the police. Companies such as Johnson & Johnson also spent money to encourage nonracial education and medical care, a direct confrontation to the then-current structures based on a racial hierarchy. Many companies such as John Deere bought homes in white areas, making it possible for blacks to assume ownership, thus challenging and eroding the Group Areas Act that zoned land by race.[18]

What was happening here was clearly the breaking of the old mould and the fashioning of a new model. This new model holds much promise for the future of business, but only if it consciously appropriates the paradigm and takes a stand when human rights are violated. Because business never did this until late in the struggle in South Africa, religious groups never trusted the motives of the signatories of the Sullivan Principles and pressured the companies to leave right up to the 1990s. There is some evidence that business has learned ethical language as, for example, in the cases of the "Levi Strauss & Co. Business Partner Terms of Engagement and Guidelines for Country Selection" policy and the "Caux Roundtable Principles for Business." Both of these codes explicitly advert to the importance of human rights in developing countries where business operations might be located. On the other hand, the ICCR members filed shareholder resolutions in 1995, asking three major multinational companies (Pepsi Co., Texaco, and Unocal) to include in their codes or policies how the corporation will deal with "decisions on investing in or withdrawing from countries where there is a pattern of ongoing and systematic violations of human rights."[19] Countries such as Burma, the People's Republic of China, Angola, Azerbaijan, Bahrain, Egypt, Indonesia, Nigeria, Saudi Arabia, and Turkey are all discussed in the Investor Responsibility Research Center (IRRC) report on the need for human rights guidelines for U.S. companies.[20]

After considering a brief history of the struggle, it is now appropriate to consider some of the factors that made the apartheid issue especially compelling in the United States.

Human Rights: An Idea Whose Time Has Come

To understand the American passion for political rights in South Africa, it is helpful to review some of the events that coalesced. Beginning in the mid-1960s, the civil-rights movement took on a whole new dimension with the black power focus, and there emerged a new identification with the fate of the poor of the developing countries. From 1957 to 1964, twenty-four countries achieved independence in Africa. The ACOA formed a Committee of Conscience Against Apartheid and led a campaign against loans by U.S. banks to South Africa. The ICCR, in the early 1970s, began a disinvestment campaign aimed at U.S. corporations and banks. Campuses and church groups joined in the program.

In 1971 the Congressional black Caucus was formed with thirteen black members of Congress. Congressman Diggs, chair of the House Subcommittee on Africa, had championed disinvestment as early as 1969.

Steve Biko was murdered in September 1977, and this event mobilized widespread identification with the black cause. In July 1977 TransAfrica was chartered as an official lobby with a special focus on developing a more progressive U.S. policy toward southern Africa. On November 21, 1984, Randall Robinson of TransAfrica began a protest at the South African Embassy and remained there until he was arrested. The protest lasted almost two years, with celebrities volunteering for a day and being arrested, events all graphically portrayed on the evening news. Over two thousand people were arrested at the embassy during the two-year protest. As mentioned above, cities, states, and counties passed selective purchase ordinances, thus making foreign policy in the face of great dissatisfaction with the Reagan policy of constructive engagement. By 1986 most of the black leaders in South Africa argued for economic sanctions and disinvestment and saw little to be gained by constructive engagement.

Finally, on October 2, 1986, after exhausting a number of tactical moves, President Reagan found his veto overridden and the Comprehensive Anti-Apartheid Act of 1986 (Public Law 99–440) became law. The law strengthened the trade embargo and banned new loans and investments in South Africa until major signs that apartheid was dismantled were in evidence. Concerned with the issue of race in U.S. foreign policy, Republican Senator Richard Lugar, chair of the Foreign Relations Committee, opposed Reagan and led the coalition with an override. The passage of this bill marked the culmination of a long struggle of the antiapartheid organizations and the African-American coalitions.

It was many of these same coalitions that mounted the campaigns that ultimately forced the more than one hundred U.S. companies out of South Africa. A pervasive feeling remained in the movements that business was only interested in reaping profits in South Africa and that the principles were a cover story.

Values and Ethical Theory

Many compelling arguments were made for disinvestment from South Africa. Thomas Donaldson made a strong argument that full disinvestment was required since there was a systematic violation of the most basic human rights.[21] Citing Dworkin, he noted that consequential goals are ordinarily "trumped" by rights considerations unless "extraordinary moral horrors" could be expected to ensue from their exercise.[22] Developing a "condition of business principle," Donaldson also stated that "transactions are impermissible unless those transactions serve to discourage the violation of rights and either harm A or, at a minimum, fail to benefit A, in consequence of A's rights violating activity."[23] Since he finds neither of these conditions present, he judges that doing business with an apartheid South Africa was wrong.

Others, however, argued that the moral course was for the companies to remain in South Africa, provided they took measures to assist the blacks in their struggle and to prepare the way for job creation and investment in the new South Africa.[24] In this teleological view which focuses on shaping a certain sort of community, Donaldson's "extraordinary moral horror" was a new black government trying to lead a country with over 40 percent unemployment and little prospect for new investment because all foreign firms and capital had been forced out. Those arguing this position, while not denying the great achievement of attaining political rights, continued to look forward during the struggle to the day when overcoming economic apartheid would be the challenge. That challenge, which is the current one, requires a well-developed infrastructure and a critical mass of multinationals to attract new investment and job creation, as well as a renewed emphasis on affirmative action. Should the quest to attain economic rights fail in South Africa, there is little hope for a democratic future and little hope for a land of peace and justice.

At present, South Africa, under its new state president, Nelson Mandela, is leading a vigorous campaign for new international investment and doing reasonably well in attracting new firms and capital. What would have happened if all foreign firms and capital had fled? (Most non-U.S. firms remained in the R.S.A., along with some fifty-four major U.S. multinationals that had signed the Sullivan Principles.) Since total disinvestment never happened, one can only speculate, but this speculation may be helpful in guiding policy in other situations, such as China and the human-rights struggle. It seems clear that in the South African experience, there was value in the international pressure provided by strategic sanctions, that is, carefully crafted sanctions designed to reach specific groups and a limited objective (for example, the cultural and sports sanctions, the denial of landing rights for R.S.A. airplanes, and the curtailing of loans from international banks). For many, it is not clear that total and comprehensive disinvestment by multinational businesses was the morally right position. As it turned out, the plurality of apparently conflicting strategies may have yielded the result sought by all. Yet the fact remains that over one hundred fifty U.S. companies were pressured to leave South Africa, and this loss has slowed the task of job creation in the new democracy. Many of the one hundred fifty that have reentered come, for the most part, with only a sales force. The many jobs that might be present with a manufacturing facility are lacking.[25] If justice is ever to be realized, job creation on a massive scale is a requirement.

In any event, the ethical arguments, while powerful, did not appear to be the singular influence on the decision for disinvestment pressures.

World Views or Assumptions

In large measure, the reason that U.S. companies in South Africa were targeted by groups wanting apartheid dismantled was because the U.S. government was so unresponsive. The government believed that the Cold War demanded that communism be fought on all fronts and this anticommunism effort required that racial concerns be either overlooked or given short shrift. Ambassador Philip Crowe summed up the government's position in 1961, in a letter to *U.S. News and World Report*: "The net of it is that South Africa has faced the issue of Communism squarely and is willing to go a long way toward combating it. Russia's threats and saber-rattlings do not scare here as they seem to frighten most of the emerging nations of the continent."[26]

Until 1989, when the Cold War environment changed dramatically, both Republican and Democratic administrations were primarily governed by global strategic interests when it came to South Africa.

Leon Sullivan relates that the major incentive he used to persuade the CEOs to accept the principles in his 1976 Sands Point meeting was that unless capitalism was perceived by blacks in South Africa as their friend and ally, communism would ultimately prevail.[27] This argument took root, for many of the companies view their presence in the country as an avenue to spread the free-enterprise system. Communism could never view even the best multinational companies as agents of development but only as instruments of dependency.

That communism was on the minds of Americans on both sides of the aisle is evident from a 1979 letter to the executive officer of the

Caltex Petroleum Corporation from Congressman Paul N. McCloskey, Jr., from the 12th District of California:

> I join Andy Young in agreement that thus far U.S. business activity in South Africa is constructive, rather than harmful to overall U.S. interests, but if apartheid continues to be strengthened and communist intrusion into Africa is enhanced as a result, Congress could very likely react unfavorably to continued U.S. business investment.[28]

The influx of troops and support from the Soviet Union and Cuba in the 1977–78 Ogaden War in Ethiopia only added to Cold War mentality and increased the U.S.-South African cooperation. Finally, only the demise of the Soviet Union allowed the situation to be normalized. However, even in 1986, Senator Jesse Helms, no doubt representing a small minority, opposed the Anti-Apartheid Act on the grounds that it aided the African National Congress (ANC), a group believed by Helms to be communist:

> What it does mean is that the bill itself gives preference in almost every respect only to those opponents of the government and those groups that are deeply committed to the Communist Party of South Africa, an organization funded and controlled by the Soviet Union. The non-Communist leaders of the blacks and non-whites are treated as though they do not exist.
>
> The fundamental flaw of S. 2701 is that its whole purpose is to force the South African Government to legitimize and negotiate a transfer of power to the Communist and terrorist movements which espouse these methods. No legislation which is not balanced, just, and constructive can hope to avert the impending disaster in South Africa. This bill fails on all three counts.[29]

Many continued to argue that, while South African black leaders espoused the communist line and accepted Soviet money, they were at heart nationalists. This was clearly shown to be the case when, at the request of the ANC, the University of Notre Dame held a meeting for the ANC to discuss new investment in the postapartheid South Africa. Held in October 1991, some seventy-five corporations sent representatives and heard Thabo Mbecki (now a vice president of South Africa), the keynoter, outline the pro-free enterprise position of his party.[30] In any event, to understand the powerful dynamic of the South African disinvestment debate, the communist versus capitalist world views must be considered.

Perhaps the most influential ideological or world-view difference was that manifested prior to 1984 when business leaders opposed any efforts by the Reverend Sullivan to challenge the South African government on apartheid. In all fairness to business leaders, the period of the South African struggle with apartheid corresponded with a major rewriting of the implicit social contract between business and society.[31] Until relatively recently, market and legal signals were the only significant social forces that caught the attention of top management. Consumer sovereignty reigned to the extent that astute management carefully tracked consumer needs and expectations and responded with the appropriate product and price to capture the market in question. Sometimes called the market capitalism model, this model had been a dominant one for more than two centuries.[32]

Today, there is a growing expectation that the social responsiveness of business must be much broader and is not optional. Church coalitions and other activist groups critical of business in South Africa attributed their opposition to their interest in advancing a more humane and democratic society, a society that respected the rights of all. Yet it was not so long ago that there was a strong social consensus that the best way for business to advance a humane society was to compete efficiently in the market. Providing quality goods and services at the best price was taken to be business's contribution to the common good. During the South African controversy, from the 1950s to the 1980s, executives were living between the times, that is, they were caught between the time when there was a strong social consensus that the market and legal signals were the appropriate way to control business activity and the time when a new consensus was emerging that broadened the social contract with business. Many business leaders were quite astute and were aware of this significant sea change in the business environment. Many were challenged about their role in Vietnam, napalm production, or civil rights, for example. Yet perhaps because of a lack of adequate models and vocabulary, they were much less adept at forging the bonds of trust with the major critics of their South African operations.

Conclusion

This chapter opened by asking a series of questions. How is it that prodisinvestment groups captured the minds and hearts of many Americans, to the extent that over one hundred fifty U.S. companies departed South Africa? Can interest groups mount that kind of pressure on other contemporary issues? How did such a broad constituency for disinvestment coalesce?

To gather together much of the material presented here, it may be helpful to use a model I have adapted from that of ethicist Ralph Potter.[33] Potter designed his model, relying on the work of Talcott Parsons[34] to understand how people come to disagree passionately over a matter of policy (see Table 1). The model suggests that four elements shape policy proposals: the definition of the situation (A); the loyalties of the decision-maker (B); the values held, which reflect the type of ethical reasoning used (C); and the world view or assumptions of the person or group involved (D).

Any policy proposal is based on certain facts or observations that are taken to be significant (A). What one takes as a significant "fact" is influenced by one's values which, in turn, reflect an implied, if not explicit, ethical theory. Our values provide the link between a descriptive observation and a normative policy prescription. Thus, if one's ethical theory focuses on helping to shape the sort of community where blacks would have marketable skills and their share of the good jobs, as well as the right to vote (C2), and one observes that international business can advance these ends (A4), then one would argue that international business should remain in South Africa and advance these important values. (This teleological stance was the Reverend Sullivan's position in 1976 but, as explained above, he was not able to persuade business leaders to challenge the South African government.)

On the other hand, if one values the right to political participation as the essential right to achieve at this time (C1), and observes that business will do little to oppose a host government in this area (A2 and A3), especially a government that opposes the Soviet communist expansion in Africa, one would conclude that the only policy that makes sense is to pressure companies to leave. The assumption here is that the departure of international businesses and the subsequent decline in the economy will serve as leverage to force the white South African government to the negotiating table. All of us have certain world views or assumptions of how the world works, as well as certain loyalties that influence our perceptions and decision-making. Table 1 is offered as a way to conceptualize how this complex process influences a policy proposal.

For church groups, a thirty-year struggle had convinced them that business leaders would do no more for South African blacks than they were pressured to do (A5). The factors that seemed to grip business leaders included a business ideology that precluded political

TABLE 1
The Substantive Elements that Shape Policy Proposals

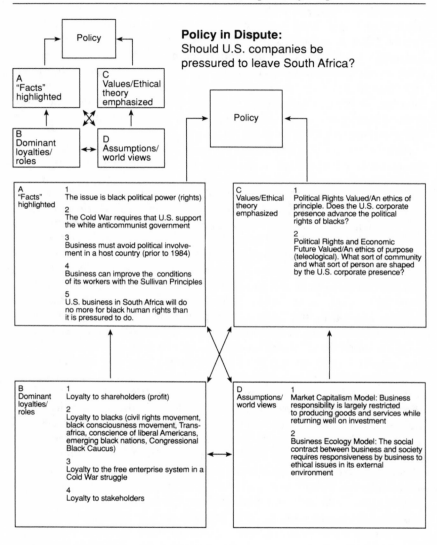

involvement in a host country, Cold War considerations, and a notion of responsibility that was largely focused on creating shareholder wealth (D1). While business leaders seemed often to be very moral individuals and to be genuinely concerned about the plight of the blacks, church groups found them to hold a world view that precluded any significant, proactive involvement that would challenge or interfere with a government in a host country.

In the mid-to-late 1980s, when business leaders finally did take an aggressive stand against the white South African government and for black economic and political liberation, antiapartheid church groups in the United States, with the blessing and encouragement of the South African Council of Churches, had already discounted business as a trusted ally in this struggle; thus, church groups pressed all the more for complete disinvestment, and the results of this pressure were largely responsible for the departure of equity investments of some one hundred fifty companies.

While there seems to be clear evidence that financial sanctions (not rolling-over loans) slowed the economy and thus hastened the move to the negotiating table, forcing the companies out of South Africa is a move questioned by many; yet it is beyond the scope of this article to render a final judgment on whether the departure of the one hundred fifty U.S. companies did, in fact, provide the crucial pressure that brought the South African leaders to the negotiating table. What is clearly true is that in the postapartheid South Africa there is a growing unemployment and consequent crime problem; had the U.S. companies joined forces with the church groups early in the struggle, many of them would still be in South Africa in more than a token manner, and their plants and equipment would be marshalled to create jobs.

Other factors noted in Table 1 were most influential in shaping a policy decision. Because of the Cold War environment, the U.S. foreign-policy establishment continued to give priority to anticommunism and thus support the white Afrikaner government rather than to antiracism and the support of the black liberation struggle. This world view angered many white liberals and African-Americans who mobilized church and other interest groups to apply intense pressure to business corporations directly rather than through the government.

With the black consciousness movement and black power concerns, there was a heightened interest by many Americans to respond to the plight of poor blacks in South Africa. This new identification with the blacks of a developing country was a most powerful shift in dominant loyalties for many Americans and may well have been the factor that pushed many Americans on the fence about disinvestment over the edge (B2).

While good ethical arguments could be marshalled for disinvestment, arguments could be made for companies remaining and advancing the welfare of the blacks. A problem here was that until rather late in the struggle, business never spoke moral language or advanced ethical arguments to promote political rights for blacks. Business leaders were perceived as being largely interested in making profits and doing only what they were forced to do in the area of social issues.

While the facts highlighted by church groups focused almost exclusively on political rights, the business leaders, unwilling to follow the lead of the Reverend Sullivan, focused only on improving the lot of blacks in the workplace. Finally, under tremendous pressure to disinvest, in the mid-1980s the companies began to speak and to work for political and civil rights but, as they were very late in joining the campaign, church groups continued to treat business efforts with cynicism and pressured even more strongly for disinvestment.

Given this analysis, demonstrating how the power of African-Americans as well as Cold War considerations were unique facts, business leaders can take some comfort in knowing that it seems unlikely that other social issues may ever blindside them again with quite the same intensity. On the other hand, this assumes that one key lesson has been learned and that is that human-rights concerns must be factored into business decisions.

What is clear is that, after 1984, human rights were factored into business decisions of U.S. multinational companies in South Africa. This is a great achievement and the Reverend Sullivan and the companies that struggled for rights deserve our praise. It is also clear that this amplification of the Sullivan Principles to include political rights occurred largely because of extreme pressure on the companies, mobilized by the ICCR and other adversary groups. There is inconclusive evidence that this move to consider human rights was based on normative theory about the role of business on the part of most business leaders. The article argues that unless our business leaders have the education to assess the ethical validity of interests presented by various stakeholders, there are slim grounds to hope that we can avoid another South African type of confrontation. If pressure is the significant motivator and not normative theory, the future is cloudy.

As indicated above, some version of integrative social-contracts theory holds much promise for answering the "says who?" question when business is asked to take a stand on a social issue.[35] In brief, this approach recognizes ethical obligations based upon consent in the local community as well as consent by "all rational contractors to a theoretical macrosocial contract." While the local community of white Afrikaners saw no problem with a norm specifying racial hierarchy (apartheid) in South Africa, the world community saw that norm as "illegitimate." It was illegitimate because it violated a "hypernorm," a principle "so fundamental to human existence" that it is found in "a convergence of religious, political, and philosophical thought."

While it is impossible to do more than outline here how integrative social-contracts theory might address the crucial issue of assessing and prioritizing the claims of various interest groups, it is clear that this issue requires much research and discussion for the future welfare of the business community.

Notes

1. D. Kneale, "Xerox Finally Succumbs to Pressure," *Wall Street Journal*, 20 March 1987, 2.

2. Interview with George Houser, 15 October 1994.

3. George A. Steiner and John F. Steiner, *Business, Government, and Society*, 5th ed. (New York: Random House, 1988): 9. See Table 1 of this article for the use of the market capitalism and business ecology models.

4. For a good discussion of social-contracts theory, see Thomas Donaldson and Thomas W. Dunfee, "Toward a Unified Conception of Business Ethics: Integrative Social Contracts Theory," *Academy of Management Review* 19(2)(1994): 252–284.

5. Jeffrey Pfeffer and J. R. Salancik, *The External Control of Organizations* (New York: Harper & Row, 1978): 106.

6. For a good discussion and illustration of the use of these strategic response patterns, see S. Prakash Sethi, *Multinational Corporations and the Impact of Public Advocacy on Corporate Strategy* (Boston: Kluwer Academic Publishers, 1994): 34–39.

7. Timothy Smith, "Whitewash for Apartheid from Twelve U.S. Firms," *Business and Society Review* 74 (1977): 59–60.

8. Letter from the Reverend Leon Sullivan to Mr. George Houser, 25 April 1977. Unless otherwise indicated, all correspondence quoted here is from the Sullivan Principles Archives, Temple University, Philadelphia, Pa.

9. Letter from the Reverend Leon Sullivan to Father Robert C. S. Powell, 5 January 1977.

10. Letter from Sister Regina Murphy and twenty-six other members of the ICCR to General Motors, 31 October 1977.

11. "Pinching Apartheid," *New Republic*,12 August 1985, 4.

12. Letter from Henry Ford II to the Reverend Leon H. Sullivan, 11 November 1977.

13. Letter from R. H. Herzog to the Reverend Sullivan, 1 November 1976.

14. Sol G. Marzullo, Minutes of a Conference Board Meeting on South Africa, 15 March 1978.

15. Elizabeth Schmidt, *Decoding Corporate Camouflage: U.S. Business Support for Apartheid* (Washington, D.C.: Institute for Policy Studies, 1980).

16. Elizabeth Schmidt, "One Step—In the Wrong Direction: The Sullivan Principles as a Strategy for Opposing Apartheid," presentation to the State of Connecticut's Task Force on South African Investment Policy, 25 February 1982.

17. See Reid Weedon, *Eighth Report on the Signatory Companies to the Statement of Principles for South Africa* (Cambridge, MA: A. O. Little Co., 1984).

18. See the *Fourteenth Report on the Signatory Companies to the Statement of Principles for South Africa* (Cambridge, MA: A. O. Little Co., 1990).

19. See "U.S. Business and Human Rights Guidelines," *Social Issue Service: 1995 Background Report* (Washington, D.C.: Investor Responsibility Research Center, 1995): 1.

20. "U.S. Business and Human Rights Guidelines," 7–15.

21. See Thomas Donaldson, *The Ethics of International Business* (New York: Oxford University Press, 1989): 129–144.

22. Donaldson, *The Ethics of International Business*, 134. See Ronald Dworkin, *Taking Rights Seriously* (Cambridge: Harvard University Press, 1978).

23. Donaldson, *The Ethics of International Business*, 133.

24. See, for example, Leon H. Sullivan, "Agents for Change: The Mobilization of Multinational Companies in South Africa." *Law and Policy in International Business* 15(1983): 427–444; and Oliver F. Williams, *The Apartheid Crisis* (San Francisco: Harper & Row, 1986).

25. See, for example, S. Prakash Sethi, "American Corporations and the Economic Future of South Africa," *Business and Society Review* 92(1995): 10–18.

26. Quoted in Les de Villiers, *In Sight of Surrender* (Westport, CT: Praeger, 1995), 10. For an overview of this policy, see P. J. Schraeder, *United States Foreign Policy Toward Africa* (New York: Cambridge University Press, 1994).

27. Interview with the Reverend Leon H. Sullivan, 21 July 1995.

28. Letter from Paul N. McCloskey, Jr., U.S. Congressman of the 12th District, CA, to the Executive Officers of the Caltex Petroleum Corporation, 16 November 1979.

29. "Additional View of Senator Jesse Helms," *Calendar No. 775: Setting U.S. Policy Toward Apartheid* (U.S. Senate Report 99:370): 23–24.

30. J. F. Siler, "The ANC to U.S. Investors," *Business Week*, 21 October 1991, 47.

31. For a discussion of the social contract between business and society, see Thomas Donaldson, *Corporations and Morality* (Englewood Cliffs, NJ: Prentice-Hall, 1982), 50–53.

32. Steiner and Steiner, 1988, 9.

33. Ralph B. Potter, *War and Moral Discourse* (Richmond, VA: John Knox Press, 1969). My use of this model was also informed by Marvin T. Brown, *The Ethical Process* (Berkeley, CA: Basic Resources, 1994).

34. For an informed discussion of what is at issue here, see C. Hufbauer and J. Schott, *Economic Sanctions in Support of Foreign Policy Goals* (Washington, D.C.: Institute for International Economics, 1983).

35. Donaldson and Dunfee, 1994.

13

Corporate Social Responsibility: Wisdom from the World's Religions

Dennis P. McCann

The historic move toward a single, globally integrated, market economy provides a new context in which to ask perennial questions about the role of moral and, especially, religious values in business and economic development. Among these questions, the most timely and yet neglected, at least within conventional thinking on business and economics, is this: What role should the world's major religious traditions play in promoting corporate social responsibility? What follows is meant to open this question for general discussion, beyond the professional concerns of theologians, religious ethicists, and specialists in the sociology of religion. It will outline in broad strokes how the relationship between religious values and economic and social organization is generally understood in the field of religious studies and why a general knowledge of comparative religious ethics may provide a useful orientation to corporate social responsibility.

Corporate social responsibility is not a prominent concept in either the literature of comparative religious ethics or of inquiries into business ethics that are in interdisciplinary dialogue with this field. This does not necessarily mean that businesses not under the sway of Western religious and moral values do not exercise corporate social responsibility. Nor does it mean that U.S.-based firms must abandon their commitments to corporate social responsibility to remain competitive in the global economy. The evidence I will present warrants neither conclusion. Instead, it suggests that the ways in which business corporations exercise corporate responsibility are a function of long-term trends that may be as diverse as the cultural histories in which they are embedded. The wisdom of the world's religions thus points out the folly of assuming that there is any single model of economic development, modernization, organizational behavior, or business ethics. Some of the non-Western religious traditions, in fact, may be more effective in promoting corporate social responsibility than we have been recently in the post-Christian West. If the so-called "good corporation" is dead, an autopsy may show that its death has less to do with the pressures of global competition than it does with our own increasingly dysfunctional values.

Laboring in the Shadow of Max Weber

The most accessible place to begin a general discussion of the relationship between religious values and economic and social organization is still Michael Novak's *The Spirit of Democratic Capitalism* (1982). Novak argued convincingly that a certain range of religious values within the history of Christianity was, in fact, creative of the "spirit" of democratic capitalism. Novak's purpose was not analytical—he meant to rally support for democratic capitalism at a time when many intellectuals, including most major theologians and Christian ethicists, had grown skeptical of it during the wearying later stages of the Cold War. Novak's audience, for the most part, did not need to be convinced of the significance of "spirit" because their question, as well as his own, was primarily theological—they were seeking to determine which social system, capitalism or socialism, was more compatible with the moral imperatives and religious world view of classical Christianity. He and they simply presupposed that religious and moral values created social systems and were not, as Marxist and other ideologies would have it, a mere reflection of economic and social arrangements based on other strategic imperatives.

It is to this basic presupposition I must turn to determine the role of the world's religious traditions in shaping the global economy, and not simply those of classical Christianity. Here, Novak rightly appreciates Max Weber's seminal work, *The Protestant Ethic and the Spirit of Capitalism* (1920), for clarifying the relationship between religious values and economic development. But he dissents from Weber's gloomy assessment of capitalism's diminishing prospects and implicitly challenges his assumption that only a specifically Protestant version of the Christian world view and ethos is capable of sustaining a capitalist model of economic development. The theological dimensions of Novak's argument are couched in the traditions of Roman Catholic thought that, in his view, provide a more useful explication of the metaphysics, as it were, of economic development, by showing how capitalist enterprise plays a role in fulfilling humanity's destiny in the Divine Life of the Holy Trinity.

Novak's Catholic celebration of the spirit of capitalism is itself a reflection of the success of American Catholics who have achieved an impressive degree of upward social mobility, especially in the post-New Deal period when capitalism became as democratic as it ever has been in this country. American Catholics became successful capitalists without transferring their religious allegiance to Protestantism. To the extent that Weber argued for an exclusive connection between the Protestant ethic and capitalism, his thesis has been refuted by the social history of American Catholicism. On the other hand, Weber was at least partly right about the historically creative role of the Protestant ethic. For the history of American Catholicism, as well as Novak's own theology, demonstrate that the dominant Protestant ethic did provide a template for social change that unleashed transformative energies within the immigrant Catholic communities that had access to it. The church in the United States transformed itself in response to the challenges of the Protestant social environment, thereby creating both a Catholic work ethic, under the aegis of "devotional Catholicism," and a complementary sense of social responsibility, faithful to the traditions of Catholic social teaching. I must insist, however, that this historic process of acculturation cannot be understood as simply tailoring religious values to fit new economic opportunities. Weber's general defense of the significance of religious values is supported by the broad contours of American Catholic social history which continues to have a transformative impact on the institutions of democratic capitalism.

My purpose is not to rehearse this argument, which is implicit in my discussion of the American Catholic bishops' economic pastoral letter, *New Experiment in Democracy: The Challenge for American Catholicism* (1987). Instead, using this relatively familiar example, I want to launch out into the unfamiliar territory occupied by the world's major religious traditions to see whether something similar to the American Catholic experience with capitalism has been under way in non-Western cultures, with similarly momentous consequences for the global economy. Here, too, one immediately encounters the eminence of Max Weber who was not content to study religion in the narrow confines of European history. Faced with the unprecedented expansion of European hegemony throughout the world that the nineteenth century had witnessed, Weber did similar ground-breaking studies on the religions of China and India. It is not surprising that, given their decadent circumstances at the time of his studies, Weber concluded that the traditional cultures of Asia and their distinctive religious world views were incapable of generating the spirit necessary for capitalist development. If South and East Asia were to develop economically, they would do so to the extent that they would abandon their inherited religious and moral values and adopt the so-called "universal ethic" characteristic of liberal Protestantism.

In reality, at least one Asian nation was already busily refuting Weber's assessment even before it went to print. I refer, of course, to Japan, whose distinct path toward modernization had begun with the Meiji restoration in 1868. By the time Weber was contemplating the fate of East Asia, Japan had selectively opened itself to European models of politics, economics, science, and technology, while adapting its religious traditions to the challenges of an urban industrial society. The success of this new model of Asian development was publicly ratified by Japan's astonishing military victories, first against China and then in 1904 against Russia, the first European state to be defeated by a non-Western power in, perhaps, half a millennium.

The history of Japan's economic development—and, increasingly, that of the rest of South and East Asia—challenges Weber's thesis in a way that is strikingly similar to what I infer from the social history of American Catholicism. The Protestant ethic (and its secular surrogates) is not the only religious and moral foundation capable of supporting capitalist economic development. Modernizing religious traditions such as those of the Japanese and of American Catholics appear to be just as effective in generating an appropriate spirit for capitalism. So Weber is wrong, if he meant to assert any ethical monopoly for liberal Protestantism. On the other hand, Japanese history tends to confirm that Weber is right about the creative role of religious values in economic and social organization, for the history of modern Japan cannot be understood apart from the history of its attempt to modernize its own religious and moral traditions.

Those concerned with business ethics in a global economy ought to be challenged profoundly by the twentieth century's unexpectedly diverse patterns of modernization and economic development. Recent history suggests that business ethics in a global economy can and ought to be religiously pluralistic and grounded in a hermeneutical perspective that takes the world's religious traditions seriously as living witnesses to the moral aspirations of humanity. Business executives who expect to make a significant contribution to the development of a global economy would be well advised to familiarize themselves with the history of religions, and business schools that are serious about business ethics ought to make comparative religious ethics a constitutive part of the core curriculum for the M.B.A. or at least, for M.B.A.s with concentration in international business. But it is not sufficient merely to preach a sermon on this topic. Such proposals require supporting evidence, and the more disruptive the changes proposed, the more compelling the evidence ought to be. In what follows, I hope to present enough evidence to encourage further study of these questions.

The Business Ethics of Classical Hinduism

Throughout the world, the dawn of civilization is generally marked by prayer. Skeptics may dismiss the pervasiveness of religion in antiquity as so much superstition, soon to be dispelled by further advances in science and technology. A more discerning view, however, is possible: Just what do the prayers that have been preserved tell us about the everyday concerns of our ancestors? Here is an ancient prayer that, I, for one, found very surprising. It is from the *Atharva Veda* (The Book of Spells and Incantations), one of the four *samhitas* (hymnbooks) containing the most ancient strands of Hindu tradition. This hymn speaks to our purposes, for it is dedicated to "Success in Trading":

> I stir and animate the merchant Indra: may he approach and be our guide and leader.
> Chasing ill-will, wild beast, and highway robber, may he who hath the power give me riches.
> The many paths which Gods are wont to travel, the paths which go between the earth and heaven,
> May they rejoice with me in milk and fatness that I may make rich profit by my purchase.
> With fuel, Agni! and with butter, longing, mine offering I present for strength and conquest;
> With prayer, so far as I have strength adoring—this holy hymn to gain a hundred treasures.
> Pardon this stubbornness of ours, O Agni, the distant pathway which our feet have trodden.

> Propitious unto us be sale and barter, may interchange of merchandise
> enrich me.
> Accept, ye twain, accordant, this libation! Prosperous be our ventures
> and incomings.
> The wealth wherewith I carry on my traffic, seeking, ye Gods! wealth
> with the wealth I offer,
> May this grow more for me, not less: O Agni, through sacrifice chase
> those who hinder profit!
>
> (*Atharva Veda*, III:15 in Embree, 1972: 38–39)

The hymn is as noteworthy for what it says as for what it does not say.
Not only are Indra (the Aryan sky warrior-king, like the Greek Zeus,
the guarantor of the moral order) and Agni (the god of fire, who,
among other things, is active in making ritual acts of sacrifice propi-
tious)—two of the most important deities in the Vedic pantheon—
invoked on behalf of money-making, but money-making, or commer-
cial-exchange relations generally, clearly is regarded as morally
legitimate and ennobling.

Noticeably absent from the hymn is any sense that business is a
morally unworthy occupation. This lack of moral ambivalence ought
to strike us as surprising if we compare it with the rather different
attitude projected in the classical period of Western civilization. Aristotle's *Politics*, for example, enshrines the antibusiness bias of the
Hellenistic aristocracy in terms of the natural law. His economics,
based as it is on the *oikos* or aristocratic household, offers a theory of
property, defined first in relationship to the *oikos* and not with reference to exchange relations in the marketplace. Understood primarily
as a means of maintaining the household, property or wealth thus has
a fixed or natural limit. Ironically, Aristotle is able to reconcile such a
limit by legitimating both slavery and warfare as natural ways of
acquiring property. Economics, or household management, thus generally is focused on developing the skills necessary to secure and
preserve the *padrone*'s rule over his slaves, women, and children.

Our focus, however, must remain on the way in which Aristotle
contends that such natural limits preclude making one's living by
commercial exchange:

> There are two sorts of wealth-getting, as I have said; one is part of
> household management [i.e., agriculture], the other is retail trade: the
> former is necessary and honorable, while that which consists in exchange
> is justly censured; for it is unnatural, and a mode by which men gain from
> one another. The most hated sort, and with the greatest reason, is usury,

which makes a gain out of money itself, and not from the natural object of it. For money was intended to be used in exchange, but not to increase at interest. And this term interest, which means the birth of money from money, is applied to the breeding of money because the offspring resembles the parent. That is why of all modes of getting wealth this is the most unnatural.

(Aristotle, 1984: 1997)

Aristotle's dim view of exchange relations, tied as it is to his understanding of natural law, was to survive the passing of the Hellenistic civilization in which it was formulated. More than the teachings of Jesus of Nazareth, Aristotle has shaped the moral skepticism about commerce that is characteristic of Christian social ethics to this day. (Cf. McCann 1994, 1989)

Commerce in ancient India labored under no such similar prejudice, but that does not mean that the Vedas contain teachings that are a functional substitute for Weber's modernizing Protestant ethic. The texts yield a picture that is far more complex, one in which economic activity is embedded in a larger scheme of human and cosmic purposes. The ideal moral order upheld by classical Hinduism consists of a series of interrelated quaternities, the most basic of which are the four *varnas*, commonly known as the caste system. Already in the *Rig Veda*, the earliest of the Vedic hymnbooks, there is the famous *Purusha-sukta* ("The Primeval Sacrifice") in which a sacred Person, "Thousand-headed Purusha," is ritually dismembered in order to create the cosmos. Here is part of that hymn:

> When they divided Purusha, in how many different portions did they arrange him? What became of his mouth, what of his two arms? What were his two thighs and his two feet called?
> His mouth became the *brahmin*; his two arms were made into the *rajanya*; his two thighs the *vaishyas*; from his two feet the *shudra* was born.
> The moon was born from the mind, from the eye the sun was born; from the mouth Indra and Agni, from the breath (*prana*) the wind (*vaya*) was born.

(*Rig Veda* 10.90, in deBary, 1958: 14–15)

The ideal division of labor symbolized by the four *varnas*—here designated as *brahmin*, *rajanya*, *vaishyas*, and *shudra*—is just as intrinsic to the cosmic order as are the passages of the sun and moon. The *brahmin* are the religious hierarchy, the *rajanya*—usually referred to as *kshatriya*—are the warrior aristocracy, and the *vaishya* are the householders, those who produce wealth, *including* the merchants. The *shudra*, of course, are those who do the dirty work.

Each of these ideal *varnas* has its own distinctive set of caste duties. While there are nine duties that are "eternal" and morally oblige members of "all four orders [equally]"—"the suppression of wrath, truthfulness of speech, justice, forgiveness, begetting one's children on one's own wedded wives, purity of conduct, avoidance of quarrel, simplicity, and maintenance of dependents" (*Mahabharata* XII:60, in Embree, 1972: 80)—the basic sense of how one fits into the cosmic order of things is tied less to this universal ethic than it is to one's distinctive caste duties. Here are those of the *vaishya*. Notice how this discourse knows no moral distinction between commerce and animal husbandry of the sort that Aristotle decreed:

> I shall now tell thee, O Yudhishthira, what the eternal duties of the Vaishya are. A Vaishya should make gifts, study the Vedas, perform sacrifices, and acquire wealth by fair means. With proper attention he should also protect and rear all [domestic] animals as a sire protecting his sons. Anything else that he will do will be regarded as improper for him. . . . I shall tell thee what the Vaishya's profession is and how he is to earn the means of his sustenance. If he keeps [for others] six kine, he may take the milk of one cow as his remuneration; and if he keeps [for others] a hundred kine, he may take a single pair as such fee. If he trades with others' wealth, he may take a seventh part of the profits [as his share]. A seventh also is his share in the profits arising from the trade in horns, but he should take a sixteenth if the trade be in hooves. If he engages in cultivation with seeds supplied by others, he may take a seventh part of the yield. This should be his annual remuneration. A Vaishya should never desire that he should not tend cattle. If a Vaishya desires to tend cattle, no one else should be employed in that task.

> (*Mahabharata* XII: 60, in Embree, 1972: 82)

Though cattle are regarded as the primary form of wealth, and the householder's expertise in animal husbandry is understood as the primary means of creating wealth, the Vaishya's duties will lead him inevitably into the commercial activities that usually are seen as the exclusive prerogative of his *varna* as such.

The exceptional circumstances in which members of the other high castes, *brahman* and *kshatriya*, are permitted to engage in commerce tend to confirm my thesis that business ethics in the Hindu tradition is role- and institution-specific and not, as in Weber's Protestant ethic, a reflection of universal moral imperatives. Here is a text that suggests how important the distinction of roles is, not just for understanding business ethics, but for appreciating the very nature of the ideal moral order. Keep in mind that the hierarchical ordering of the *varnas*, in Vedic theory at least, reflects the natural ordering of the various parts of the Purusha's cosmic body:

> Among the several occupations the most commendable are, teaching the Veda for a Brahmana, protecting the people for a Kshatriya, and trade for a Vaishya.
>
> But a Brahmana, unable to subsist by his peculiar occupations just mentioned, may live according to the law applicable to Kshatriyas; for the latter is next to him in rank.
>
> If it be asked, "How shall it be, if he cannot maintain himself by either of these occupations?" the answer is, he may adopt a Vaishya's mode of life, employing himself in agriculture and rearing cattle.
>
> But he who, through a want of means of subsistence, gives up the strictness with respect to his duties, may sell, in order to increase his wealth, the commodities sold by Vaishyas, making however the following exceptions.
>
> He must avoid selling condiments of all sorts, cooked food and sesamum, stones, salt, cattle, and human beings,
>
> All dyed cloth, as well as cloth made of hemp, or flax, or wool, even though they be not dyed, fruit, roots, and medical herbs;
>
> Water, weapons, poison, meat, Soma, and perfumes of all kinds, fresh milk, honey, sour milk, clarified butter, oil, wax, sugar, Kusa-grass;
>
> All beasts of the forest, animals with fangs or tusks, birds, spirituous liquor, indigo, lac, and all one-hoofed beasts.
>
> (*Manu Smriti* X: 80–100, in Embree, 1972: 94)

The extraordinary detail in this list of exceptions suggests two things: (1) that modern India's initial preference for an extraordinarily complicated system of commercial regulations seems to go back a long way; (2) that the specific items in which non-*vaishyas* are forbidden to trade are not prohibited because they are universally immoral as, say, we might regard trafficking in illegal drugs. Castes higher than *vaishya* cannot trade in these items—even if they are forced to abandon their caste duties and go into business—because illegitimate contact with them may incur a penalty for ritual impurity.

The four *varnas*, however, merely scratch the surface of Hindu business ethics. Each of the three higher castes, which alone participate fully in the religious life of classical Hinduism, exhibits an ideal pattern of occupations—the four *ashramas*—that define still further the moral order distinctive of each stage of life. The four *ashramas*—student, householder, retiree, and homeless wanderer or *sannyasin*—spell out how the various stages in life participate in the common pursuit of the four normative goals of human existence. The four goals—*dharma* (the pursuit of virtue or preservation of the moral order), *artha* (wealth), *kama* (sensual pleasure), and *moksha* (ultimate liberation)—suggest that the ultimate meaning of life consists in overcoming *samsara*, the wheel or, if you will, the treadmill of rebirths. This lofty, but bleak account describes the human predicament as a potentially infinite series of lifetimes, in which each person struggles to liberate him- or herself from this world by achieving nirvana. Nirvana should not be confused with the Heaven longed for by orthodox Christians; nirvana is the cessation of *samsara*, the void in which there is no further necessity of rebirth. *Moksha*, the ultimate goal, means finally overcoming the world as we know it. The higher castes are closer to this goal; they are reborn to their higher status precisely because of the degree of success they have had previously in living the *dharmas* assigned to them.

I find this to be an astonishingly powerful religious vision. But we cannot pause here to contemplate its varied ethical implications. Since our focus is on religious resources for business ethics, we must confine ourselves to the penultimate goals, especially *artha* and *kama*, the pursuit of wealth and pleasure, and their overriding significance in the *dharma* specific to the householder stage in life. The Hindu householder, like the Hellenistic *padrone*, presides over an extended family and its dependents. No question: this is also the template of traditional patriarchy. But the patriarchal household, like it or not, was the central economic institution in this society. Upon the householder devolves the responsibilities of management, which are inevitably a mixture of religious, familial, and business duties. Social responsibility, including whatever care the destitute were likely to receive from their neighbors, was incumbent upon the householder who possessed the means of helping others precisely because he was skilled at creating and preserving wealth.

The following text suggests the ideal of selflessness proper to the stage in life devoted to *artha* and *kama*:

A householder should perform every day a Smriti rite. . . . He should
  perform a Vedic rite on the sacred fires. . . .
Offering the food oblation, offerings with the proper utterance,
  performance of Vedic sacrifices, study of the sacred texts, and honoring

guests—these constitute the five great daily sacrifices dedicated
respectively to the spirits, the manes, the gods, the Brahman, and men.
He should offer the food oblation to the spirits (by throwing it in the air)
out of the remnant of the food offered to the gods. He should also cast
food on the ground for dogs, untouchables, and crows.
Food, as also water, should be offered by the householder to the manes
and men day after day. He should continuously carry on his study. He
should never cook for himself only.
Children, married daughters living in the father's house, old relatives,
pregnant women, sick persons, and girls, as also guests and
servants—only after having fed these should the householder and his
wife eat the food that has remained. . . .
Having risen before dawn the householder should ponder over what is
good for the Self. He should not, as far as possible, neglect his duties
in respect of the three ends of man, namely, virtue, material gain, and
pleasure, at their proper times.
Learning, religious performances, age, family relations, and wealth—on
account of these and in the order mentioned are men honored in
society. By means of these, if possessed in profusion, even a shudra
deserves respect in old age.

(*Yajnavalkya Smriti*, I:97–116; in Embree, 1972: 87–88)

Clearly, the pursuit of wealth traditionally enjoined upon the Hindu
householder is anything but a pretext for possessive individualism.

I have suggested that classical Hinduism's role of specific ethics of
dharma may be a more promising point of departure for business
ethics than the classical Western heritage enshrined in the texts of
Hellenistic philosophers like Aristotle. Not that Hindu *dharma* is
morally superior to Greek *arete* (or virtue ethics), but that in our
Western penchant for ethical universalizability, we—or at least some
of Aristotle's disciples, notably the influential philosopher Alasdair
MacIntyre—have tended to decontextualize Aristotle's comments on
money-making as if they were meant, not as prudent advice to future
padrones, but as an eternally valid judgment on the ethical merits of
careers in business as such. Aristotle can be read plausibly either way;
the Hindu tradition, however, suffers from no such equivocation. A
virtuous life in business is not only *not* an oxymoron, it is the specific
way in which *vaishyas* fulfill their religious duties and, by implication,
their moral duties to the rest of society, beginning with their own dependents.

Such a perspective, however, is still a far cry from the Weberian
version of the Protestant work ethic. The ultimate goal of life, seeking

the *moksha* that overcomes *samsara*, clearly suggests the otherworldly asceticism that Weber regarded as a barrier to capitalist development. But the penultimate goals in life—*dharma, artha*, and *kama*—are also given their due, and in a manner that strikes me as more encouraging to business than comparable traditions in the classical antiquity of the West. Why, then, did not the spirit of capitalism first emerge in India? One could cite India's long history of colonial oppression, to be sure, beginning with the Moghul Empire and, later, the hegemony of the British East India Company, and culminating in the British Raj that reserved to itself control over modern India's economy.

Weber, however, was less impressed by the political history than by the typical patterns of Hindu social organization. He felt that modern capitalism required a degree of impersonalism in business relationships that could be sustained only on the basis of a universal ethic that, in a biblical sense, was no respecter of persons. Business was best kept separate from family affairs; favoritism based on kinship or other forms of social dependency necessarily would inhibit successful economic performance. The Protestant ethic, in his view, provided the key to capitalist development, not simply because of its fresh perspective on worldly affairs but because it encouraged covenantal forms of association that, in principle, were open to strangers. Business enterprises could be hived off from the patriarchal household and managed on the basis of impersonal, contractual agreements, a universal framework of commercial law that embodied, at least in part, the covenantal moral imperatives of Protestant Christianity.

Weber, therefore, remained pessimistic about the future of modern capitalism in Asia because he could find nothing in the traditional cultures of India and China equivalent to the Protestant ethic. Nevertheless, modern capitalism, as we have seen, has found a home in Asia and has become successful enough to be globally competitive, not just as a major exporter of manufactured goods but as an alternative model to our customary thinking about economics and business management. What Weber regarded as most likely to retard capitalist development in Asia, namely, the various cultures' primary commitment to business organization based on kinship and other forms of social dependency, now strikes many observers as the secret to Asian economic success. We turn, then, to East Asia where the religious significance of kinship is as well documented as the successful economic performance of its corporations. Is there a connection between the two?

Capitalism and East Asian Family Values

East Asia's extraordinary record of economic growth is not news and has not been news for the past quarter of a century. What such growth means for the global economy, and how it is reshaping the prospects for U.S. economic development are important strategic questions whose answers will determine, as they are already determining, the parameters for future discussion of corporate social responsibility. My immediate concern, however, is with the religious dimensions of the East Asian challenge. To what extent is East Asia's success based on cultural factors that, inevitably, are religiously rooted? How do religious values continue to shape the meaning of economic activity in this region and the forms of business organization in which it is carried out?

Empirical inquiry into the nature of an "East Asian Development Model" tend to presuppose the so-called post-Confucian hypothesis. This theory explores a possible link between the powerful and pervasive influence of Confucianism upon what has been characterized as East Asia's Sinitic civilization and the region's distinctive patterns of modernization and economic development. The Confucian influence is particularly apparent in Japan and the newly industrializing countries (NIC), heretofore restricted to the "four little tigers," South Korea, Taiwan, Hong Kong, and Singapore but now also including much of coastal China, Viet-Nam, Malaysia, Indonesia, and Thailand. The hypothesis asserts that a modernized form of Confucianism—what Robert M. Bellah aptly called "bourgeois Confucianism" (Berger 1990, 7)—is as important for understanding the distinctive success of the East Asian development model as is the recent political and economic history of the region. If the hypothesis is confirmed, it will tend to reinforce the argument made so far regarding Weber's views of capitalism and religious values, but it will also show how modernizing inherited religious traditions, rather than abandoning them entirely, can actually work to enhance a nation's prospects for economic development.

There are few direct affinities linking classical Hinduism with Confucianism, but both religious perspectives tend to legitimate the household as the central economic and social unit in society. The bedrock of Chinese cultural tradition is emphatically this-worldly and apparently knows nothing of the otherworldly concerns governing classical Hinduism's pursuit of *moksha*. Sacred powers, gods, and goddesses, including the living spirits of dead ancestors, exert a powerful influence upon this world. They are as real, and just as unpredictable, as we are. Religious practice therefore seeks to establish a mutually beneficial accommodation between the sacred and the profane, a harmonious balance of power that is thought to reflect the will of Heaven (*T'ien*), the ultimate—though hardly personal—embodiment of the cosmic order itself (*Tao*).

The moral emphasis in Confucianism is unmistakable. The core of ethical concern is expressed in the concept of *hsiao* or filiality, which is the ideal governing the nucleus of social relationships in the Chinese household. *Hsiao* is to be realized in all five of these relationships: children to their parents; subjects to their ruler; wife to husband; younger brother to older brother; younger friend to older friend. Each of these, obviously, is hierarchical, involving a subordinate and a superior; yet each also involves mutual obligations and mutual respect. Indeed, the whole of social ethics can be understood as a "rectification of names," insofar as each of these relationships carries its own objective standards. To achieve right relationship one must recognize what is at stake in the name given it. The *hsiao* that a subject owes his ruler, for example, is implicit in what it means to be subject and what it means to be ruler.

Confucian ethics thus emphasizes the thread of continuity linking the reciprocities operative in the five basic relationships. The Chinese nation as a whole was the Emperor's extended family, and the patterns of mutual obligation characteristic of the relationships of children to their parents were expected to set the moral tone for imperial government. The following text suggests the universal scope of *hsiao*:

> The Master said: "Formerly the illustrious kings governed the empire by filiality. They did not dare neglect the ministers of small countries—to say nothing of their own dukes, marquises, earls, counts, and barons! Thus, they gained the readiness of all the countries to serve their former kings. The rulers did not dare insult the widows and the widowers—to say nothing of officials and ordinary citizens! Thus, they gained the grateful love of all the people in the service of their former princes. The heads of families did not dare mistreat their servants and concubines—to say nothing of their wives and children! Thus they gained the readiness of the people to serve their parents. Accordingly, while living, parents enjoyed all prosperity; after their death, sacrifices were offered to their spirits. In this way the world was kept in peace and harmony; calamities did not arise, nor disorders occur. Such was the world government by filiality of the former kings."

The Odes say:
  "They gave an example of virtuous conduct
  And all the nations submitted themselves."
                    (*Hsiao Ching*: VIII; in Camenisch, 1991: 174–175)

Thus, in the Sinitic civilization, political ethics—at least as an ideal—tend to conform to the norms embodied in the household or extended family. Just the opposite tendency seems to be apparent in our own society, where the ethical expectations governing family life in our post-Christian society seem increasingly dependent upon our continuing experiment with political democracy and human rights.

Asian family values, as commonly discussed in analyses of East Asia's strategic strengths in the global economy, are the pervasive and enduring heritage of the Confucian ethic of *hsiao*. To be sure, modern Japanese business corporations are not simply an extension of the premodern Sinitic household. But the link between the two has been documented in various studies, and that link is highly suggestive of the ways in which modernizing religious traditions are economically significant. One such study is Koichi Shinohara's "Religion and Economic Development in Japan: An Exploration Focusing on the Institution of *Ie*" (Shinohara 1983, 167–178). *Ie*, like its Chinese cognate, *jia*, refers to house or household, in a sense roughly equivalent to the classical Greek, *oikos*, the Latin, *domus*, and the Spanish, *casa*. As Shinohara asserts, "*ie* is best understood as the basic unit of communal life and consists of all those who live under one roof and eat meals prepared in the same kitchen" (1983: 168). He opts here for a broad definition, in order not to restrict the *ie* to blood kinship as such. Adoptions are common within the traditional *ie*. To preserve continuity within the household, it is customary for a widow to remain within her former husband's *ie*, in order to raise the children there. Typically, the *ie* is internally differentiated, as subordinate branches of the family (*bunke*) can be established in relation to the main branch (*honke*), whose head (*kacho*) retains substantial control of the entire household's property. Though the *ie* developed historically in the premodern period and is clearly documented in the mid-Tokugawa period (eighteenth century C.E.), its survival in modern Japan until after World War II is admirably conveyed in Tanizaki's splendid novel, *The Makioka Sisters* (1957).

The religious and moral values embedded in the premodern *ie* came to dominate modern Japanese business practices by a process of cultural diffusion. Shinohara argues that the internal differentiation of *honke* and *bunke* within the *ie*, and its distinctive approach to household property, provided the model for the prewar Japanese enterprise groups known as *zaibatsu*. The *ie* structure, in other words, always was an economic unit; the major change was from a village-oriented agricultural system to an urban industrial economy. As the power of the traditional households declined, Japanese industries increasingly took up, first, the social functions of the *ie* and, later, its distinctive pattern of religious and moral values (1983: 174). It is little wonder, then, as Hamabata has shown (1990), that in many Japanese firms there is an extraordinary degree of continuity linking religious, familial, and business concerns. Religious rites are exercised and social responsibilities discharged, quite naturally, within the firm itself, to a degree that defies modern Western assumptions about the boundaries separating the sacred from the secular. Policies considered typical of Japanese corporations, e.g., lifetime employment, wage distribution based on seniority, management by consensus, and an egalitarian atmosphere within the firm, are shown by Shinohara to be expressions of the enduring influence of the *ie* as a template for Japanese social organization.

Shinohara helpfully concludes his analysis with a parting shot at Max Weber. From a Weberian perspective, because the modern Japanese corporation reflects the social logic of the traditional *ie*, it ought not to succeed—at least, not when measured against any rigorous standard of economic performance. It lacks the impersonalism characteristic of a company of strangers whose relationships are primarily contractual; it will be debilitated by nepotism, Weber would have predicted, and typically will pursue policies that are economically irrational. Japan's impressive economic success may, however, suggest—as it does to James Fallows in his recent book, *Looking at the Sun: The Rise of the New East Asian Economic and Political System* (1994)—that our own assumptions about what is and is not economically rational are arbitrary and at least as derivative from inherited religious and moral norms as any alternative system. Fallows makes a distinction between an autonomous and a "culturally embedded" economy which, within the limits of neoclassical theory, is a contradiction in terms. Japan's economy is culturally embedded in the sense that it is organized to fulfill certain "noneconomic" purposes, the chief of which is national security, broadly understood. Its corporations, as we have seen, are not only a reflection of Asian family values, but an effective instrument for preserving them. This system may be economically irrational; but why does it perform so well in the global economy?

Shinohara's essay responds most effectively to Weber's fears about nepotism. He shows that, even in its premodern reality, the *ie* was geared to successful economic performance. The custom of adoption allowed the *kacho* to designate an heir, either when he lacked a son (*yoshi*) of his own or when his heir already had shown signs of being grossly incompetent. The household's collective future, including its accumulated property, was not to be frittered away by someone who showed no inclination to live by the ethic of *hsiao*—known in Japanese as *ko*. As Shinohara comments, managing the affairs of the *ie* involved "a significant level of economic rationalism" (1983: 172). Though the social responsibilities of kinship were exercised through the *ie*, family ties were not allowed to threaten the *ie*'s own survival. Such an approach to economic performance is seen clearly in Japanese firms, where a manager is not likely to be fired for his failures, but he is also not likely to be given anything else of much importance to do. Clearly, there are ways to keep most people productive, even in a system guaranteeing lifetime employment. Tenured professors should have little difficulty imagining how this is done!

Reinventing the Good Corporation

This brief sketch of some of the resources for business ethics to be discovered in the religious and moral traditions of South and East Asia, among other things, ought to provide enough distance to highlight the irony involved in the alleged death of the "good [U.S.] corporation." If the good corporation is dead, it is not because the competition has killed it but because we have allowed it to die for lack of imagination about the nature of the challenge we face in the global economy. The challenge is not about which nation can make the most microchips or which can protect more of its strategic industries, but about whose traditional values are deep and resilient enough to capitalize on the positive benefits of modernization while resisting its corrosive effects on our humanity.

The good corporation, it turns out, was not simply a strategy for outflanking the labor unions or an expression of the largesse that flowed from the United States' fleeting dominance over the global economy after World War II. The good corporation, whether we knew it or not, was also an expression of certain cultural values in which, apparently, many Americans no longer have the collective will to believe. The irony, of course, is that the good corporation is being dismantled in the name of economic exigency, as if the rigors of competition with, especially, the East Asian system were forcing us to revoke the economic securities that once afforded "good jobs" for the majority of U.S. workers. But as the data I have surveyed suggest, the competition that is beating us is characterized by its own model of the good corporation. It is hard not to think of the Asian challenge in terms of Western cultural decline, religious apathy, and moral confusion.

I have no quick fixes to offer for reviving the good corporation in the United States. I do, however, suggest a conclusion. The good corporation will not be revived by redoubling our efforts to remake this society according to the rigorous axioms of neoclassical economics. Even in business circles, those who once hailed the promise of superior competitiveness through reengineering are now bemoaning the "anorexic corporation" that is too weak, in terms of the accumulated experience and skills embodied in its personnel, to respond to new opportunities. Anyone with a lick of common sense could have predicted the likelihood of this outcome, but those business strategists addicted to the formalisms of neoclassical economics are not known for their common sense. There is an alternative, of course; but taking it seriously would mean dispelling the illusion that economics is a value-neutral science, universally valid without reference to any historical or cultural context. The challenge afforded by our East Asian competitors might lead us to rediscover the cultural embeddedness of our own ways of thinking about economics and business, and the enduring roots of our thinking in Western religious traditions. It might inspire us to cultivate those roots anew, so that we might learn once again what we mean to each other, what we owe to each other, as members of a company of strangers. Whether we like it or not, the original template for the good corporation remains biblical and covenantal. We can revive the good corporation, and make it competitive once again, only if we learn how to use that template effectively.

Bibliography

Aristotle. *The Complete Works of Aristotle: The Revised Oxford Translation*, vol. 2. Jonathan Barnes, ed. Princeton: Princeton University Press, 1984.
Beeman, William O. "Patterns of Religion and Economic Development in Iran from the Qajar Era to the Islamic Revolution of 1978–79," in James Finn,

ed., *Global Economics and Religion*. New Brunswick: Transaction Books, 1983: 73–103.

Berger, Peter. *The Capitalist Revolution: Fifty Propositions about Prosperity, Equality, and Liberty*. New York: Basic Books, 1986.

Berger, Peter, and Hsin-Huang Michael Hsiao, eds. *In Search of an East Asian Development Model*. New Brunswick: Transaction Publishers, 1988.

Buultjens, Ralph. "India: Values, Visions, and Economic Development," in James Finn, ed., *Global Economics and Religion*. New Brunswick: Transaction Books, 1983: 17–34.

Camenisch, Paul F. "Chinese Religion: Introduction and Readings," in John Dominic Crossan, ed., *Religious Worlds in Comparative Perspective* (Department of Religious Studies, DePaul University, Chicago). Dubuque, Iowa: Kendall/Hunt Publishing Company, 1991: 141–202.

Camenisch, Paul, and Dennis McCann. "Christian Religious Traditions," in Clarence C. Walton, ed., *Enriching Business Ethics*. New York: Plenum Press, 1990: 63–84.

Carmody, Denise Lardner, and John Tully Carmody. *How to Live Well: Ethics in the World Religions*. Belmont, California: Wadsworth Publishing Company, 1988.

de Bary, Wm. Theodore, ed. *Sources of Indian Tradition*, vol. 1. New York: Columbia University Press, 1958.

Dolan, Jay P. *The American Catholic Experience: A History from Colonial Times to the Present*. Garden City, New York: Doubleday, 1985.

———. *Catholic Revivalism: The American Experience, 1830–1900*. Notre Dame: University of Notre Dame Press, 1978.

Embree, Ainslie T., ed. *The Hindu Tradition: Readings in Oriental Thought*. New York: Random House/Vintage Books, 1972.

Fallows, James. *Looking at the Sun: The Rise of the New East Asian Economic and Political System*. New York: Pantheon Books, 1994.

Frankel, Francine R. "Religio-Cultural Values, Political Gradualism, and Economic Development in India," in James Finn, ed., *Global Economics and Religion*. New Brunswick: Transaction Books, 1983: 35–66.

Hamabata, Matthews Masayuki. *Crested Kimono: Power and Love in the Japanese Business Family*. Ithaca, NY: Cornell University Press, 1990.

Leahy, John T., and Aminah Beverly McCloud. "Islam: Introduction and Readings," in John Dominic Crossan, ed., *Religious Worlds in Comparative Perspective* (Department of Religious Studies, DePaul University, Chicago). Dubuque, Iowa: Kendall/Hunt Publishing Company, 1991: 437–512.

McCann, Dennis P., *New Experiment in Democracy: The Challenge for American Catholicism*. Kansas City, Mo.: Sheed and Ward, 1987.

———. "Accursed Internationalism of Finance: Coping with the Resources of Catholic Social Teaching," in Oliver F. Williams, Frank K. Reilly, and John W. Houck, eds., *Ethics and the Investment Industry*. Savage, Md.: Rowman and Littlefield, 1989: 127–147.

————. "Hinduism: Introduction and Readings," in John Dominic Crossan, ed., *Religious Worlds in Comparative Perspective* (Department of Religious Studies, DePaul University, Chicago). Dubuque, Iowa: Kendall/Hunt Publishing Company, 1991: 13–68.

————. "Toward a Theology of the Corporation: A Second Chance for Catholic Social Teaching," in Oliver F. Williams and John W. Houck, eds., *Catholic Social Thought and the New World Order*. Notre Dame: University of Notre Dame Press, 1993: 329–350.

————. "The World's Parliament of Religion, Then and Now: From Social Gospel to Multiculturalism," in Harlan Beckley, ed., *The Annual of the Society of Christian Ethics*, 1993: 291–296.

————. "Doing Business with the Historical Jesus," in Jeffrey Carlson and Robert A. Ludwig, eds., *Jesus and Faith: A Conversation on the Work of John Dominic Crossan*. Maryknoll, N.Y.: Orbis Books, 1994: 132–141.

Napier, Ron. "Interrelationships of the Economic and Social Systems in Japan," in James Finn, ed., *Global Economics and Religion*. New Brunswick: Transaction Books, 1983: 179–194.

Novak, Michael. *The Spirit of Democratic Capitalism*. New York: Simon and Schuster, 1982.

O'Brien, David J., and Thomas A. Shannon, eds. *Catholic Social Thought: The Documentary Heritage*. Maryknoll, N.Y.: Orbis Books, 1992.

Read, Kay Almere. "Buddhism: Introduction and Readings," in John Dominic Crossan, ed., *Religious Worlds in Comparative Perspective* (Department of Religious Studies, DePaul University, Chicago). Dubuque, Iowa: Kendall/Hunt Publishing Company, 1991: 69–139.

Shinohara, Koichi. "Religion and Economic Development in Japan: An Exploration Focusing on the Institution of *Ie*," in James Finn, ed., *Global Economics and Religion*. New Brunswick: Transaction Books, 1983: 167–178.

Stackhouse, Max. *Creeds, Society, and Human Rights: A Study in Three Cultures*. Grand Rapids, Mich.: Eerdmans Publishing Co., 1984.

————. "The Hindu Ethic and the Ethos of Development: Some Western Views," *Religion and Society*, vol. 20 (December 1973): 5–28.

Strain, Charles R. "Japanese Religion: Introduction and Readings," in John Dominic Crossan, ed., *Religious Worlds in Comparative Perspective* (Department of Religious Studies, DePaul University, Chicago). Dubuque, Iowa: Kendall/Hunt Publishing Company, 1991: 203–279.

Tanizaki, Junichiro. *The Makioka Sisters (Sasame Yuki)*. Translated by Edward G. Seidensticker. New York: Alfred A. Knopf, 1957.

Weber, Max. *The Protestant Ethic and the Spirit of Capitalism*. Translated and edited by Talcott Parsons. New York: Charles Scribner's Sons, 1958.

————. *The Religion of China: Confucianism and Taoism*. Translated and edited by Hans H. Gerth. New York: The Free Press, 1951.

————. *The Religion of India: The Sociology of Hinduism and Buddhism*. Translated and edited by Hans H. Gerth and Don Martindale. New York: The Free Press, 1958.

Part IV

The Socially Responsible Corporation: Converting Theory into Practice

"Bob, we weren't born yesterday. We know what the principles of this company are. We know what our own personal principles are. We know where that extra million will go—into the pockets of some of those generals. We told them we would not take the order."

I said, "Dan, it thrills me even more that you did the right thing. Thank you very much for having done the right thing."

Then I said, "Let's continue the discussion. You have said you won't take the order at the $11 million price. Let's just hypothesize that the generals come back to you when they've thought it over and say, 'Oh, you didn't understand. We were just expressing an option. You'll get the order for $10 million.' "

I reply, "We won't take it at $10 million."

"Well," Dan said, "we were kind of wondering what might happen if there had been a change in their representation."

I continued, "Further, Dan, we will not ever quote to that government. If the government changes we will quote to a new government in that country."

He said, "Whoa. You carry this thing way beyond what we thought would be the handling of this relationship."

I said, "It's very simple. Dan, we know now those people play footloose. The people they've done business with probably had to play footloose to get the business so if we take a contract they will assume we play footloose too. Now, all of a sudden, our integrity is beginning to erode. Some people will think we don't stand for absolute impeccable standards of conduct of doing business."

He said, "Thank you very much. The gang will know that before we go home for dinner tonight."

Corporate employees reacted to this with mixed feelings. We had already, in effect, covered all our fixed overhead of the almost $200 million we were going to do with other customers. My salary had been absorbed as had all of our fixed costs. The gross profit on the $10 million would have been something in the order of about $3 million, maybe even $4 million, and would have actually turned to a net profit for just that one last order. The consequence of our decision was that our employees were not going to receive over $100 per person out of the profit-sharing. The profit report of the corporation was going to be less, assuming we had made a 5 percent profit on the business that had already been taken into account. This probably would have raised us to an 8 percent after-tax profit. Those are big numbers. Should we not be swayed by those things? Not a bit. We made so much more money honorably over the next twenty years while that anecdote was still fresh in people's minds. I tell this story in tribal storytelling meetings once in a while with some of the people in our training sessions. They also hear other examples.

I respectfully suggest that, as we were taught by our parents or teachers, we simply practiced the Golden Rule, which is not that hard to do. That is why I dare to say it is not a challenge, in my estimation, to deal with the issue of responsibility if, indeed, one of the subdefinitions of that is to act ethically or responsibly or to treat people with respect. I respectfully suggest also that there are many role models who are practicing this constantly.

We now turn to the subject of a company's competitiveness and how it affects its responsibility to society. Our companies have to be competitive but so must the organization. You are competitive one person at a time, counterpart to counterpart. If Kobyashi-San of NEC is smarter than I am, how can we be competitive? If the foreman of your competitor is smarter than yours, how can you be competitive? We have concluded that the only way to be competitive is to make sure every one of our people is as smart or smarter than the smartest competitor we have anywhere in the world. As a consequence, we are investing a tremendous amount of our resources to that end. Incidentally, training does not cost us any money. That is a heresy I firmly believe. If we train somebody in January, he or she will use the information so effectively by March that, in terms of efficiency, we probably get it back in the same quarter.

We are not only helping people to make better products but we teach our people better overall problem-solving processes and how to learn faster than others. That is going to be a distinguishing characteristic of a better corporation. We are teaching the people fundamentals that, frankly, they have not learned adequately from the educational systems that apply to families, neighborhoods, schools, as well as on the job. In the meantime, we get to be more competitive as a commercial institution, creating more wealth, investing in more things, creating more stable jobs (incidentally, jobs that are going to be lifetime jobs). I love to hear about presumed new fads like virtual corporations and why people will not work for one company for extended careers. If our competitors embrace those principles we are going to overwhelm them because our people want to belong. They want to belong to a relevant family. They want to do things inside our house. They want to have distinctive, related competencies that allow them to control their own destinies within an institution whose destiny is common to theirs.

There is a phenomenon going on in American industry—I hope it will happen in education and other places as well—and that is the phenomenon of *teaming*. In our company now, almost all employees cycle through team memberships. Ten or twelve people who have a line of sight to a given issue come together. We represent a mixture of skills and interests, have been trained in problem-solving, have very significant education, and go to work and solve the problems. If we find that an occasional team seems to have a bias about a given class of people, we rearrange the teams and employees discover that is not a very smart way of doing things because we are not getting as good a result as possible from our team efforts. The interesting thing is that if you go after a solid business result, people of goodwill automatically will chose the right way to do it because, among their peers, they want to look as though they are doing right. They discover the teams next door get the best results if they go by only the highest principles, which becomes a reinforcement phenomenon.

Incidentally, these team efforts can be extremely important in the macro sense in terms of democracies. Motorola now manufactures products in China; eventually, we will have a thousand teams there, with ten people on each—ten thousand people. They will go home and tell their families about the value of working on teams and making consensus decisions and how they followed the advice of a boss after they argued with him. What will that do to the political climate in China? In twenty-five or fifty years it will have a big effect.

The social consequences are evident. The education and training program that aims at accomplishing a good business result coincidentally makes the individual a better family person and a better citizen.

It is also possible through consultation and even advocacy to help others' social responsibilities. For example, a year or two ago I was privileged to speak at a conference attended mostly by the citizens of India. It was appropriate for me in my message to graciously admonish the Indian officials. Their attention to modest incremental improvements in their bureaucracy was not what was essential to help them bring their country into an economic environment that could help produce higher incomes. I suggested that they focus on the interests of customers, not of government employees. If customers were served better, more business would be done, more income would be earned, and government officials would have more reasons to carry out their other well-intentioned endeavors.

So many societies in the world cry out for improved economic stature. Too often those who counsel the leadership of those countries fail to understand the significance of investment. Such people seem to think all that matters is to start with apparent social benefits before creating the ability to earn them. Thus, companies like ours try their best to convince such developing countries to understand the basic principles of economic development and the need to create an environment hospitable to private investment. Only if that environment is hospitable is it ultimately possible to provide the other social goods.

There is an old saw that says you cannot achieve happiness by simply getting up in the morning and deciding that will be your active purpose for the day. All of us have come to know we must engage in constructive activities that day. It is possible, as a result of having achieved those worthy purposes, that we will be rewarded indirectly with a sense of satisfaction that might even be counted as happiness. So it is with intentions to do social good. It is hard to afford many social goods without having worked to achieve the wealth-creating results I have described. But it is immensely satisfying to know that when such responsibility is demonstrated, so many more of our good intentions can be fulfilled.

I believe there is a very strong, and growing stronger, majority of American business leaders who are practicing high principles in domestic and international trade of their own volition. They recognize it is the smartest and right way to do it. Coincidentally, in recent years federal legislation—the federal Corrupt Practices Act—sets limits on unethical conduct. Had that law existed in 1950, we would have been guilty of violating a federal law if we had done that extra million dollar pricing in the South American country. So, although some businesspeople may cite the law as the reason they behave ethically, I know right from wrong and practice what is right, regardless of the law.

One might question this by naming the many counterexamples. Obviously, there are some obfuscations—should you bribe the customs officer so your goods can pass through? We do not do it but some people justified that as necessary because it is the only way the customs officers make enough money. But we think you can stand on an absolute.

Questions and Answers

Question: You talk about business and that one of its common purposes is to raise wealth. How do you redistribute that wealth? For instance, I understand Motorola has a project going on right now called Iridium, a network of telecommunication satellites and, once the fixed cost is clocked down, there is clear profit. Could Iridium be used for the benefit of poor, Third World nations? For instance, could the Red Cross, World Hunger Coalition, the relief efforts in Somalia, Ethiopia and Bosnia have the use of this instantaneous communication equipment you will have in orbit?

Galvin: You began your question by asking how we redistribute our wealth. That is done, in effect, by the very nature of business. The term *distribution of wealth* has a certain connotation to it so I want to walk away from the idiom by saying that our employees are paid a more than fair compensation. They, in turn, pass that through society by their purchases, their options, their elections, and their investments. Our suppliers (we indeed use people on the outside) do half the business with us so they send out their roots of wealth. Incidentally, an interesting experiment many companies engage in (to illustrate how that wealth is distributed) is, sometime in a small town, to pay everyone who works at your factory with silver dollars, and watch the effect around town when your employees start to pay their grocery bill and their barber, etc. The corporate people say, ''Wow, look at the effect. This thing multiplies all over the place.'' But one of the main things you have properly sensed is that we use some of our wealth to plow back into our institution to make it bigger but make it better and, every once in a while, a company can be fortunate enough to think up the type of system I have just described, which offers the promise of bringing the communications to people who have never had it before. Because of our investors in India, in the Soviet countries and in Africa, we expect that when this system goes operative in 1998, people who have all manner of other social responsibilities, concerns and problems will have communications for the first time. However, they will be obliged to pay a fair price for that. It is not something you give away. It has a value. It will earn more money for the people who work in Iridium as well as for those who receive the service. So great values come from this class of situation. You have, in effect, projected a significant social benefit from the investment and the redistributing of the investment process.

Incidentally, we start industries; we do not just start businesses.

Question: How do you ensure that your moral stance and concern for responsibility to society is implemented within the corporation, and are there instances in which certain corporate values, for instance, return on investment or hiring of minorities, might clash with one another because there are some moral stances, at least in the short run, that are more expensive than other decisions?

Galvin: Over the last twenty-five years there have been no hurdles of the nature of who we hire or what country we go to for good, honest, well-educated people. However, we do have a bias. We cannot go to a country where the people are illiterate. That is a big problem. But if the people are literate and competent, whatever their color or dress, we invite them into our situation.

I do not wish to represent that we are unique but, No, I do not know of any inhibitor in companies like ours that represents anything other than an occasional act of individual fraud. We do pick up some flat tires once in a while and that person will do something illicit and we have to investigate. Then either we are able to cure the individual in some fashion or our Code of Conduct just washes him or her right out of our company.

Question: What do you feel is the role of business in assisting public primary and secondary education to improve? We have heard many negatives about the U.S. education system in comparison to other countries.

Galvin: The question is so significant and the answers so many that I can give you only a hint of the class of thinking we apply to that issue. First, if the company is not working very well, if it is not creating some wealth, probably it has not got much elasticity to work on the problem at all. That is what has happened to corporations such as IBM and General Motors in the last few years. Many people have had to go back to the drawing board.

But in our case, for example, we have the elasticity and the funds— because we are earning satisfactorily—to have professionals working on the issue of the administration of school districts. Now that may not be a hot button to you. You may think we should be concerned about teaching teachers to teach math, but the point is that diversity allows us to attack many aspects of the problem. We are working on the administration part. Why? Well, we are alleged to be rather competent on the subject of quality management so we can show a school district how it can operate much more efficiently. We are trying to persuade some of the administrators to make some changes. If they do, they will have a little more money left to train people to teach mathematics. We are taking a bite of the apple and endeavoring to make an impact. I guess my generic answer is that all of us ought to take as big a bite of the apple as we can, where we are welcome, and try to be supportive.

Question: You mention educating your own people in problem solving. How do you do it? Workshops? Three-week sessions? Once a week? What sort of materials do you give them? Have you developed your own materials? Are there books or do you hire people who have the techniques already?

Galvin: We require formal, classroom training for all our people up to a certain number of days per year and, depending on each of our duties, we target what seems to be the most relevant. I will take you back a few years when, in effect, we defined what we call "manufacturing literacy." We determined that all the people in our new factories must understand English because English is the language of the computer, and I am speaking of an American-based situation. Now we can do the same in Japan in Japanese. But our people had to understand English—we had a very large number who did not. They had to understand some algebra, they had to understand certain principles of statistical quality control, and they had to be able to enter and take output from the computer—some dexterous skills. We gave them training in creative thinking, in problem solving, and gave them a variety of techniques such as Pareto diagrams, fishbone diagrams, and various process diagrams. We gave them a whole bunch of tools and gave everybody the same. Now, I learned some parts of them better than you did, you learned some others better than I did, and we get on the same team.

I say, "Well gee, why don't we use a Pareto diagram?"

But I've forgotten what a Pareto diagram is and all of a sudden you say, "We just distribute the data round this way. Oh, there's our problem, isn't it?"

"Yeah. Let's go solve it."

So they learn on the job but we teach them very practical things. I have given you the manufacturing. We teach vice presidents too.

Question: Do you have your own internal teachers?

Galvin: We have an entity we call Motorola University which is a bit of an extension of the word but we dare to do that because we are probably researching some subjects that are quite advanced compared to what is happening in any other university in the world. We have a corporate-managed and a corporate-resourced education system and we spend hundreds of millions of dollars a year through a ledger system. Incidentally, I do not think it costs us any money because we get that money back almost instantly if we teach contemporaneously to the application of the material. The process works and our people like it. Most of our people want to go to school because they want to be smarter. We have a few hardnoses once in a while. Some little manager does not think he or she can give people up so they revolt and get over to the course because they do not want to be left behind.

Let me give you a circumstance we think is unique, and organizations like this could debate as to whether or not our principles are correct. A few years ago we said to ourselves, "Our people, for the most part, do not wish to suffer in an environment where there is a proliferation in the trading and use of drugs." We had tried introductory drug testing, meaning testing people when they applied for a job, but decided that was not enough. So, a few years ago, we put into place a very controversial policy which may or may not be a good piece of social action—we engage in random drug testing of all our employees. I have been tested three times. My name is pulled out of the hat and I am tested. We have a minority of our people, extremely well-educated people, who are incensed because they think this is voiding their private rights. I think they make a very good case, but we still maintain that principle because I think it is right, most of my associates think it is right, and most of our people think it is right.

The people who are the minority in our company want to argue about it every day. We do not waste our time arguing about peripheral issues, and drug testing is a peripheral issue to us. We decide either to do it or not, and this takes away the ambiguity. Then the company creates wealth and goes on to do the other things that are quite evident to meet the right social responsibilities. The minority will still argue about whether or not we have voided their constitutional rights but, so far, we are hanging in there. We have this kind of problem but, to me, it is not critical, just a two-hour issue some afternoon. We make the decision, go on from there, and never debate it again.

Question: I sense you have succeeded in imbuing your fellow professionals and colleagues at the company (with all good opportunity for humor, of course) with the importance of taking each other very seriously and in believing deeply that you have hired very good people who empower each other. It seems to me your commitment to doing things the right way comes from a belief in each other as human beings that must permeate Motorola. We need more of this in our universities, we need it in our companies. Please comment on this.

Galvin: Well, that was a very generous statement. It was certainly a sincere compliment and I thank you for that.

It is probably easier for us to do because we are a collected society, we are aggregated literally within our four walls and we can propagate some common interests. We can build on success and the success is oriented to our creating wealth. Our people talk about creating wealth.

Mostly they talk about serving the customer, perfection, etc. We have convinced our people that some day they might deserve to be recognized as the finest corporation in the world. Wow! That is something worth aspiring to. Coaches do that with their teams; so do college presidents.

But let me give you an anecdote that you professionals will have to wrestle with and teach us whether or not these things are going to mature into major league phenomena. It is about this thing called *problem-based education.* I am not an educator but there is a pony in there somewhere.

Motorola's growth is going to require, in our estimation, that we start hiring at the age of fourteen. We will have to identify people at that age so they will be ready by the time they are thirty-five, at the rate of hundreds per year, to become presidents of businesses that we are going to be spawning over the next twenty-five to forty years. Now, you might say, How are you going to get at that? Well, we have an experiment. We are running summer camps on our properties for the children of employees. Very discriminating. Children or cousins or grandchildren, they have to be related to the employee. The kids who come range from age eleven to sixteen, but we will use fourteen. When these kids are recruited by their parents or another family member to come to the camp for one week (currently, they only come for one week) right in the middle of the summer, you can imagine how excited they are about that. They would like to send their moms and dads off to camp instead! They come to the first day of camp—and we know how to receive them in a nice, friendly and youthful way—and by ten o'clock that morning we have thrown a problem at them.

We say, "Hey, we're having trouble getting the last hundred million for our Iridium project. Here's who has promised to invest in it and would you please figure out how we can find $100 million for this business."

The kids say, "Well, how do you do that?"

We say, "Well, you've got to start figuring it out."

I am not going to walk you through the whole thing but they say, "Well, let's see. You've an investor in Japan, one in Russia, one in the Mid-East and so on. I guess we could see if there are some other places in the world."

"Well, that's not a bad idea. What other places?"

"I don't know."

Some kid says, "Well, how about Brazil?" The other kid says, "Where's Brazil?"

Notice what is beginning to happen. They have to get a map and figure out where Brazil is. In effect, we have given them a recipe as to how they can get data, if they want it. So they start asking for data, they start bringing in material, they sub-set the problem—one bunch of kids does this, another group does that, some people start adding up numbers.

At the end of the first day, all the kids go home at five o'clock. At the end of the second day, the moms and dads have to wait for them until about 5:20. At the end of the third day they have to go in and drag the kids out after six o'clock. At the end of the fourth day, the kids say, "We haven't finished yet. You've got to let us finish because we've got to give a report to the big bosses tomorrow at two o'clock."

What I am attempting to illustrate is that we are not making school exciting enough.

Question: Mr. Galvin, it is obvious that your religious formation in your early life has had a great impact on your business practices and, in many ways, it seems to me that our talk about being ethical in business has more to do with our religious formation than with any kind of formula in ethics. One of the concepts we learn as Christians is forgiveness and, in your pursuit of excellence and quality, how much tolerance is there in the corporation for making mistakes and how much forgiveness can you actually practice in your corporation in your pursuit to create wealth?

Galvin: My father had so many elements of wisdom; he was really a remarkable person. This is shorthand but I think you will find substance. He said, "I don't mind a man who is dumb. I just can't stand a man who is numb." Therefore, there was tolerance for making a mistake and we make a lot of mistakes back on the ranch. How do we learn except by driving into cul-de-sacs and having to turn around and come back out?

The man who made the single biggest mistake in our corporation, Elmer Wavering, said to my father, and my father supported him so therefore it was his responsibility too, "I'll take us into the heater business for cars." We made a lot of heaters but had to recall them all. They were a big mistake. Nobody got hurt but it was a terrible business experience at a time when the company was doing about $100 million. We lost probably $10 or $15 million on it. That is big league stuff. Mr. Wavering became president of the company eventually, even though he made that mistake. So we are very tolerant of people who make the right kinds of mistakes, meaning they are trying to do something. But if somebody says, "I paid that fellow off down in the Chicago Police

Department because I thought that was good for the company because we'd get an order," that guy will not be around by the end of the afternoon.

Question: When a company's survival is at stake and a business deal is offered, such as the one from the Latin American company, how does a company deal with that kind of ethical problem?

Galvin: Our company has faced those real issues and I know we will face them again. We will make some human errors in the leadership of our company and when that happens, the governing factor ultimately has to come down to the survival of a piece of the institution and that piece of the institution has to be able to afford itself. You cannot subsidize an imperfect institution for long. If it is a short-term matter, a year or two, we will subsidize, we will move people around, we will create jobs and do all manner of things like that. But if it is a big failure, if we have another heater situation, then probably a lot of the people who work in the heater business would not have jobs for a lay-off period of time. We would hope we could call them back after we had corrected the problem six months or a year later. We do have to be practical about the survivability of the institution and there are financial constraints. I think all institutions have to be practical if they are to remain healthy. Even though it is a poignant event for the hundreds of people who might be affected, if you talk to the balance of the people in an otherwise healthy institution, they recognize these practical realities. So it is a compromise.

15

The Hershey Story: Vision and Leadership for a Socially Responsible Corporation

William Lehr, Jr.

This is the story of one corporate business, how it started, and how it goes about balancing the demands of generating shareholder value with a socially responsible and ethical approach to business.

There is a maze of choices in the business world. One eloquent writer—beloved by children and parents everywhere—succinctly states a course for success: "You have brains in your head. You have feet in your shoes. You can steer yourself in any direction you choose. You're on your own. And you know what you know. And YOU are the guy who'll decide where to go." The writer, of course, is Dr. Seuss and the message is the great balancing act—dealing with a maze of life choices while choosing the best path to success.

A corporation faces a similar maze. It has a large and diverse pool of employees, each one able to choose a direction and chart a course for the company. How do companies ensure that they stay on course in a responsible and ethical manner while providing an adequate return on investment for their shareholders? This has been an increasingly complicated issue for many major corporations. At Hershey Foods, we celebrated our centennial in 1994 and, in our case, the issue is clear because the groundwork has been set over our one-hundred-year history. It is important to understand our past to appreciate fully the success of Hershey Foods today.

The Story of the Founder

Milton S. Hershey, our founder and one of America's greatest entrepreneur-philanthropists, failed many times before finally achieving success. As a risk-taker, Milton Hershey was the essence of entrepreneurialism. As a philanthropist, he wanted to provide others with a better start in life than he experienced, and to that end gave away all of his wealth.

His name, of course, is synonymous with success. In the late 1800s, however, the road to success for Milton Hershey was littered with one failure after another. He was a man of modest beginnings. Born in the town of Derry Church, Pennsylvania—today Hershey or *Chocolate Town, U.S.A.*—Mr. Hershey inherited two strong traits from his parents. The first was his father Henry's inclination to dream big dreams. The second personality trait was Milton's deep-seated appreciation for hard work, which he inherited from his Mennonite mother, Fannie. Milton was nineteen years old when he took his dream and his work ethic to Philadelphia to make candy by night and sell it by day. The business did not flourish, and he failed, owing his relatives hundreds of dollars.

Milton failed many times in several different cities. Finally, he managed to borrow some money from his aunt one more time. He again started making candy by night and selling it by day. The candies he made were called *Crystal A* caramels. The caramels became a success, due to a large order from an English importer.

By the 1890s Mr. Hershey had become the toast of the town. His company, the Lancaster Caramel Company, covered a city block. The chocolate product line included sweet chocolate bars and novelties, along with cocoa and baking chocolate. Mr. Hershey had become wealthy, and done so with his integrity, sincerity, and simplicity of character fully intact.

In 1899 a group of rival caramel manufacturers approached Mr. Hershey with plans for a giant merger to control the industry. Although he was not interested in merging, Mr. Hershey did agree to sell his business for $1 million, a lot of money in those days. But he retained the right to make chocolate.

Back then, milk chocolate was considered a luxury item—handmade, expensive and sold in specialty shops. Mr. Hershey was confident that he could not only mass-produce milk chocolate, but make it affordable for everybody. He returned to his hometown to turn his vision into reality.

In June 1905 the Hershey Chocolate Factory began operations.

Three years later Mr. Hershey, who had reached the age of fifty-one, was widely regarded as a captain of American industry.

Milton Hershey also was a leader in social and corporate responsibility. Because he believed in the value of education, Mr. Hershey and his wife founded the Hershey Industrial School in 1909 for orphan boys. This institution was destined to become a pivotal force in the company's drive for success. Now known as the Milton Hershey School, it sits on 10,000 acres in Hershey, Pennsylvania, and provides more than one thousand children, whose family lives have been disrupted, with the opportunity to receive quality education and care. In fact, while we have approximately eighty thousand stockholders, the school is Hershey Foods' largest shareholder. Through the Hershey Trust Company, it owns about 41 percent of Hershey Foods' common stock, controls about 77 percent of the corporation's voting shares, and is a direct beneficiary of Hershey's success. The dividends of this company go directly to educate, clothe, feed, and care for the students.

Mr. Hershey was not a philosopher. He seldom spoke about his beliefs, but we do know that Mr. Hershey shunned dishonesty, laziness, inattention to duty and, most of all, disloyalty. Loyalty was a two-way street in Mr. Hershey's book. If the breadth of a man's true greatness is best measured in the darkest of hours, then Mr. Hershey's brightest moment had come during the Great Depression. He charged forward instead of retrenching and created six hundred jobs for a massive construction program in the town. It was another Hershey risk. He and his workers built an arena, a stadium, a hotel and a community center. Today, these facilities stand as testimony to the vision and heart of Milton Hershey. It was through this construction that people could keep working during the bleak years of the Great Depression. Even Hershey's chocolate sales, though lower than during the 1920s, produced substantial profits.

Milton Hershey died in 1945 at the age of eighty-eight. Since his death, the company he founded has changed from one-person dominance to team leadership and team management. Yet Milton Hershey remains a living presence for the company he built. His insistence upon honesty, integrity, and quality—in the products he made and the people he employed—continues to be felt at all levels of the organization.

The Ethical and Social Legacy

Because of our heritage, we are keenly aware of the importance of balancing many interests in our pursuit of a profitable, thriving, and growing business. Today, many formal programs and systems are in place at Hershey Foods, emphasizing social responsibility and ethics. Bear in mind that these are the organized structures; what makes them work so effectively at Hershey Foods is the culture and informal traditions handed down over the last one hundred years.

At the heart of all of our efforts is the Corporate Philosophy and Mission Statement. In fact, the first item in our corporate philosophy states that we shall "protect and enhance the Corporation's high level of ethics and conduct." In 1976, Hershey formally adopted a written Statement of Corporate Philosophy to reinforce the already much-acknowledged importance of balancing our desire for profitable growth with our obligations to our various constituencies—to our shareholders, our employees, our customers, our consumers, our suppliers and the community at large. We developed five key corporate policies to guide our employees in the ethical and legal realm. They cover the following areas:

Use of Corporate Funds and Resources
Conflict of Interest
Antitrust Law Prohibition on Price-Fixing
Trading in Hershey Foods and Other Related Securities
Personal Responsibilities of Employees

A major challenge for a company the size of Hershey is to ensure that employees understand the corporate philosophy and the key corporate policies. Every year we send a copy of the statement and policies to our salaried employees, asking them to read the documents and certify their compliance by signing and returning a card.

But that is just the start of our efforts to educate salaried employees on the importance of conducting business in an ethical manner. We provide employees with an ethics booklet entitled "Guidelines for Ethical Business Practices." This booklet contains a letter from the chief executive officer, stating:

High ethical standards and proper business conduct are critical elements that should be integrated into everything that we do at Hershey Foods. Over the years we have done an excellent job in developing and maintaining traditions of quality and excellence, and it's up to all of us to ensure that Hershey Foods continues to be a company that people trust and rely on, not only for our products but for the way we do business.

We have also produced a videotape in which our CEO, senior vice-presidents, and general counsel discuss the key corporate policies.

Managers are requested to show the videotape and discuss the policies at staff meetings.

Ethics awareness and education is a part of Hershey's in-house training and development programs. In fact, we have specific courses in Valuing Diversity, Hershey Heritage, and Ethics Awareness. The Hershey Heritage program was developed to educate employees about the Milton Hershey School and Mr. Hershey's legacy. Since we look for every opportunity to enhance awareness, our new manager-training program features a segment on ethics awareness as well.

We recognize that it is difficult to communicate about ethics and that often there are a lot of questions but few clear-cut answers, that there are a lot of gray areas. So we encourage employees to discuss ethical issues and questions with their managers, members of senior management, or the offices of the corporate secretary or the general counsel. Through continued communication, we hope to increase awareness that Hershey is not just saying the right things, but expects employees to do the right things. No communication effort can be successful without two important ingredients. Good role-models are critical. A senior manager must not only be willing to say he or she is committed to the ethical conduct of business, but is expected to demonstrate it in his or her own behavior day in and day out. In other words, he or she must "walk the talk." The second step is to ensure appropriate action if a violation occurs. Our philosophy is that the remedy must be immediate and firm.

Our Preventive Law Program fully integrates legal questions with the ethics of business. We encourage our employees to ask not only whether it is legal but whether it is ethical. Is it the right thing to do? Since, in most cases, ethical norms are more stringent than legal norms—at least in Pennsylvania Dutch Country where our senior management and almost half of our fourteen thousand employees are located—getting good legal compliance is relatively easy. Integrity and fair-dealing are much more important than a detailed knowledge of some complicated legal principles. The bottom line here is that the basic decency and integrity of management, professionally and personally, is the foundation of a successful preventive law program.

While internal communications are an important part of our overall program, we do not stop there. We know that we must practice what we preach, so we try hard to behave in an ethical manner with our employees, our consumers, and our neighboring communities. That we have been selected as one of the one hundred best companies to work for in the United States is no fluke. We pay our employees fairly and provide them with competitive benefits and a whole range of programs, making the corporation an employee- and family-friendly place in which to work.

We are aware of the pressures on employees in balancing their work and home responsibilities, so Hershey offers flexible work arrangements such as leaves of absence and alternate work schedules. Appropriate child-care also is of concern to many dual-career and single-parent families. The company has facilitated the construction and operation of a new child-care center in downtown Hershey, within easy reach of almost 50 percent of our employees. We offer a referral service also to provide information on child-care centers in other local communities.

In addition, the company understands that physical and mental wellness are very important. Independent and confidential counseling services are available to employees in parenting, alcohol, aging, stress, and drugs, and the company is pioneering a wellness-incentive program.

Many of our employees complement their professional development through continuing education. Hershey promotes these efforts by providing tuition reimbursement. Other employees support education through financial contributions to their alma maters. Hershey offers a higher education gift-matching program on a two-for-one basis.

Although Hershey has these policies and programs, we have not lost sight of the fact that we are here to provide a good return for our stockholders. We realize the need to balance our employees' well-being with the shareholders' interests and the company's business demands. In the long run, this is best for all parties. Hershey is a lean and focused company, operating in a very competitive environment.

With respect to our consumers, Hershey takes a similar role in developing socially responsible policies. For example, the corporation has a formal advertising policy that states:

> The Corporation has an obligation to communicate in an appropriate manner with the public about its products. Hershey Foods is not attempting to be a corporate censor for the American public. However, it does wish to encourage programming and publications which attempt to maintain high standards of taste. Of particular importance are programs and media directed primarily to youth. Specifically, advertising will be avoided in programs and publications which contain graphic and unnecessary violence, explicit sexual situations, excessive use of vulgarity or profanity, glamorization of drug or alcohol use, and sensationalism involving delicate and controversial social subjects.

We do not advertise on MTV, even though substantial sales dollars could be at stake, because the programming on MTV sometimes does not mesh with Hershey's goals for wholesome, family entertainment. On the other hand, we have supported public television programming, including "What's in the News," an educational TV program for elementary school children nationwide.

We also encourage social responsibility through our formal Charitable/Contributions Program. As a corporation, we recognize that we have an inherent responsibility to be a good neighbor and corporate citizen. It is corporate policy to make voluntary contributions in support of worthy educational, health, human service, civic and community, and arts and cultural organizations. Our goal is to make aggregate contributions at a level approximating those of other responsible businesses, particularly manufacturers in the food industry.

We encourage our employees to get involved in their communities. Many of our employees serve on boards of charitable and nonprofit organizations. In the spirit of our founder, Hershey supports and recognizes employees who perform volunteer service in their communities on their own time. This recognition takes the form of grants to nonprofit agencies when employees volunteer one hundred hours of service annually.

We try also to improve the local communities, particularly in funding programs for children, which is another direct link to our founder's legacy. For instance, Hershey Foods sponsors a Youth Concert Program to foster musical appreciation among elementary school children. Hershey Foods is the sole funding sponsor of Hershey's National Track & Field Youth Program which provides boys and girls between the ages of nine and fourteen with a physical-fitness opportunity where they can jump, run, and throw a softball. More than four million children participated in the program in 1993. Hershey Foods Corporation is the largest volunteer corporate employee fundraising group in the United States for the Osmond Foundation's Children's Miracle Network.

We, and our employees, are strong supporters of the United Way. We tailor many of our contributions on a local level. For example, we have contributed to playground improvements in many plant site locations, and we donate food products to Second Harvest Food Bank affiliates nationwide.

I have been talking about employees and consumers and our philanthropy programs, but this is not an all-inclusive list by any means. I could go on to cite numerous examples, in particular, Hershey's record on the environment, which is a strong one. We have an environmental-compliance policy where we not only strive to meet existing environmental laws and regulations, but to exceed those levels where possible. We believe that we have an obligation to protect and preserve the environment for ourselves, our children, and future generations. The policy also states that "we will continue to conduct our business activities in a manner which will not adversely affect the environment, which will ensure the health and safety of our employees, our consumers and the communities in which we operate."

The environment is taken seriously by employees. Individual offices have partitioned waste receptacles for recycling. On a large scale, Hershey recycles office paper, aluminum, and glass. In the largest chocolate factory in the world—our main Hershey plant—80 percent of the items we once sent to landfills is now diverted to secondary use. For example, cocoa shells are sold for mulch, food scraps are used for animal feed, and even the smallest batteries are recycled.

Our efforts reach beyond the confines of the buildings, however. The company received an environmental award for the design and construction of our corporate office complex which was completed in 1991. The award recognized us for our sensitivity to the natural landscape and the care taken in minimizing any environmental impact to the surrounding area. We get good marks routinely from various organizations that rate corporations on social responsibility. The Council on Economic Priorities publishes a guide for consumers, entitled "Shopping for a Better World," to help them select products made by companies whose policies and practices they support. The book rates companies on ten factors, including charitable contributions, minority advancement, disclosure of information, community outreach, environment, family benefits, and workplace issues. In the most recent edition, Hershey was listed as one of the council's top-rated consumer products companies, stating appropriately that our "record on social responsibility is as sweet as . . . chocolate."

I have presented these examples not merely so that you may appreciate our efforts but to illustrate the seriousness given to social responsibility and ethics in everything we do at Hershey.

Let me return to the subject of ethics. Why do we try to act this way in everything we do? I have talked about Milton Hershey and our history, our culture, and our programs but these are meaningful only if our senior management and our employees really believe in this approach to business. I can honestly tell you that is the case. We do believe it is the right approach.

Like the rest of corporate America, we are not immune to the temptation to take shortcuts, a temptation that increases as competition intensifies. In an environment of employee cut-backs and internal competition for fewer available jobs and promotions, the desire to take the easy way, not necessarily the right way, dramatically increases. However, we understand and believe also that the consequences of unethical conduct are severe. A good name and reputation for fairness and quality that have taken a company a hundred years to build can be destroyed in one day. Therefore, we believe our commitment to ethics must be as strong, if not stronger than ever. Quite simply, we know it makes good business sense.

We have been fortunate to have had strong, ethical leadership since the days of Milton Hershey. The first employees in our organization worked hard and put in long hours, earning modest wages. They believed in Milton Hershey and in what he was trying to achieve. Like Mr. Hershey, they believed in making the highest-quality product and in making sure that consumers got the best value for their money. They believed in his commitment to the highest standards of honesty, fairness, and integrity. They were inspired by his imagination and drive, his ceaseless labor, and his caring heart. They served with deep loyalty.

These very positive, early role-models and their values and beliefs are intertwined within our corporate culture and provide a vision for our current employees to follow. It may sound corny and it may take a new employee a while to understand but, invariably, just about every one does, making Hershey a very special place in which to work.

Business Responsibility

What does this all add up to? It is a nice story, but you're in business to make money for your stockholders. As our organization has grown, we have seeded and reseeded with the addition of new people and new skills. In striving to meet the everyday challenges of a business whose sales total nearly $3.5 billion, we have managed to enjoy bottom-line financial success, warranting stockholder confidence and an increasing stock price. We are number one in market share in North America in both chocolate and confectionery and in branded pasta products.

Our successes over the past few years have earned Hershey a strong position in the financial community. To put this in perspective, here is an indication of Hershey's stock performance over the past ten years. In short, if you have been a stockholder during this time, your investment would have grown appreciably. If you had invested $1,000 in Hershey's stock at the close of 1983 and reinvested all dividends, the total return on your investment would have been 503 percent, or a compound annual growth rate of 19.7 percent. That $1,000 would be worth more than $6,000 today. By comparison, the same investment in the Standard & Poor's 500 would have yielded a growth of 298 percent or a compound annual growth rate of 14.8 percent. We like to believe that our stock price is a score card reflecting investors' perceptions of our business strategies, our abilities to execute those strategies, and our overall approach to business.

Even with the continued expansion and diversification Hershey Foods has experienced, we remain firmly committed to the vision of our founder. Today, our senior management and employees are very much dedicated to continuing the financial success of the company, while adhering to the highest standards of fairness and integrity. All of us at Hershey have had the good fortune to work for a company that—like the man who founded it—judges its success by more than the money it earns. We look forward to our next one hundred years.

16

How One Company Is Socially Responsible

David W. Fox

Since the Northern Trust may not be a household name for many of you, I begin with a description of my company to put my remarks in a better perspective.

> Northern Trust Corporation is the third-largest bank in Chicago. We are the thirty-eighth largest bank holding company in the United States, with banking assets of about $17 billion. We are, however, among the top five banks in the country in terms of personal and corporate trust activities, with over $480 billion of trust assets under custody and administration. We are the active investment manager for about $80 billion of those assets, and are one of only three major banks in the country which derives the bulk of its revenue from the trust business. We earned a record $168 million in 1993, representing about an 18 percent return on common shareholders' equity.
>
> Northern was founded one hundred five years ago in Chicago, which is still our headquarters. We employ sixty-six hundred people at forty-three locations in six states and in London. Until 1960 we were largely privately held for the first seventy-one years of our existence, and we are unique among major U.S. banks in that our employees own almost 20 percent of our stock.

The rapid pace of change impacting corporate America certainly does not allow one to be complacent about management practices or competitive strategies. Everywhere, companies are being forced to change, for competitive reasons, or at least to question their traditional

277

beliefs and ways of doing business. Downsizing, rightsizing, delayering, reengineering, and process improvement have become the mantras of corporate management. Initially, these actions were focused on companies saddled with heavy debt service through leveraged buyouts, and they had no choice if they were to survive. Now, however, we see highly successful companies taking similar steps, based on their view of the future pressures they must meet if they are to remain successful.

These wrenching changes and the inevitable ones yet to come are having a profound effect on the historical social contract between the company, its people, and the communities in which it operates. We are clearly in the midst of a structural change in business, quite apart from the normal recession and recovery cycles that we have experienced in the past. One recent survey by an independent pollster indicated that 40 percent of the people in this country are worried about their jobs; normally the figure is 4 or 5 percent, according to that same pollster's previous polls. If true, it has serious implications for morale, corporate loyalty, quality of work and, ultimately, our competitiveness. Admittedly, sharp reductions in the workforce have immediate cost-benefits, creating a mean and lean company, well-positioned to compete on a cost basis, at least on a short term. Institutional investors will applaud, the stock price will rise, and management incentive will kick in handsomely.

However, is it the right thing in the long term? The answer is not yet clear. I am not in any way suggesting that corporate layoffs may be unnecessary. A company cannot continue to employ the same number of people if its products or services are not selling, or its cost structure has been allowed to grow disproportionately to its revenue. If it must downsize to survive, then it must. I am simply saying that corporations need to think very carefully about the long-term impact of potentially destroying a corporate culture that has evolved over decades and that may have been a major factor in attracting the best and brightest people to it. Job security is not the issue. No one is guaranteed employment, nor should they be. The issue is how employees are viewed within a company. Are they a valuable asset or simply an expense, just another cost of production?

Technology plays an enormous role in our business. Approximately $50 billion in financial transactions flow through our bank each day, and we are initiating and settling investment securities trades and foreign-exchange transactions in sixty global markets around the clock. It is a given that our clients expect us to have the computer systems and technology to meet their needs, and we do. But so do some other providers. Therefore, the one factor that consistently differentiates Northern in the marketplace is its people, because computers do not listen to clients and solve their problems—people do. Computers do not build relationships that stand the test of time—people do.

In short, Northern's philosophy of people management is critical to our success because of the belief that people are the essence of what makes Northern a special place to work and to do business. Our objective is to create an atmosphere of mutual trust and work satisfaction that translates into superior service for clients. Our mission of unrivaled client satisfaction can be achieved only if Northern employees are inspired to that level by their knowledge that their well-being has a similar priority. Does that mean that we have never laid off people nor will have to in the future? Of course not. We are subject to the same business pressures felt throughout the world. But it does mean that we will try to control staff growth and other expenses when times are good and so minimize the impact on people should things turn against us. It also means that through training and broad-banding of job descriptions, we will make every effort to improve employees' skill mix and relocate people in the corporation. It is by no means an easy or perfect solution, nor is it always successful. But our people know that the intent is there.

At a time when values all around us seem to be torn apart and people's bedrock beliefs are challenged, even more pressure is placed on a corporation to develop or retain its own value system. A recent *Fortune* magazine article noted that this would be a real switch from the conventional wisdom that society promotes sound principles of behavior while businesses pursue only their own interests. The article was not suggesting that corporate America lead an ethical renaissance, but that values such as candor, integrity, taking responsibility, being accountable, investing in education, and respecting diversity can be fostered within the corporate environment. It is a notion with which I not only agree but that I believe is critical to the well-being of U.S. business over the long term. Community and people issues need equal time and emphasis in any corporation's strategic process, but they do not always get it. If superior service execution is the key to competitive advantage, and I believe that in my business—financial services—it is, then specific people strategies and policies must be linked to business operating plans.

Corporate Citizenship in the Communities

As for the communities we serve, it should be remembered that while corporate support of charitable causes is important, employment is also a socially responsible act. That was the principal motivator in our decision five years ago to construct an $80 million operations center in Chicago rather than in the more economically attractive suburbs. It kept our workforce intact and preserved twenty-two hundred jobs for the city of Chicago. It reflected our belief that a healthy employment base is important to Chicago and to Northern's long-term viability.

Equally important is the support we give to other community needs, such as early intervention programs for preschool children, health clinics, and efforts to rebuild or revitalize neighborhoods. We have, for example, over thirty different lending programs to promote home ownership in low- and moderate-income areas of our city. Much of our support is directed toward self-improvement programs designed to break the cycle of dependency, one of our most successful being our adopt-a-school program. We cannot resolve all these issues by ourselves but we can make a difference in local neighborhoods. In the longer term, I believe that the trend may be in collaborative ventures and joint efforts with others to help solve problems that no company alone is willing or able to undertake. We should not get trapped into the notion that cash is the only method of support. Even companies under cost pressures can contribute volunteers and services that are sorely needed and can create, as well, enormous personal satisfaction for their employees.

There is also a practical business aspect to all this. More and more, when we are competing for business from governmental agencies, endowments, foundation funds and corporations, we are asked to outline what we are doing about the social problems in our communities. Our clients want to feel they are placing their business with a socially responsible company.

I mentioned the importance of people in Northern's ability to compete, and our pension, 401K, ESOP, and medical plans are designed to help our employees create a reasonable and cost-justified level of financial peace of mind.

Of growing importance in recent years have been our "Work and Family" programs where we feel we are on the leading edge in responding to employee needs. These needs vary by age and economic status, and we try to assess those things that are affecting the ability of our people to perform their jobs. We do this from surveys, by benchmarking other companies, and by listening to employees who come to us with issues.

Our employee-assistance program came about when we recognized that people were being distracted by elder-care issues, gangs, drugs or alcohol abuse, or domestic violence and did not know where to turn. Employees motivated our decision to construct in our new operations building a corporate child-care center, the first of its kind in downtown Chicago.

Education assistance, an adoption program, and flexible work schedules are all ways in which we try to show Northern people that they matter to us and that we want to strengthen our relationship with them. We are very proud of the fact that for the last four years Northern has been included in the top one hundred companies in the United States for working mothers.

While we know how much our "Work and Family" programs cost, we do not spend a lot of time determining how much we should spend. We prefer to be driven by the needs as we see them and then keep them in reasonable proportion to our overall benefit programs. When it comes to cost-cutting we have avoided reducing the "Work and Family" programs because their positive impact on morale and motivation far outweighs their cost. We believe also that our ability to attract and retain top talent is positively influenced by programs that underscore the importance and needs of people. Of course, the company must be profitable to support its employee programs, but our view is that profitability is more likely than not to be achieved through motivated people.

Some might ask, is the secular change that U.S. business is undergoing eroding the traditional employee notion of corporate loyalty? Very possibly. Does that mean we should just accept it as a fact of life and do nothing about it? I do not think so. While things have changed, we need to find new ways to forge ongoing links with our people. Events may prevent us from providing the traditional definition of job security but we can work to provide job enrichment through training, open communication, and programs that show that people are important to us. When a market changes or product development lags or a competitor gains an edge, that is when a business can use all the help it can get from employees who feel they are part of the team.

There are also those who suggest that secular change makes the socially responsible corporation a vanishing species. I do not accept that, nor do I think we can afford to let it happen. Companies under cost pressures must find ways to concentrate what resources—either human or financial—they can afford on those issues most important to them and their communities. It may mean much more selectivity but using cost pressures as a reason to abandon the playing field will, in the long run, undermine the foundation and the markets on which U.S. business depends for survival.

17

The Value of Corporate Values

W. Douglas Ford

I learned much about values and social responsibility when I was a student at the University of Notre Dame, in the class of 1966. I heard a lot about Christian values and the importance of being a good neighbor and setting a good example. I must have learned those lessons well because I have referred to them often during my twenty-four years at Amoco Oil Company.

As evidenced by so many noted speakers and symposium participants, there is obviously considerable interest—a vested interest, I hope—in exploring the value of corporate social responsibility in a rapidly changing, global marketplace. I say vested interest because, as business citizens, companies such as Amoco are integral parts of the communities in which they operate.

Amoco shares each resident's concern for a healthy social and economic environment in our communities because, without it, a business cannot grow and prosper any more than the individual can.

The high standard of living enjoyed by most Americans results from the combination of a strong business sector and a society that continually strives to enrich the lives of its people. Our values establish the playing field on which we live and work, as individuals and as local businesses. But what makes those values meaningful is how high we set our standards. For corporations, managers, and communities to succeed, the standards must always be set very high.

The main objective of U.S. business is to make a profit for its investors by producing and/or providing quality products and services at reasonable prices. However, I do not think we can achieve that objective if we do not set high standards and then value, recognize, and live up to our corporate responsibilities. Sometimes that is easier said than done because there must be a realistic balance between a company's economic and social responsibilities.

Unfortunately, some people believe that the resources of large corporations—especially oil companies—are limitless, that we have an infinite amount of money, and the ability to be society's caretaker. The fact is, of course, we do not and cannot possibly undertake all the social responsibilities that some think we should. Although we do have an obligation to help meet the needs of our communities, our support must also reflect our strategic direction and our business success or profitability. Nevertheless, I can assure you that the growth and expansion of the business sector in general, and my company in particular, depend to a considerable degree upon our acceptance as good corporate citizens.

Even when we are restructuring and downsizing, as Amoco and many others are doing now, we continue to have responsibilities to our local communities. For example, when economic realities forced Amoco to close its refinery in Casper, Wyoming, in 1991, we did not turn our back on the facility's two hundred ten employees or on the community. On the contrary, the employees received counseling and support services through our Employee Assistance Program. Most employees were offered the opportunity of transferring to another Amoco location, and those who chose not to relocate received severance pay based on years of service, as well as company-supported medical and life insurance for twelve months and help in finding new jobs. In addition, with the help of local contractors, we are actively remediating environmental problems that remain on site, and we continue to help maintain nearby Soda Lake which is recognized as one of the premier breeding grounds for waterfowl in Wyoming.

Despite these efforts to be responsible corporate citizens, there are times when reduced profitability limits what we can do. However, even when the economy and our budgets are relatively tight, we can still find ways to give back to our communities through employee volunteerism, business-school-community partnerships, and other local initiatives. Such efforts are important because the people in our communities have a direct stake in our activities, in terms of employment, environmental quality, support services, and community betterment. Their perceptions of us have a direct bearing on our ability to function in those communities as viable operating facilities. Therefore, it is essential that we have, and do our best to meet, corporate social-responsibility goals that help shape those perceptions. For example, Amoco and its service stations, refineries, and other facilities want to be known as fair employers, reliable suppliers of quality products, having skilled and environmentally conscious managers, and as active promoters of community interest. Our reputation is based on consistently achieving these goals and communicating such credible performance to the public. However, like a shadow, our corporate persona is always with us, and it is always very fragile. People have an opinion of us, whether we want them to or not. At any given point, the public—or different segments of the public—feel more or less favorable toward our operations, based on perceptions that sometimes are good, sometimes not so good. But the sum of these attitudes and perceptions is our public image.

Understandably, the community wants to feel confident that we care as much about them as we do about our employees. They want to know what goes on behind our plant gates, they want to be sure that they are safe in their nearby homes, and they want assurances that we are responsible caretakers of their environment. The days of operating a facility that no one knows or cares about are long gone. Instead of being viewed simply as the corner service station or the refinery at the other end of town, as we were in the 1960s and earlier years, today we are an important, highly visible part of the community. As a result, our mission, vision, and especially our values are reflections of how we want to operate and how we want to be viewed by our various publics, including employees, customers, shareholders, and the general public.

According to Amoco's mission statement, we are

A refining, marketing and transportation company. We provide high-quality petroleum products and related services that meet or exceed the expectations of our customers. We operate and invest to achieve profitable growth and a superior return on the assets employed, while providing *safe, fulfilling employment* and respecting *the environment* and *the communities in which we work.*

According to our vision statement,

We will be the superior competitor—achieving excellence in everything we do and becoming *the standard by which others are judged.*

With regard to Amoco's values and responsibilities, we have identified them: integrity; people; technology; environment, health, and safety; business relationships; and progress.

1. We insist on honest, fair, and trustworthy behavior—or integrity—in all our activities.
2. We respect the individual rights and dignity of all people because our individual and collective actions and talents create our competitive advantage.
3. We believe that technology is a key to the success of our organization.
4. We pledge to protect the environment and the health and safety of employees, the users of our products, and the communities in which we operate.
5. We are committed to customer satisfaction and mutually beneficial business relationships.
6. We challenge ourselves to continually improve—or progress.

While I believe that our mission, vision, and values are central to renewal and our long-term success, I believe that our values, in particular, have real consequences. Values are powerful. They define our standards and our aspirations. They have the potential to change our expectations of ourselves and, ultimately, our behavior, and they can change the perceptions and realities of how we are viewed by others. Amoco's values, along with a wide array of strategic initiatives, really are changing the way we think and work. But we must remember that these values are not cast in bronze, which means we must make many judgment calls as we conduct our day-to-day business, at all times making sure that the standards are set high enough.

Contrary to the attitude that once prevailed in the business sector, we know now that we need to have a strong external, as well as internal, focus. We need to reach out and be involved in our communities and we must want those communities to know who we are. Instead of keeping to ourselves behind plant walls, we are opening our gates to the community. We are shaping and telling our own story, now, before someone else tells it for us in a less-than-factual manner at a less-than-appropriate time. As many businesses have already discovered, the window of opportunity that allows you to tell your side of the story can close rapidly. Once public perception has been formed, it can be extremely difficult to change.

On the other hand, when the community has confidence and trust in your operation and you have a good public image, you will have a much better chance of maintaining that positive relationship when you need it the most. For example, if you have already established a close working relationship with the various government and public-service agencies in your community, your normal business and crisis-response efforts will go a lot more smoothly than if you are a stranger. This is especially true in today's global marketplace, where English-speaking Americans sometimes find themselves trying to conduct business at international locations, with no particular knowledge of either the language or the culture. Fortunately, however, the times are changing because the corporate sector now has a better understanding of cultural diversity and the important role it plays in our rapidly changing world.

Valuing diversity is ethically the right thing to do. But it is also the smart thing for business to do. In the United States, the workforce and marketplace are increasingly diverse. As we globalize our operations, we will encounter more and more diversity among our employees, our suppliers, our host governments, our neighbors and, most importantly, our customers. That is why Amoco's management created our Diversity Advisory Council which is working to increase our understanding of different cultures and to bring more diversity into our workforce as a source of competitive advantage.

Whether you live and work in South Bend, Indiana, or Mexico City, you need to know and understand more about your employees, your customers, and your community. It is particularly important to have a good working relationship with your local leaders, including the mayor, local legislators, and representatives of the fire, police, and other city departments. These people will either be your best supporters when there is a problem or when antagonists want to discredit what you have done for the community. If you are a stranger, they may well be your worst enemies.

Although our communities' needs are often small, our support means a great deal. Each year, for example, Amoco refineries send representatives of local fire departments to the Texas A&M Fire-Training School, where they work side by side with some of our employee-volunteer firemen. The experience is always positive because they learn to work together as a team, and they increase their knowledge of each other's capabilities. As a result, Amoco benefits and so do the local communities.

We encourage our employees to get involved in all aspects of community life, from schools and civic groups to local government, even though they may have no direct connection to Amoco. We do so because we believe that such involvement helps the community and helps Amoco build a long-term, positive reputation in that community. For instance, at our Texas City refinery, more than one hundred fifty

employees have volunteered their time to an Amoco group called
Avenues in Education, which provides people instead of funds to
local school districts. The volunteers conduct refinery tours, scientific
demonstrations, career presentations, tutoring sessions, and many
Junior Achievement activities that help the students get a better
education. At the same time, Amoco earns a reputation as a company
that cares.

Amoco refineries also have what we call community involvement or
citizens-advisory committees, which consist of employee volunteers
who develop and maintain a dialogue between Amoco and the community. In this way, the community knows what Amoco is doing, and we
know what the community is thinking. By acting with integrity and
treating everyone with respect, these Amoco employees are helping to
build the community's confidence and trust which, in turn, adds value
to the company.

In addition, the Amoco Foundation has geographic contributions
committees that are empowered to decide on requests for contributions
from local organizations and make funding recommendations to the
foundation. Throughout this process, the committees discuss community issues, their alignment with corporate values, and the involvement
of Amoco volunteers in local educational, cultural, and community-
service groups. Subsequently, our employees are recognized for do-
nating their time and talent to the organizations, and the organizations
receive small grants from local refinery budgets or larger grants from
the foundation.

Although, historically, we may have tried to be all things to all
people, the Amoco Foundation now directs more than half of its
contributions to communities where our employees and retirees live
and work and to organizations where Amoco people volunteer. In 1993
the Foundation and Amoco's operating companies donated a total of
$25 million to nearly a thousand educational, community-service, and
cultural organizations, with about 60 percent of that amount going to
local schools, colleges, and other community groups. However, since
our foundation also now recognizes that money alone is not the
answer, more support and recognition are being given to Amoco
volunteers whom we consider very important extensions of our financial support.

A good example is Amocares—concerned Amoco retirees engaged
in service—which encourages Amoco retirees and their spouses to
become actively involved in volunteer leadership and service. Although created with the help of an Amoco Foundation grant to the

National Retiree Volunteer Coalition, Amocares depends more on people than on dollars. By using the skills and expertise developed over a lifetime, the retirees are helping to make things a little better in their communities, through projects such as one-on-one mentoring in the schools and renovating shelters for the homeless.

Being active in the community also is good training for current and future managers, especially as we move to more participative forms of management. For example, most community activities involve taking on new responsibilities and learning to work as a team member instead of as the boss, which is good experience that helps Amoco employees do a better job. We believe such active participation in community service is one of the most important investments of time and modest sums of money we can make. It is an investment that will pay long-term dividends in public acceptance and goodwill and, therefore, it is one of the keys to our long-term success.

Another key to Amoco's success is our pledge to protect the environment, which will require spending more than $2 billion or about 50 percent of our total capital expenditures between now and the year 2000. All thinking people in the oil industry and U.S. business in general realize that clean air, land, and water are essential. We are committed to correcting past environmental problems and establishing effective environmental safeguards for the future.

However, Amoco is concerned about environmental regulations and huge expenditures that often are not cost-effective nor based on good science and do not always achieve the desired goals.

While Amoco is committed to abiding by the Clean Air Act and other environmental regulations, we believe that the soundest environmental policy is one based on the best information that science can offer. We believe such a policy should also balance costs with actual environmental benefits and set national goals while allowing free-market forces to determine the strategies best suited to meeting such goals. Amoco believes that its responsibility is to help develop this environmental policy by working with instead of against the Environmental Protection Agency and other governmental bodies. Unfortunately, exercising that responsibility in the United States has not always been easy. Relations between the petroleum industry and the government frequently have been adversarial because it often seems that the nation's environmental agenda has been shaped more by legal, political, and ideological considerations than by what is truly needed to protect the environment.

This is not the case in Canada, Europe, or Japan, where environmental standards are very strict but, typically, are established by a process of consensus-building among industry, government, and the public. In today's global marketplace, we must remember that these international neighbors are also our competitors, and that their regulations may accomplish their environmental goals more cost-effectively than ours. The challenge, therefore, is to find a better way to deal with environmental issues, one that provides solid scientific information as a basis for policy-making and regulation-writing, one that encourages cooperation rather than confrontation, and one that ultimately produces real environmental results.

Amoco is particularly proud of having recently found such a better way by working closely with the EPA during an unprecedented, cooperative study of emission management and reduction methods at our refinery in Yorktown, Virginia. The Yorktown pollution prevention study was the first joint effort of its kind carried out at an operating refinery. It lasted two years and involved more than two hundred people from thirty-five organizations; an independent peer review committee, chosen by the EPA, provided oversight of the results. Among those results were some surprises. For example, to comply with Clean Air Act regulations, Amoco was required to spend $54 million over four years to reduce airborne hydrocarbon emissions from the refinery. However, the Yorktown study showed that Amoco could have reduced those emissions by virtually the same amount for only $10 million—if we had been allowed to implement scientifically sound alternatives. In other words, it is possible to be socially responsible and competitive, to the mutual benefit of our shareholders, our customers, and our local communities.

Amoco has a long tradition of looking for and finding new and better ways to protect the environment. For example, we have marketed unleaded gasolines for nearly eighty years, or three decades before the EPA mandate of 1974. We are an industry leader in developing gasoline-vapor recovery systems and a used-oil recycling program for our service stations. In 1990 we became the first U.S. oil company to offer compressed natural gas (CNG) to the motoring public, which can now get CNG at Amoco stations in eleven states and Washington, D.C. Besides responding to the Clean Air Act, which will require most vehicle fleet-owners to begin using alternative fuels in the late 1990s, we are selling CNG in response to growing consumer interest in cleaner-burning, more cost-effective, domestically available fuels. In addition to protecting the environment, Amoco believes that CNG represents a good business decision, in terms of both the United States and international markets.

However, as we enter a new era of aggressive, global competition, doing business in those international markets will present some interesting challenges and opportunities for all of us. The downfall of communism has opened many new markets in Eastern Europe. China has opened its doors to international investors, and other countries in Asia, Latin America, Africa, and the Middle East are actively seeking new markets for their products. Our world is changing in ways that profoundly affect where we do business, with whom we do business, and how we do business. This can put a strain on our corporate values. Such change can be perilous if you are not expecting it, if you are not prepared to deal with it, or if you are not very adept at coping with it. But change also offers opportunity if you are ready and able to take advantage of it. Sometimes, though, even when you think you are ready, doing business in the global marketplace can be a little like walking a circus high-wire—without a net. At Amoco, we believe it is important to understand that we cannot change a country's culture or ideologies, just as it is important not to compromise our corporate values.

Based on recent experiences when exploring new markets in Mexico, Russia, and China, I know there will be many challenges in the years ahead. However, I am confident that socially responsible corporations such as Amoco will remain viable in this global marketplace if we continue to apply Christian values to our day-to-day operations. Despite downsizing, higher operating costs, and other economic pressures, I can assure you that the business sector still recognizes the value of corporate values, which is why I am optimistic about the years ahead.

18

Chevron's Ethical Commitment

James N. Sullivan

I graduated from the University of Notre Dame in 1959. My oldest son, Mark, graduated in 1982, and my daughter, Helene, graduated from St. Mary's College and Notre Dame a year later. Like all families, we have our differences. But we also have a great deal in common. I am talking about values which, to me, are the root of social responsibility. Both of my children have strong values that were planted at home, and developed and cultivated in college. Mark is a chemical engineer and also works at Chevron. Helene, on the other hand, majored in Italian and International Studies, and works for a nonprofit group that assists the families of people with Alzheimer's and other related brain impairments. You might conclude that my son has chosen to be a capitalist, while my daughter is in a profession that helps people, and you would be partially right. However, my son has devoted many hours to helping others. For example, through Notre Dame's Center for Social Concerns, he served for a year as a full-time volunteer at a group home for disturbed children. Today, he does a great deal more volunteer work in the community where he lives. My daughter has demonstrated that she has as keen an acumen for business as anyone in the family. I would call both these children socially responsible. Both contribute to society in a very direct way, one by helping to produce a vital consumer product, one by assisting people in need; both also perform public service outside their jobs as much as their time allows. They have a keen interest in the world around them and their roles in the world, and have opportunities every day to exercise their personal values.

To me, these same qualities define social responsibility at the corporate level. A socially responsible company must, above all, do its job, thereby providing quality goods and services for its customers, jobs for its employees, financial return to its stockholders, and other benefits such as tax revenues, contributions, and volunteerism in the community.

Social responsibility also dictates that a company do these things in an ethical way, taking every possible action to prevent harm to people or the environment. A socially responsible company has an obligation to reach out and help people beyond standard business boundaries. Outreach can take the form of community leadership, charitable contributions, volunteerism, or more creative approaches. Third, a socially responsible company must be adept at monitoring; it must be alert to and respond to the change in priorities of customers, employees, neighbors, and stockholders. Finally, a socially responsible company must show support for personal values. It must demonstrate a sense of intolerance for shortcuts, half-truths, and shady compromises. It must recruit, reward, and promote only workers who demonstrate high levels of integrity.

These are the requirements for social responsibility. Meeting them is not always easy. Society's needs are multiplying, even as most corporations are scaling back in size, humanpower, and resources. Social issues are becoming more global and more complex, but I do believe that corporate social responsibility is alive and, in some cases, thriving in the form of creative solutions, new partnerships, and the continuing respect for individual values.

The following are a few examples of how Chevron is demonstrating its social responsibility in the 1990s. I said a responsible company must, above all, do its job. Chevron's job is to find and produce petroleum, to manufacture, to sell and to transport petroleum products in more than ninety countries worldwide. One of these countries is Papua, New Guinea, where, in 1992, we became the first company to produce and export crude oil. Our producing fields are deep and high in the country's mountain rain forest. Entire villages in this region were unknown to the outside world until the early 1900s. Many of the people practiced subsistence farming. As a result, land ownership is a tremendous priority, one for which the villagers are willing to fight each other, and they do, with poisoned spears. Our challenge has been to do a job without unduly disrupting lifestyles of these New Guineans.

For more than five years before we started producing oil, we sent teams of employees on foot and in dugout canoes to the scattered villages. Their job was to talk with more than one hundred separate, and often competing, landowner groups to establish boundaries, to forge agreements for renting land, to set up hiring and training, and to open lines of communication. One of the interesting facts you learn from going to the highlands of Papua is to discover that each of these hundred tribes has its own language—roughly four or five hundred separate recorded languages. There is no common language, other than pidgin English, so you can imagine the difficulty of bringing together in one house a group of tribal leaders, each speaking his own language, to try to negotiate and tell them what we were doing and to establish boundaries. We needed an interpreter to go from their tribal language to pidgin, and then from pidgin to English. It was an amazing feat. How do you compensate a tribe for knocking down some of their trees and taking a right-of-way through their property? How do you put together a formal contract to do that?

We took many other measures to preserve the local culture, such as having land near our project designated a protected area for wildlife. We voluntarily buried a one-hundred-ten-mile-long pipeline to the coast rather than lay it above ground, which would have forced us to clear a permanent new path through the rainforest.

Working in undeveloped countries like Papua requires creativity and the ability to build alliances. We have applied these principles closer to home in our contributions and outreach programs. Corporations have never been in the business of giving money away. We do, however, invest money in the communities where we operate, but the recent recessions have put a stranglehold on the budgets for most contributors; 1992 and 1993 were the first years in modern times in which total U.S. corporate cash contributions to charitable causes declined. However, business still plays an important role as a catalyst and underwriter for social improvement.

At Chevron, for example, more than one-third of our $25 million in annual contributions and matching funds goes toward education—from university grants to an ambitious program that helps elementary school youngsters at risk of dropping out. But our research and outreach assistance goes beyond writing checks. One of Chevron's most successful programs is an all-day symposium that we put together to help about six hundred San Francisco Bay area nonprofit companies do their jobs better. We provide speakers and workshops, using experts from our own company and outside consultants, on topics ranging from accounting software to strategic planning.

At Chevron we try to be a pulse-taker. We watch and respond to social trends, both in our own backyard and abroad. For example, in neighborhoods near our refineries, our chemical plants, and our storage terminals, we have seen increased grassroots concerns over issues of safety, toxins, and emergency response. Increasingly, we find that meeting routinely with local citizens is an effective way to show that we share these concerns and are acting responsibly. It is really just a matter of communication.

On a broader scale, we factor a wide range of sociopolitical and environmental issues into our business decisions. One global issue that is very important to me is the changing covenant between corporations and their employees. Like nearly every large U.S. company, Chevron has found downsizing imperative to stay competitive. We have eight thousand fewer employees than we did in 1990, leaving us with a current workforce of about forty thousand. Robert Samuelson has suggested that downsizing makes companies lose their compassion, their sense of responsibility for employees. I disagree. I feel our sense of responsibility actually has increased, but in a new and different way. The old paradigm may have been that companies rewarded loyal employees with steady promotions and lifetime employment. The new model places higher priority on shared goals, partnerships, and realistic options.

For example, Chevron now has career-enrichment programs designed to help employees identify and develop their most marketable skills, to understand and manage change, and to understand and value diversity. These programs help employees to be more prepared and fulfilled in their work, as well as helping them to have a better chance of finding a good job if they leave Chevron. For people whose jobs have been eliminated, we first try to redeploy them into other jobs within the company but if that fails, we try to soften the blow with generous voluntary severance programs and outplacement counseling. Over a thousand of our employees (these are surplus employees) have been redeployed in new jobs within the company over the past two years. In former days they would have been terminated, and we would have had to hire, at great expense, and train one thousand other employees. So we have taken people across boundaries that have not before been broken, barriers that said if the upstream part of the company hired an engineer, he could not be an engineer in a refinery but only in the producing field. She could be a petroleum engineer but not an engineer in a chemical plant.

Finally, we have launched a new companywide effort to ensure that employees get what they need to do their best work. We believe that for employees to do their best work we need open communications—up, down, and sideways—that we require strong, talented, skilled leadership, and that we need to have equitable treatment of all our employees.

We recognize that the commitment of our employees is critical to our success, so how do we replace this lost loyalty and build commitment? We decided that building a committed employee team will be one of our eight corporate strategic intents; it was the highest priority of our eight strategic intents in 1993 and will continue to be so until we fulfill our vision of a committed team.

Working with care and concern, reaching out to communities, and noting and responding to shifting trends are three critical elements to being socially responsible. But they lose much of their impact if we do not also encourage our employees to adhere to high standards of honesty and integrity. We do this in a number of ways: by selecting and promoting candidates with strong personal values (we also have a deselection process); by having detailed written principles of business conduct; and by having a system of internal controls to ensure that our principles are enacted. One of these controls is our network of internal audits that monitor safety and environmental compliance. Another is our performance-management process which gives employees the right and obligation to participate in their own career planning. We also created a toll-free U.S. hotline that gives all employees a risk-free way to report possible violations of law or company policy, which is one more way we empower our employees to do what they feel is right. Ultimately, that is what corporate responsibility is about—doing the right things as an institution and creating an environment in which employees can do the same.

Corporate social responsibility is not dead any more than personal values or individual responsibility are dead. After all, every businessperson is first a person, and personal values are still the backbone of any socially responsible company.

19

Henkels & McCoy—Our Story

Paul M. Henkels

I have been asked to talk about some of the pressures the present business atmosphere visits on a company. First, however, let me tell you about Henkels & McCoy. We are seventy-one years old; we are in engineering and construction; we normally employ between five and six thousand people. We have a very large investment in equipment: 1.2 pieces of major equipment for every employee. Henkels & McCoy is known, and has been known since my father started the business in 1923, for quality and integrity.

Telecommunications is one of our largest fields of endeavor; we are the only significant union contractor operating in a milieu of nonunion contractors. We have noticed in the last several years, in addition to the intense pressure on prices and deregulation in the industry, the way the telecommunications industry has changed. First is the tremendous downsizing of companies like AT&T, GTE, Ameritech and the other Baby Bells—many of them are half the size they were. Among other things, it gives one a feeling, an idea, of how bloated they really were when they were monopolies. We have also found out some other things about these companies, some of which are our biggest customers: they are not as nice as they used to be. At industry conventions, in bygone times, everyone was friendly with everyone else. Now when we go to conventions and meet officers and other employees of companies that were monopolies in their own areas but are no longer, we find they are not as friendly with their industry brothers and sisters as they used to be. They have become competitors with each other.

We have had a good history with one of the large companies we work for, probably one of the twenty largest companies in the United

States. We have worked continually for them since 1949, developing them over the last several years into our largest customer. That is, up until this year [1994]. We operate nationwide and have worked for all the subsidiaries of this company. Several years ago they started a partners-in-quality program whereby, if our company were to achieve a certain rating in the quality of our work, we would receive a price advantage of one or several percent over competitors who might not have attained as good a quality.

At the beginning of 1993, however, a strange thing happened, one that was totally out of character with partners-in-quality or with our forty-five years' experience in working for them. They decided to change the way they would contract their work. Instead of doing it through each of their individual statewide operating companies, they would contract over a large geographical area. Further, it would be by single-source, three-year contracts, winner take all. This was for engineering and construction, covering regions such as the Midwest, the Southwest, and the East, and was a big change. We took their bid tenders as they issued them early in 1993 and submitted our best prices for each section of the country as required. After they had received prices from everybody all over the country, they did a very startling thing. They took the prices we and others had submitted in good faith and then sent a letter to all their bidders, thanking them for their price information and asking for everyone's final prices! They enclosed what they called "sample prices" for guidance. What they had done was go through the long list of unit prices submitted by every contractor and had carefully selected the lowest for each item. This was the information they gave back to all bidders. Then they told us they wanted our best bid. Ethics in business? We debated whether to rebid at all but eventually we submitted new prices. We ended up with maybe 20, 25 or 30 percent of the work in areas where we had often done one-half or two-thirds of it, and done it well. For us, it caused a great amount of dislocation with many problems but, fortunately, we are diversified, so we were able generally to keep our employees, people who had been loyal to us, by placing them in other situations.

Now, at Henkels & McCoy, we know the telecommunications contracting business. We know this business better than anybody else in the country. We know the prices, we know the costs, and we know that some of the successful bidders cannot do the work at the prices they had bid. Apparently one competitor's plan (a big winner in the competition) was to go back to the mom-and-pop companies and the other contractors that had been working for this owner and try to hire those contractors at lower prices than they had been getting. It appeared as though they intended to subcontract all the work. They were not totally successful. In fact, they even approached us for prices in many areas. We gave them the prices we had bid originally and, generally, they turned us down. To get the work done, occasionally they had to contract with us at our prices, which gave us a small measure of satisfaction considering the amount of work we lost.

We could have bid some of the lower prices if we had been willing to compromise our quality. We could also have obtained work from some of the successful contractors at their prices if we had been willing to compromise our quality. For example, if you are burying cable, you are doing it with a trencher or, more directly, with a cable plow. Sometimes it is specified that the cable be buried twenty-four inches, sometimes thirty inches, sometimes forty-two inches. Unless an inspector is there to observe, which is not often, he does not know how deep a cable has been buried. We could have taken a chance and subcontracted from some of the successful bidders and maybe gotten away with burying that cable twelve or eighteen inches. However, our company has a reputation for quality and integrity, and we were not going to do that. Among other things, we were not going to tell our people to work with lower standards; we have other work that has been gained through our good reputation, and we would suffer greatly if we started to compromise our quality.

Where this is going to go, how it will play out, I do not know. We are still in the midst of it. Our plan, however, is to try to ride out the storm and hope the competition will learn a hard lesson and that prices will improve. We have suffered through these cycles before when price governed everything, and we have come out all right. We are not sure that such will happen in time because there are some players out there who, although they might be new to the game, have deep pockets. But we will give up neither quality nor integrity because it is so important to our company and all our work. We know that there is a market for quality, and we are going to persevere with it. We think we have always paid our people a little better than our competitors, and we will continue to do so. We are basically union, and we think we can continue also to handle that. We think we have a chance eventually of getting back much of this work. We believe that ethics in business pays, but there is one essential thing in making it pay and that is competence. If we have confidence along with our competence, we believe our integrity and quality will eventually triumph. We shall see.

Index

About the Center for Ethics and Religious Values in Business

The Notre Dame Center for Ethics and Religious Values in Business seeks to build bridges among business, business studies, and the humanities. Its programs are designed to strengthen the Judeo-Christian ethical foundations in business and public policy decisions by fostering dialogue between academic and corporate leaders, and through research and publications. The Center is under the codirectorship of John W. Houck (business), professor of management, and Oliver F. Williams, C.S.C. (theology), associate professor of management College of Business Administration.

Publications and activities of the Center include:

Full Value: Cases in Christian Business Ethics (1978)
"Quite successfully juxtaposes the power of the Christian story, in its biblical immediacy, to concrete problems Christians in the world of business are likely to meet."

—Michael Novak

"Religious traditions provide, as these writers observe, a story, for example the Christian story, which informs our moral outlook, creates our moral vision, sustains our moral loyalties, and nurtures our moral character."

—James M. Gustafson

The Judeo-Christian Vision and the Modern Corporation (1982)
In 1980 the Center hosted a national symposium bearing the same name, about which the *New York Times* reported "there would be no facile resolution to the conflict between the values of a just society and the

307

sharply opposing values of successful corporations." Further, the *Los Angeles Times* contrasted "the competitive success-oriented style necessary for corporate promotion with the traditional Christian view of the virtuous person."

Co-Creation and Capitalism: John Paul II's "Laborem Exercens" (1983)

The symposium, Co-creation: A Religious Vision of Corporate Power, was presented in 1982, focusing on Pope John Paul II's encyclical letter, *Laborem Exercens. Newsweek* characterized the conference as a "free marketplace of ideas" exploring a religious vision of corporate power.

Catholic Social Teaching and the U.S. Economy (1984)

In December 1983, the Center assisted the U.S. Bishops' Committee charged to write a pastoral letter on the economy by convening a three-day symposium, Catholic Social Teaching and the American Economy. The *Los Angeles Times* observed: "About one-third of the major speakers represented conservative viewpoints, the remainder voiced moderate-to-liberal positions." The *New York Times* reported that "contentiousness is commonplace here at Notre Dame. . . . And when dozens of business leaders, theologians and academics lined up against each other at the university this week, the debate over the economy was fought as hard as any gridiron encounter." More than two hundred fifty people attended the meeting, including the five bishops who were to draft the letter.

The Common Good and U.S. Capitalism (1987)

Catholic Social Teaching and the Common Good was the theme of a 1986 symposium to explore the possible retrieval of the notion of "the common good" in philosophical-economic discourse. Ralph McInerny saw the concept of the common good as needed "to draw attention to flaws in our economic thinking and policies as well as to make positive suggestions that will be manifestly in line with our tradition." *New Catholic World* wrote: "a collection of eighteen essays . . . by social scientists, theologians, philosophers, business faculty, and television producers. The essays represent different points of view from both theoretical and practical perspectives. . . . It would be a valuable contribution to Catholic social teaching if all it did was to make people aware that a concept of the common good once was alive and well. It does much more than that."

Ethics and the Investment Industry (1989)

The 1987 symposium focused on ethics in the investment industry. Much has been written in the eighties about the misdeeds of actors in the investment community; suggestions for legislative reform abound. Very little has been said about the ethical vision and institutional bonding that form the context for a humane capitalism. It is these themes, as well as the appropriate market and legal aspects, that were explored at Notre Dame. *America* said of *Ethics and the Investment Industry* that it "will be an important reference for future participants in the international business community."

A Virtuous Life in Business: Stories of Courage and Integrity in the Corporate World (1992)
"I highly recommend *A Virtuous Life in Business: Stories of Courage and Integrity in the Corporate World.* . . . This book is not only valuable, it is readable and gets progressively better."

—*Commonweal*

Catholic Social Thought and the New World Order: Building on One Hundred Years (1993)
"With the recent demise of the Marxist alternative to capitalism, Catholic social teaching has assumed the role of the major international force challenging free enterprise to be more humane."

—*National Catholic Register*

Other publications by the Center include:

The Making of an Economic Vision (1991)
Matter of Dignity: Inquiries into the Humanization of Work (1977)
The Apartheid Crisis (1986)

as well as articles appearing in *California Management Review, Business Horizons, Theology Today, Business and Society Review, Horizons, Journal of Business Ethics* and the *Harvard Business Review*.

About the Contributors

Gerald F. Cavanagh, S.J., is academic vice president, provost, and professor of management at the University of Detroit Mercy. He holds a B.S. in engineering, graduate degrees in philosophy, theology and education, and a doctorate in management from Michigan State University. He was ordained a Catholic priest in the Society of Jesus in 1964. Reverend Cavanagh has lectured at Stanford, Harvard and Berkeley, has given ethics workshops for business and university people, and has consulted on federal legislation affecting business. He is the author of numerous articles and five books, including *American Business Ethics*, 3rd edition (1990), *American Business Values in Transition* (1976), *The Businessperson in Search of Values* (1976), and co-author of *Ethical Dilemmas in the Modern Corporation* (1988), *Blacks in the Industrial World: Issues for the Manager* (1972, 1974).

Richard T. De George is University Distinguished Professor of Philosophy and professor of business administration at the University of Kansas. He received his Ph.B. from the University of Louvain, Belgium (1955), and his M.A. (1958) and Ph.D. in philosophy (1959) from Yale University. He was a Research Fellow at Yale, Columbia, and Stanford Universities and the Hoover Institution, the Charles J. Dirksen Professor of Business Ethics at Santa Clara University (1986), and is a specialist in Russian and East European thought. Professor De George was president of several academic organizations, including the American Philosophical Association and the Society of Business Ethics. He has written widely in the field of applied ethics and has published sixteen books, including *Competing with Integrity in International Business* (1993), *The Nature and Limits of Authority* (1985), *Business Ethics* (1982), *Ethics, Free Enterprise and Public Policy* (1978).

311

W. Douglas Ford was named president of Amoco Oil Company, Chicago, in 1992, having been with the company since 1970. He is responsible for Amoco's refining, marketing, and transportation activities. He has served in a variety of managerial positions in Amoco's refineries throughout the United States. Mr. Ford holds a bachelor's degree from the University of Notre Dame and a Ph.D. from Northwestern University, both in chemical engineering.

David W. Fox is chairman, chief executive officer and a director of Northern Trust Corporation and its principal subsidiary, Northern Trust Company, Chicago. He joined the bank in 1955. He received a B.S. degree from the University of Notre Dame and an M.B.A. from the University of Chicago. He served as an officer in the U.S. Marine Corps from 1953–1955. He is a director of the Federal Reserve Bank of Chicago, USG Corporation, and is a public governor of the Chicago Stock Exchange. Mr. Fox is also a director of the Chicago Council on Foreign Relations and a member of the advisory board of the J. L. Kellogg Graduate School of Management at Northwestern University.

Robert W. Galvin started his career at Motorola in 1940. He held the senior officership position in the company from 1959 until January 1990, when he became chairman of the Executive Committee. He continues to serve as a full-time officer of Motorola. He attended the University of Notre Dame and the University of Chicago and is a member, and was recent chairman, of the board of trustees of the Illinois Institute of Technology. Mr. Galvin has been awarded honorary degrees and other recognitions, including election to the National Business Hall of Fame; in 1991, he received the National Medal of Technology. Motorola is the first large company-wide winner of the Malcolm Baldrige National Quality Award, presented by President Reagan at a White House ceremony in November 1988.

Ronald M. Green is the John Phillips Professor of Religion at Dartmouth College, director of Dartmouth's Ethics Institute, and professor of business ethics at Dartmouth's Amos Tuck School of Business Administration. He holds a Ph.D. in religious ethics from Harvard University, and has taught there and at Stanford University. Professor Green serves on the board of directors of the Society of Christian Ethics and is a Fellow of the Business Enterprise Trust. He has written five books as well as many articles in theoretical and applied ethics, and has been a consultant or lecturer on business and organizational ethics. His publications include, *Kierkegaard and Kant, the Hidden*

Debt (1992), *Religion and Moral Reason* (1988), *Religious Reason: The Rational and Moral Basis of Religious Belief* (1978), *Population Growth and Justice: An Examination of Moral Issues Raised by Rapid Population Growth* (1976).

Paul M. Henkels is chairman of Henkels & McCoy, Inc., in Blue Bell, Pa.; he joined the company in 1947 after graduating from Haverford College with a B.A. in engineering. Under his direction, Henkels & McCoy has grown to include 18 divisions and subsidiaries that engineer and construct facilities for gas transmission and distribution companies, electric utilities, telecommunications and data providers and users, and industrial corporations. He is past chairman of the board of trustees of St. Joseph's University, a member of the board of trustees of Chestnut Hill College and of the Academy of Applied Electrical Sciences, and a member of Temple University Hospital Board of Governors. He is also co-chairman of the REACH Alliance (Road to Educational Achievement through CHoice).

John W. Houck is professor of management and co-director of the Notre Dame Center for Ethics and Religious Values in Business. A former Ford and Danforth Fellow, he has earned both an A.B. and a J.D. degree from the University of Notre Dame, an M.B.A. from the University of North Carolina-Chapel Hill (1959), and an LL.M. from Harvard University (1963). He is also a Fellow of the Royal Society for the encouragement of Arts, Manufactures & Commerce. Professor Houck has lectured and conducted workshops on the role of religious and humane values in business. He has written numerous articles and reviews and has published ten books, including *Catholic Social Thought and the New World Order* (1993), *A Virtuous Life in Business: Stories of Courage and Integrity in the Corporate World* (1992), *The Making of an Economic Vision* (1991), *The Common Good and U.S. Capitalism* (1987), *Full Value: Cases in Christian Business Ethics* (1978).

William Lehr, Jr. is vice president, secretary and associate general counsel (securities) for Hershey Foods, with whom he has been since 1967. He is a 1988 graduate of the Stanford Executive Program, and holds a B.A. degree in business administration from the University of Notre Dame (1961). He also received a law degree in 1964 from Georgetown University. For two years prior to joining Hershey, Mr. Lehr served in the U.S. Army at Fort Story, Virginia, where he rose to the rank of captain.

Dennis P. McCann is professor and chair of the Department of Religious Studies, co-director of the Center for the Study of Values, and Senior Fellow at the Center for the Study of Values in Modern Society at DePaul University in Chicago. In 1992 he became the first annual holder of the Wicklander Chair in Professional Ethics at DePaul. He received his S.T.L. in theology from the Gregorian University in Rome and his Ph.D. in theology from the University of Chicago Divinity School. Professor McCann has served on the board of directors of the Society of Christian Ethics and is a member of the editorial board of the *Journal of Religious Ethics*. He is the author of *New Experiment in Democracy: The Challenge for American Catholicism* (1987), *Christian Realism and Liberation Theology* (1981), co-author of *Polity and Praxis: A Program for American Practical Theology* (1990), and co-editor of *On Moral Business: Religious and Theological Perspectives on Business, Ethics, and Society* (Grand Rapids, Mich.: Eerdmans Publishing, 1995).

Michael Novak is a theologian, author, and former U.S. ambassador, and holds the George Frederick Jewett Chair in Religion and Public Policy at the American Enterprise Institute in Washington, D.C., where he is also director of social and political studies. He has served as an advisor during Democratic and Republican administrations. In 1956 he was graduated from Stonehill College and, in 1958, from the Gregorian University in Rome. Mr. Novak continued theological studies at Catholic University and at Harvard University where he received an M.A. in 1966. He has received numerous awards, including the annual Anthony Fisher Prize for his book, *The Spirit of Democratic Capitalism*, presented in 1992 by former British Prime Minister Margaret Thatcher. In March 1994 he received the Templeton Prize. His publications include *The Catholic Ethic and the Spirit of Capitalism* (1993), *This Hemisphere of Liberty* (1990), *Free Persons and the Common Good* (1989), *Will It Liberate? Questions about Liberation Theology* (1986), *The Spirit of Democratic Capitalism* (1982, 1992).

James E. Post is professor of management and public policy at Boston University where he has taught since 1974. He also holds a J.D. degree. He has written widely on the role of business in society, public policy issues, and public affairs management, and has consulted with a wide variety of private-sector firms in the United States, Europe, and the Pacific Rim. His professional activities include associations with the World Health Organization, Population Council, National Wildlife Federation, and the Corporate Conservation Council. Professor Post is a trustee of the Foundation for Public Affairs. Recently, he was named research director, Business & Society, at the Conference Board, a leading business research organization that studies economic and management trends. He is the author of twelve books, including *Corporate Behavior and Social Change* (1978), and co-author of *Business and Society: Corporate Strategy, Public Policy, Ethics*, 7th edition (1992), *Private Management and Public Policy* (1975).

Howard F. Rosen is executive director of the Competitiveness Policy Council in Washington, D.C., a federal advisory commission reporting to the President and Congress. He has served also as an economist in the Research Department of the Bank of Israel in Jerusalem and in the Bureau of International Labor Affairs in the U.S. Department of Labor. Mr. Rosen received his M.A. in economics from George Washington University, focusing on issues relating to international trade and employment, macroeconomic policies, structural change, immigration, and labor market adjustment. He is the author of "Assisting US Labor Market Adjustment to Freer Trade under NAFTA," *North American Outlook*, Vol. 4, No. 1–2, National Planning Association, Sept. 1993; "Can American Industry Compete: Focus Must Be on Longer Term," *San Diego Union*, Feb. 24, 1991; and co-author of "Economic Issues in the Arab-Israeli Peace Process," *Economic Insights*, Institute for International Economics, Vol. III, No. 1, Jan./Feb. 1992; *Trade Policy for Troubled Industries*, Policy Analyses in International Economics 15, Washington, D.C. (1986).

Robert J. Samuelson has been a contributing editor with *Newsweek* since 1984, and is one of the magazine's most recognized writers for his biweekly column analyzing and reporting socioeconomic issues. He also writes a syndicated biweekly column for the *Washington Post*, the *Los Angeles Times*, the *Boston Globe*, the *International Herald Tribune*, and other papers. Mr. Samuelson holds a B.A. in government from Harvard University, and has earned many journalism awards, including the National Headliner Award for Consistently Outstanding Feature Column on a Single Subject (1992), National Headliner Award for Best Special Interest Column (1987), Champion-Tuck Business Journalism Award and Gerald Loeb Award for Commentary (1986), Loeb Award (1983), National Magazine Award (1981).

S. Prakash Sethi is professor of management and acting director of the Center for Management at Baruch College, The City University of New York. He is well known for his research and writings on business ethics, corporate social responsibility, corporate strategy and public policy, international business, and private enterprise and Third World economic development. Recently, he was appointed the first economic policy adviser to the National African Federated Chamber of Commerce and Industry in South Africa. Professor Sethi was profiled in the *New York Times* as one of the country's leading scholars in business strategy and public policy. He has published numerous articles and twenty-three books, including *Multinational Corporations and the Impact of Public Advocacy on Corporate Strategy: Nestlé and the Infant Formula Controversy* (1994), *Up Against the Corporate Wall* (1991), *Business and Society: Dimensions of Conflict* (1987), *South African Quagmire: In Search of a Peaceful Path to Democratic Pluralism* (1987).

James N. Sullivan is vice chairman of the board of directors of Chevron Corporation, responsible for worldwide refining, marketing, and chemical operations; for certain operating companies (Chevron Land & Development Co., Chevron Research & Technology Co., Chevron Shipping Co., and Chevron International Oil Co.); for Chevron's participation in 50 percent-owned Caltex Petroleum Corp; and corporate staff functions, including environmental affairs. In 1959 Mr. Sullivan received a degree in chemical engineering from the University of Notre Dame and began his career with Chevron in 1961. He is a director of the American Petroleum Institute, the California Chamber of Commerce, the U.S. Chamber of Commerce, and is a trustee of the University of San Francisco.

Lee A. Tavis is the C. R. Smith Professor of Business Administration and director of the program, "Multinational Managers and Developing Country Concerns" at the University of Notre Dame. His research and teaching are focused in the areas of business planning models and the potential contribution of multinationals to development in Latin America, Africa and Asia. He has published books and articles in the management/financial area and on the developmental role of multinational corporations, and is co-editor of a four-volume series originating from the program: *The Pharmaceutical Corporate Presence in Developing Countries* (1993), *Rekindling Development: Multinational Firms and World Debt* (1988), *Multinational Managers and Host Government Interactions* (1988), *Multinational Managers and Poverty in the Third World* (1982).

Marina v.N. Whitman is the Distinguished Visiting Professor of Business Administration and Public Policy at the University of Michigan.

From 1979 until 1992 she was an officer of the General Motors Corporation, first as vice president and chief economist and later as vice president and group executive for public affairs. Prior to her appointment at GM, Professor Whitman was a member of the faculty in the Department of Economics at the University of Pittsburgh. She received her M.A. and Ph.D. degrees from Columbia University, and is the recipient of numerous fellowships, honors, and awards. She is a member of the board of directors of Browning-Ferris Industries, Chemical Banking Corp., Procter & Gamble, UNOCAL, and serves on the boards of Harvard and Princeton Universities. She is the author of many articles and several books, including *International Trade and Investment: Two Perspectives: Essays in International Finance* (1981), *Reflections of Interdependence: Issues for Economic Theory and U.S. Policy* (1979), *Government Risk-Sharing in Foreign Investment* (1965).

Oliver F. Williams, C.S.C., is co-director of the Notre Dame Center for Ethics and Religious Values in Business, and on the faculty of the Department of Management at the University of Notre Dame. He researches and teaches in the areas of business, society, and ethics. He holds a Ph.D. in theology from Vanderbilt University and had the experience of a research year at Stanford University Graduate School of Business. He is the former chair of the Social Issues Division of the Academy of Management. Reverend Williams is the author of *The Apartheid Crisis* (1986), co-author of *Full Value: Cases in Christian Business Ethics* (1978), and co-editor of *The Pharmaceutical Corporate Presence in Developing Countries* (1993), *Catholic Social Thought and the New World Order* (1993), *A Virtuous Life in Business: Stories of Courage and Integrity in the Corporate World* (1992), *Ethics and the Investment Industry* (1989), *The Judeo-Christian Vision and the Modern Corporation* (1982).

J. Philip Wogaman is senior minister of the Foundry United Methodist Church in Washington, D.C., a position to which he was appointed in 1992. From 1966 to 1992 he was professor of Christian ethics at Wesley Theological Seminary in Washington, D.C., where he continues to serve as affiliated professor. His Ph.D. and M.Div. degrees are from Boston University and his B.A. is from the University of the Pacific. Reverend Wogaman was a delegate to the United Methodist General Conference of 1988 and 1992, and a member of the World Methodist Council from 1986–91. He has served as president of the Society of Christian Ethics of the United States and Canada, and is a member of the American Theological Society. His publications include *Christian Ethics: A Historical Introduction* (1993), *Christian Moral Judgement* (1989), *Christian Perspectives on Politics* (1988), *The Great Economic Debate* (1977), *Faith and Fragmentation* (1985).